WORK

WORK

The Last 1,000 Years

Andrea Komlosy

Translated by
Jacob Watson
with
Loren Balhorn

VERSO
London • New York

This paperback edition first published by Verso 2024
First published in English by Verso 2018
First published in German as *Arbeit. Eine globalhistorische Perspektive*
© Promedia Verlag/Vienna, Austria 2014
Translation © Jacob Watson and Loren Balhorn 2018, 2024

The moral rights of the author have been asserted

1 3 5 7 9 10 8 6 4 2

Verso
UK: 6 Meard Street, London W1F 0EG
US: 388 Atlantic Avenue, Brooklyn, NY 11217

versobooks.com

Verso is the imprint of New Left Books

ISBN-13: 978-1-78663-413-9
ISBN-13: 978-1-78663-412-2 (US EBK)
ISBN-13: 978-1-78663-411-5 (UK EBK)

British Library Cataloguing in Publication Data
A catalogue record for this book is available from the British Library

The Library of Congress Has Cataloged the Hardback Edition as Follows:

Names: Komlosy, Andrea, author.
Title: Work : the last 1,000 years / Andrea Komlosy ; translated by Jacob K.
  Watson with Loren Balhorn.
Other titles: Arbeit. English
Description: London ; Brooklyn, NY : Verso, 2018. |
Includes bibliographical
  references and index.
Identifiers: LCCN 2017051518 | ISBN
9781786634108 (hardback)
Subjects: LCSH: Employment (Economic theory) –
History. | Labor – History. |
  Work – History.
Classification: LCC HD5701.5 .K6613 2018 | DDC
331.09 – dc23
LC record available at
https://lccn.loc.gov/2017051518

Typeset in Minion Pro by MJ & N Gavan, Truro, Cornwall
Printed in the UK by CPI Mackays

Contents

Introduction

This volume is a comparative, intercultural, global history of working conditions and labour relations in human society – in short, a history of work, with a particular focus on the ways different relations and conditions have been interconnected throughout history.[1]

The historical reconstruction and depiction of these interconnections assumes the existence of simultaneously existing combinations of different labour relations. Such an approach rejects the notion of a linear, progressive sequence of modes of production, along with the conception of work that such thinking would entail. Rather, we will concentrate on the wide variety of activities that have served people's survival and self-discovery over time. The term 'work' encompasses both market-oriented and subsistence activities; it includes human activity for the sake of naked survival and also the satisfaction of desires for luxury or status, as well as activities for the sake of cultural representation or demonstrations of power and faith. The separation of workplace and home – of working hours and free time – remained the exception for most of human history, only becoming widespread during the Industrial Revolution through the centralization of gainful employment in the factories and offices of the industrialized West at the end of the eighteenth century. Yet this new life-world failed to become a daily reality for all people in industrial society, where work life was shaped by peasant agriculture, handicrafts, house and subsistence work, and by a wide range of activities allowing people without regular employment to get by. It was even less true of regions in and outside Europe where large factories initially played no role – or, in the course of 'catch-up industrialization', a non-dominant role – in which factory work remained only one gainful form of work among countless subsistence activities carried out in the context of the household and family unit.

The simultaneity and combination of different labour relations are depicted in this volume across six historical epochs, defined by representative years (1250, 1500, 1700, 1800, 1900 and today).

The year 1250 stands for the growth of urbanization and exchange of daily staples in connection with the formation of a Eurasian world system,[2] the dynamics of which were dominated by Latin Europe in the West and imperial Mongol expansion in the East. Robbery, looting and the kidnapping of skilled workers by nomadic horsemen deprived these conquered territories of value, but neither the Mongols nor the European powers succeeded in controlling interregional divisions of labour. Among the artisans of Europe's cities, a tool- and quality-oriented understanding of work began to emerge, distinct from the exhausting labour workers knew from home and farm life.

The year 1500 signifies Western European expansion in the form of plantations and mines in the emerging American colonies. The labour provided by indigenous populations and slaves in extracting and processing raw materials flowed into Western European industry, which concentrated primarily on the production of finished goods. A division of labour emerged within Europe as well, between the Western, industrialized regions and the Eastern agrarian zones which supplied timber and foodstuffs. In the Eurasian context, however, the centres of commercial production were located in Western, Southern and Eastern Asia – European merchants, trading companies and their respective states did their utmost to participate in the Asian spice and commodity trade. To do so, they relied on silver plundered from American mines.[3]

Around 1700, merchants introduced the putting-out system alongside the self-sufficient households in the countryside and the guild craftsmen in the urban centres. These merchants did not limit their inventory to goods produced on-site, but rather ordered wares from rural producers, thereby tying them into a large-scale division of labour under their central control and opening up commodity chains of varying size and scope. Asian craftsmanship retained its status as the world's best, with Indian cotton textiles imported into Europe, Africa and America by the British East India Company. African slave traders accepted Indian textiles as payment, while American plantation slaves wore cotton clothes made from Indian fabrics. The new capitalist world system absorbed manifold local working conditions into one unequal, international division of labour under Western European direction.[4]

In the 1800s, the Industrial Revolution shifted control over global commodity chains to the Western European countries (first Great Britain, followed by other European states), centralizing industrial production in mechanized factories. Mechanization brought wage labour out of the house and workshop and into the factory, contributing to a completely new experience of what it meant for many people to 'go to work'. From the workers' perspective, factory work meant dependency on a waged income; following an initial period of crude exploitation, workers united to improve wages and working conditions. Employers, on the other hand, viewed labour power as a cost factor which enabled capital accumulation in the form of value, created by appropriating wage labour. Housewives became appendages of their husbands, as their contribution to the family's survival and thus the company's creation of value was not regarded as work. Despite the intrinsic antagonism between labour and capital, the two would become closely intertwined over time. While this new conception of work spread quickly throughout Europe and was soon codified in labour legislation during the nineteenth century, industrial producers in Asian regions persisted in forms of artisanal and decentralized production: the multiple incomes and sources of subsistence provided by rural households allowed Asian commodities to compete with factory goods despite lower levels of productivity. Wage labour was also connected to the overthrow of feudal servitude and serfdom, which in turn fostered a productivity-oriented discourse discrediting the slave trade. New forms of personal dependency, more intensely mediated by the market, arose to replace serfdom and slavery over the course of the nineteenth century.

Only after 1900 would this narrowing of the conception of work to gainful employment outside the home finally become dominant on a global scale. Economists' predictions that wage labour would successively replace all forms of work rooted in earlier modes of production (such as housework, slavery, subsistence agriculture and artisanal crafts) never materialized. Nevertheless, this new, restricted conception of work as wage labour's implantation into legal codes, state planning and the demands and political imaginary of the labour movement itself solidified its pre-eminent position in twentieth-century discourse. Although a wide spectrum of other life-sustaining and income-generating activities continued to exist, value creation linked to these activities was ignored by this narrowed conception.

The flexibilization of labour relations began to accelerate in the 1980s, triggered by the crisis of industrial mass production, as what were once considered 'normal' working conditions became increasingly uncommon in the industrialized countries as well. This development has blown the debate over what constitutes 'work' wide open. Many established patterns, ideas and terms no longer apply. This lacuna has helped large, increasingly global corporations roll back the labour standards and social welfare systems built up by social democracy and social partnership in Western Europe and by the communist parties in the East, while trade unions and workers' parties seemingly look on helplessly. On the one hand, the collapse of state socialism in Eastern Europe and China's market reforms have seemingly banished the social question from public discourse and made social issues taboo, while, at the same time, a global precariat has begun to emerge. Today, we are faced with the challenge of developing a new conceptual basis for debates on the future of work. This book is a contribution to those efforts.

The volume opens with several short chapters introducing various conceptions of work and labour, controversies surrounding them, and the terminology used to talk about them. This foundation serves as an analytical instrument, underlying the book's chronological depiction of the history of work as well as discussions of long-term trends.

Each period begins with an overview of the political and economic foundations of the contemporary world system, as well as the most significant developments in each epoch. This is followed by observations on how working conditions are combined, first at the level of the individual household. Specialization, divisions of labour and interregional exchange are then discussed, before, third, divisions of labour and combinations of working conditions are examined on a broader scale. Finally, our line of inquiry turns to long-term changes in the small-scale, regional and global combinations of working conditions. For this purpose, findings are used from a study conducted by the International Institute of Social History (Amsterdam), which collected data on diverse forms of work across five periods from 1500 to 2000, thereby complementing qualitative with quantitative perspectives.

A depiction that does justice to the particularities and perspectives of all regions concerned must, for practical reasons, necessarily remain fragmentary. Global history is understood in this periodization not in the sense of a complete and uniform assessment of changes in work in all parts of the world, but rather as a relational history that traces these changes from one particular regional perspective. In this way, transregional trade relations, commodity chains and labour migration reveal the outlines of a multi-level system as it evolves from the observer's specific location. This system spans (depending on context) so far outward that work in one place can only be understood in relation to work somewhere else. Workforces, households, companies and political regulatory agencies are all treated as actors in this analysis.

In our depiction of local and regional relations of exchange and trade, we prioritize the Central European standpoint. From here we develop European and global perspectives, as genuine multi-perspectivity would only be possible in cooperation with researchers contributing expertise from all parts of the globe. Approaching global history as a relational history from one standpoint is by no means a recent invention: most works of world and global history depart from a Western European or at least Western perspective, the key figures and development parameters of which are taken as the basis for gauging how other regions of the world measure up. This basis often serves to categorize other regions as backward, deviant, deficient or underdeveloped. Eurocentric universalism has been confronted in recent years by a multi-focal perspective, which takes seriously the authority and autonomy of the global South. However, the states and regions of Central and Eastern Europe, belonging to neither the West nor the South, are often forgotten in this attempt to balance the scales. Accordingly, this volume takes as its local frame Central Europe, comprising geographically the Holy Roman Empire, or Greater Germany and the Habsburg Monarchy, and the modern states which arose in their wake. Since the dynamic of European expansion shifted from the Mediterranean to the Atlantic in the seventeenth century, Central Europe has occupied a semi-peripheral role in the capitalist world system. It differs not only from the Western states and regions, but also from its geographically and historically linked neighbours in Eastern and Southern Europe. From the eastern colonization of the high Middle Ages to the European Union's more recent eastward expansion, a continuity of imperial and later supranational intervention extends from the German-speaking core into the neighbouring regions in the east, which also face Russia and, in a previous era, the Ottoman Empire on their own eastern flank.

The German-speaking regions of Central Europe differ from the rest of what is traditionally regarded as Western Europe in many respects. While the Western European great powers dominated world trade and overseas colonies, Central European expansion was restricted to the East and South. Many observers tend to overlook intra-European power and development differentials, not least because the middle of the continent was incorporated in the political West after the Second World War, and the Federal Republic of Germany soon rose to equal status among the leading states of the EU. Unanimously, these states participated in stylizing Europe as a paragon of economic development, political liberty and universal values, from which no one would want to be excluded. Whoever neglects to share or strive for these values is considered un-European, while Europe's handful of remaining overseas territories are viewed unproblematically as parts of their European mother countries. This volume seeks to make readers aware of these intra-European differences and commonalities, as a contribution to a broader conception of global relational history as such.

1.

Terms and Concepts

Work is a familiar, everyday word; everyone knows what it means. Upon closer inspection, however, work proves to be quite the linguistic chameleon: everyone has their own, nuanced definitions, which themselves are in constant flux. Older ideas continue to resonate even as new concepts of work emerge, leading to coexisting, distinct concepts of, as well as attitudes towards, work.

Fundamentally, this book deploys a broad conception of what constitutes work, addressing the wide spectrum of forms of work performed in households and families, for landlords and bosses, in one's own business or as wage labour for someone else.[1] Whether this work is paid or unpaid is another matter, as is the question whether said work can even be monetized in the first place. A large portion of socially necessary work, the work of giving birth and raising children, is simply priceless – even if individual tasks in this category have been transformed into forms of gainful employment. Compulsory labour (the feudal lord's corvée, for instance) or tribute offered to a landlord either necessitated, or was itself, a form of work. This work was not remunerated but instead extracted from subjects through coercive means rooted in the social differences of feudal societies.

Many factors dictate who does or does not do certain kinds of work in a given society. Every society assigns different tasks to men, women and children; to old and young; lords and peasants; the propertied and the propertyless; natives and newcomers; refugees and guests. We ought to be wary of viewing the division of labour that defines today's Western lifeworld in its Western and Central European manifestation as universal, mistakenly transferring it to previous eras or other regions of the world. How work is distributed and what is even considered work have always been subject to radical change and transformation, and it would be mistaken to exclude certain labour relations or working conditions a priori.

Our interest lies in the historical understandings of work as were characteristic of specific periods, regions, societies or social milieus. It turns out that what society considered work and rewarded as such was and remains subject to radical change over time. Much of what was previously or elsewhere considered work has since been removed from today's language in the global cores of the world economy. The concept of work that equates work with paid labour and dominates our way of speaking first emerged in the nineteenth and twentieth centuries in the developed industrial countries. Industrial society's entire economic and sociopolitical order was based on a definition of work as non-domestic, paid, legally codified, institutionalized and socially safeguarded employment.

In today's post-industrial transition, the promise of social and individual self-assurance through work and labour has been destabilized. The idea that work only connotes gainful employment no longer corresponds to the diversity of deregulated labour relations replacing the relatively fixed, coherent worker identities and biographies of wage labourers in the former industrial countries. This specific understanding of work should be considered the product of particular regional and historical circumstances.

This chapter addresses this specific notion of work's historical development, first tracing periods and turning points in European history before discussing the perspective's limitations, structured around two questions for each epoch:

1   What was and what was not considered work?
2   How were various occupations and tasks recognized and evaluated, in terms of what these activities produced and who performed them?

THE EUROCENTRIC GRAND NARRATIVE

In the classic, eight-volume *Historisches Lexikon zur politisch-sozialen Sprache in Deutschland*, historian Werner Conze provides a concise and pointed contextualization of work within historical development.[2] He begins with the disdain for work harboured by the ancient Greeks, contrasting it with the dual character that work acquired in the Judaeo-Christian tradition. This ambivalence between work as joy and burden was sidelined by the apologetics for progress espoused by capitalism's early theorists, who stylized work and labour as such as the source of all value, wealth and national growth. Critical voices began to decry reducing work to a commodity determined by cost, time, money and earnings at the turn of the eighteenth to the nineteenth century. A diverse variety of currents called for conservative Christian social reform, utopian socialism, or – perhaps most radically – socialist transformation of capitalist industry. Through observing a series of historical cross-sections, Conze works out the continuities which led to the overlapping of older and newer understandings of work irrespective of possible ruptures and breaks between them.

Conze's work is an apt and concise expression of the Eurocentric grand narrative that has shaped labour historiography since Max Weber's fundamental texts of the modern age, *The Protestant Ethic and the Spirit of Capitalism* and *Economy and Society*.[3] No researcher investigating historical conceptions of work can afford to ignore this narrative, given the massive body of literature adhering to this representation.[4] Cross-sectional studies also provide deeper insight into individual epochs, while objections to the narrative's monumentality, critical observations, and scholarly controversies tend to follow their specifications.[5] The following overview outlines the key elements generally found in this version of the story.

In the Greek *polis* (fourth century BCE), manual and paid labour were treated with disdain. This attitude applied to both the arduous tasks (*pónos*) necessary for survival carried out in the domestic unit of life and production, and the *oikos* (the stem of the word 'economy') of peasants, day labourers and slaves. Women's work generally fell into this category, but received no specific mention. The work of unpropertied freemen as artisans or merchants was also disdained, although the manual craftsmanship or skill (*érgon*) necessary to manufacture their products ensured their work a better reputation. The next ranks in the feudal hierarchy were occupied by various businesses and arts which were not regarded as work in the true sense. Free citizens distinguished themselves by the fact that they neither worked nor engaged in business, but rather dedicated themselves to education and taking part in political life. This far worthier activity was called *praxis*. The ideal, however, was only reachable with slaves and other unfree household members around to ensure personal livelihoods and public infrastructure more generally. Slaves were viewed as tools, relegated to their fate by their natural limitations. The wives of free men and free citizens were regarded as people rather than mere tools, albeit people whose responsibility for lesser duties resulted from their natural condition.

The writings of the Greek philosophers handed down a social and value system for posterity, forming the basis of physical labour's negative connotation and social contempt of all that had to do with domestic activity – also in terms of the words which would later influence how language around work developed. According to the aforementioned philosophers, the negative sides of economic life extended to chrematistics, i.e. profit-making business, which was contrasted to the household subsistence economy. This contrast between *oikonomia* and chrematistics is also reflected in the differing attitudes towards money, which clearly have their origin in the social differentiation of the *polis* and the need to finance wars and foreign trade, leading to the emergence of the concepts of use value and exchange value. Today, it is difficult to understand how a positive reference to the self-sufficient household could coexist alongside such disdain for the necessary activities performed by slaves and women. The debate concerning the legitimacy of profit and accumulating money clearly shows that the *oikos* lacked the cohesion often attributed to it by ideology.

The Roman Empire inherited many Greek concepts and ideas. Labour (*labor*) out of pure necessity (*necessitas*) contrasted with the noble arts (*artes liberales*) based on the honour (*honor*) and prudence (*prudentia*) of the free man. Unlike the Greek *polis*, the epitome of worthy activity shifted from community service to private activities. Open disdain for work faded, albeit not entirely. Free men's agricultural labour in the Roman peasant tradition was spared the contempt generally associated with work. Skilled crafts which produced finished works (*opus*) rose in social esteem as well. Judaeo-Christian notions of work, which began to emerge in the first century under the Roman Empire, ultimately broke with the ancient view. Basing itself on *pónos* (Greek) and *labor* (Latin), work was again understood as suffering and hardship which people had to bear, constituting a form of heavenly punishment as part of their 'expulsion from Paradise'. On the other hand, however, work was also anointed with God's blessing, and every form thereof – regardless of activity or social rank – was thus transformed into a service to God. Western and Central European feudal society was split into the functional divisions of clerics (*oratores*), knights (*bellatores*), and labourers (*laboratores*), in which all social groups obtained dignity through work equally. Initially, only peasants were considered *laboratores*, but artisans and intellectuals came to be regarded as such as well over the course of ongoing social differentiation. From this idea came the notion of the 'third estate', which supports society through its work, and which later on will call the entire order into question. Thus notions of work and labour were wrested from contempt and turned into virtues (*virtus*), while productive creativity is reflected in the production of an individual work (*opus*). This demonstrates how work was given the dual character of painstaking burden overlaid with creative achievement, a characterization that would last until the economization of the eighteenth century.

In the Middle Ages, the combination of *ora et labora* ensured that heavy, unpaid or poorly paid labour was positively connoted in the divine order of things. Medieval monasteries relied on the Christian work ethic and developed the monastic economy based on monks, laypeople and peasant subjects motivated by Christianity into a highly effective economic unit. In fact, idleness (*otiositas*) was now treated as a vice, only tolerated among those unable to perform any kind of work whatsoever.

The scholasticist philosophy of St Thomas Aquinas, on the other hand, drew on Aristotle by placing the tranquillity of a *vita contemplativa* above the *vita activa*, the 'active life'. Mendicant orders, whose members lived off the alms that active citizens donated to compensate for their lack of godly devotion, were thus considered a legitimate way of life. Withdrawing from a life of work was no sin, as long as one's *otium* – a Latin term denoting a form of leisure or free time – was tied to divine service.

Artisanal labour received a heightened degree of social appreciation with the emergence of craftsmen and merchant guilds in the medieval towns of the twelfth and thirteenth centuries, derived not from toil and pain or prayerful transcendence but from a calling to a profession. Another step towards the recognition of a work ethic came with the urbanization and commercialization of society characteristic of early capitalism. Whether the Reformation was a driver or rather an expression of socio-economic upheaval is a key distinction between idealist and materialist approaches to historical change. Regardless, in terms of popular understandings of work, its result was that doing nothing – whether the parasitic life of the nobility and clergy or the poor begging for alms – was denounced as sinful idleness. This shift can be understood as the beginning of a work-centred society, in which the diverse activities of all of its members are increasingly obliged to take on the traits of active production and strenuous exertion. With technical specialization arose a demand for quality, which also made prior training a prerequisite to pursuing a profession.

Thus the Judaeo-Christian idea of work, a Janus-faced juxtaposition of burden and fulfilment, continued to be upheld under Protestantism, and was only overcome with the philosophy of the Enlightenment, which accompanied capitalist transition. Work's dual nature was relieved of its connection to toil and burden under this new conception. The Scientific Revolution of the sixteenth and seventeenth centuries understood work, labour and technology as the conditions by which man subordinated nature, while both untapped regions of the world and women and indigenous populations were subsumed as part of this nature. Relevant virtues in the pursuit of happiness were diligence, commitment and industriousness. The toilsome character of painful and laborious work associated with religious obligations thus faded into the background, confronted by a secular understanding of work liberated from its dual character. The Judaeo-Christian ideal of toilsome effort continued to resonate in terms of self-image and common parlance in everyday life as *ora et labora*, but work was now freed of ambiguities in the philosophy of utilitarianism and its national economic implementation, mercantilism. Work now made the worker 'happy' and 'free'.

Conze considers the transition to capitalism, termed 'economization' (*Ökonomisierung*) in the language of eighteenth-century scholars, to be the decisive break in the history of work. 'In the future, work would be assessed as productive activity, basically all activities falling under this definition were designated as "work" and measured by their economic effect.'[6] Work now became a factor of production. Rather than merely sustain one's existence, work was to create and accumulate capital. The science of work began as a lesson in happiness. The principle of capital accumulation was, according to German economist Johann August Schlettwein, that '[t]he amount of enjoyable things ... must be multiplied incessantly ... the happier the whole society will be ... procure and reproduce these materials for the people's happiness ... distribute, transform and process, and redistribute the processed; these are the two great operations confecting human society's happiness.'[7] Adam Smith identified work as the real source of wealth in *An Inquiry into the Nature and Causes of the Wealth of Nations* (1776), underlying all value and serving as the true measure of exchange value for all goods.[8] The fallacy that only views work in basic industry, processing and distribution as 'productive', while considering all other services 'unproductive' (i.e. they 'seldom leave any trace or value behind them, for which an equal quantity of service could afterwards be procured'), did no harm to how the concept of work was remoulded; in fact, it was later corrected to incorporate the tertiary sector into value-adding activities.

David Ricardo took up Smith's conception of work and made it the basis for his theory of value. Work became the sole factor of production, as the combination of 'living labour' with work previously carried out (often referred to as materialized labour) that came to bear as capital: 'The value of a commodity, or the quantity of any other commodity for which it will exchange, depends on the relative quantity of labour which is necessary for its production, and not on the greater or less compensation which is paid for that labour.'[9] This resulted in the 'natural' price of a commodity, emerging both from the conflict of interest between wages and profits and from the supply of and demand for labour power, ultimately determining market prices and market wages. As neutral forces of production, value-creating labour was decoupled from both its social environment and its religious–ethical connotation, trapped in a Judaeo-Christian understanding of 'virtue through toil'. To free up additional labour power, restrictions on free movement and non-economic access to servile labour were gradually rolled back. Work was the source of growth, its connection to the national economy the key to growing the gross national product, and the more growth the better. Organizational, legal and technological measures were deployed to maximize the exploitation of labour. The virtuous dichotomy of toil and fulfilment in artisanry (i.e. the work process in conjunction with that work's final product) was replaced by an optimistic faith in growth and progress that continues to animate capitalism even today.

The economization of work in the liberal world view, which understood freedom and liberty as independent from social responsibility, did not occur without the emergence of opposition and alternative models, most of which were inspired by the experience of industrial work in the early factories of nineteenth-century capitalism where limitations on the exploitation of labour were practically non-existent.

The reservations of the ancient and Judaeo-Christian traditions lived on and thrived in the era of industrial capitalism, despite work's absolutization as the source of progress. These constituted the foundation of a conservative critique of industrial work, rooted in notions of feudal–patriarchal responsibility for workers and an artisan–guild relation to manual labour, as formulated by Friedrich von Schlegel (1772–1829) or Novalis (1772–1801) and well received by Russian authors. The conservative critique found philosophical expression in Romanticism, which was particularly prevalent as an intellectual current in the European regions not counted among the pioneers of industrialization. These conservative currents relied on the ideals of feudal hierarchy, the self-reliance of small producers to provide for their own basic needs, and sociopolitical reforms in place of revolution.[10]

The same classical and Judaeo-Christian traditions, however, would also form the basis of early socialist ideas, which began to grow into a political programme in their own right during and after the French Revolution. Not social rank and property, but rather work and need alone entitled citizens to take part in the happiness and prosperity of society. There are, of course, immense differences between the sociopolitical utopias of Gracchus Babeuf, Henri de Saint-Simon, Robert Owen, Charles Fourier, Louis Blanc and others – not to mention their practical implementation in various social, cooperative and communitarian industrial, residential and housing projects.[11] Common to all of them, however, was the centrality of work in their conceptions, which was divided up among the members of the community and thought to constitute the foundation for the exchange of commodities as well as the precondition to benefiting from the collective's prosperity. Despite their radical criticism of exploitation, they shared the economists' euphoric understanding of work and the euphoric view of progress this entailed, but linked it with the ideal of equality: 'Man stops exploiting his fellow man; but in association with others, he is exploiting the world and subjecting it to his power.'[12]

Georg Wilhelm Friedrich Hegel transferred the tension between work as burden and as joy to the dialectic of alienation and emancipation, thereby forming an analytical basis with which to grasp the estrangement (*Entäußerung*) associated with slavery and exploitation.[13] Hegel assumed that only through work could individuals achieve actualization, inhibited by servitude and serfdom. Estrangement and alienation inevitably generated desires on the part of the worker or servant (*Knecht*) to overcome dependency and exploitation.

Karl Marx followed Hegel, borrowing the Hegelian dichotomy of alienation and actualization for his *Economic and Philosophical Manuscripts* but shifting his reasoning from the idealist to a materialist level. Marx sought to do away with the alienation characteristic of work in capitalism and replace it with an association of free individuals in which active work led people to develop and discover their own capacities (actualization). Unlike conservative and early socialist thinkers, Marx did not call for a return to the modesty of the old guild hierarchies, but rather for the socialization of modern industry and technology. Despite sharing the early socialists' vision of social equality and rejection of private ownership of the means of production, Marx relied on liberal economism in his understanding of development: in his view, only technological development driven by the expectation of future profits decoupled work from traditional restrictions and, in the form of modern industry, instigated growth dynamics in the forces of production which would eventually come into conflict with the relations of production. One way out of this conflict was to overcome liberal-capitalist private property and build a free, socialist society in its place.

Despite the highly divergent social and political points of reference and aims separating liberals, conservatives and utopian and Marxist socialists, they shared a conception of work linked to commodity production, value creation and exchange value. This view did not necessarily mean that activities necessary for immediate survival, such as domestic and subsistence work, were not seen and acknowledged. However, they were generally regarded as a part of nature, supposedly a natural property of women in the ideology of the bourgeois family, or, on the other hand, as exceptions and relics of pre-capitalist modes of production and living, which would pass from the natural world into the economic sphere through either commodification (liberals) or socialization (socialists). As for exceptions to this rule, Charles Fourier can be singled out for advocating free love, a division of housework, and equal participation of women in the labour market and public life in his *La nouveau monde amoureux* (written around 1820, first published in 1967) or *La fausse industrie*.

Anchoring this new form of work in the minds and language of the population required a radical change in lifestyle. Urbanization, industrialization and proletarianization separated more and more people from their means of production: at the turn of the nineteenth to the twentieth century, wage labour and gainful employment became the central sources of survival, personal identity and social mobility in industrialized countries. Legal, administrative and scientific measures helped to bolster this notion of work. This flattening of the concept also affected unproletarianized populations and those living in regions where factory-based industry had not, or had only partially, taken hold. Maintaining stable gainful employment also came to be considered a primary component of social security, particularly when jobs became scarce at certain times and in certain regions. Labour organizations' calls for job creation and full employment further reflected the conflation of work with gainful employment characteristic of industrial society. When women's movements denounced exclusion from or discrimination within the workplace and called for full inclusion, they also contributed to the consolidation of the new concept of work. The same is true of national-liberation movements and independent, post-colonial governments, which promptly adopted the notions of work inherited from their former oppressors in their efforts to accelerate development.

LIMITS OF THE EUROCENTRIC NARRATIVE

This is, in short, the Eurocentric telling of the story of work to the present day. First introduced by the Industrial Revolution at the beginning of the eighteenth century and bolstered through scientific and legal codification one century later, this was now a work-centred society in which identity was determined in equal measure by the glorification of work and occupation as a source of status and income, and by the simultaneous exclusion of all non-commoditized forms from the very concept of work. This division justified excluding non-value-adding labour from the history of work almost entirely.

Of course, the rigour and conclusions of this grand narrative were repeatedly called into question, giving rise to scholarly controversies and alternative conceptions. Recent studies contradict the idea that antiquity knew no purposeful, rational economic behaviour, that medieval monastic communities only pursued virtuous worship rather than profit, and that the conception of work as laborious activity which only becomes worthy through God's grace survived the economic praises of 'finding happiness in work' to the present day.[14] The intellectual history underlying the narrative also changed in light of empirical social-scientific studies, which brought forth new evidence by outlining specific working conditions and labour relations beyond the dominant lines of interpretation.[15]

Fundamental objections have been raised to the linearity and inevitable purposefulness (teleology) with which these developments are portrayed, as well as to a general failure to integrate spatial and temporal dimensions.[16] The scheme's linear sequence from antiquity to modern conceptions obscures the diversity of actually coexisting alternatives, countertendencies, labour relations and discourses at each historical juncture, obscuring some aspects entirely. The exclusive focus on Europe as the global core can only be interpreted to the effect that the European example was considered groundbreaking, universally valid and therefore upheld as a model and benchmark for other regions of the world, as explicitly postulated by philosophy and history since the European Enlightenment. Friedrich Schiller devoted the inaugural speech of his professorship in Jena to the question 'What Is, and to What End Do We Study, Universal History?' (1789). Hegel saw the European nations as the embodiment of the 'world spirit', the objective spirit of world history. In these philosophers' perspective, non-European peoples were characterized as children: 'tribes which surround us at the most diverse levels of culture, like children of different ages gathered around an adult, reminding him by their example of what he used to be, and where he started from.'[17]

No regionalization of ideal types was carried out in the European narrative. Without explanation, the narrative travels from ancient Athens through Rome to medieval Italy, France and Central Europe, before migrating to North-Western Europe in the early modern period without addressing the shift in economic and intellectual centres and regional inequality that prevented peripheral regions from developing themselves along the lines of the core's model. The respective core appears *pars pro toto*. Northern, Eastern and South-Eastern Europe and the Celtic fringes do not appear at all. Interactions between European and non-European regions – such as influences on Europe from the Islamic world, the Crusades, European expansion, proselytization and colonialism – are absent. Another objection concerns the priorities set in perceiving the ancient, medieval and early modern periods mostly through cultural-historical perspectives and intellectual histories, while economic discourse only emerges with the capitalist revolution and the rise of national economies.

This reflects another myth, namely that the transition to a rational, secular world view was a genuinely European invention. Instrumentally rational and thus predictable economic activity, the bedrock of modern capitalist enterprise, constitutes the link between the Enlightenment myth and that of free labour's Western triumph.

The general understanding of work was only destabilized in the last quarter of the twentieth century, as digitalization and the relocation of industrial mass production to developing countries began to threaten the widespread job security first eroded by the world wars but ultimately reaffirmed during post-war reconstruction. Changes in the working environment associated with deregulation of labour laws in the old industrialized countries and the reorganization of global commodity chains are no longer compatible with the old concept of work. Underpaid labour and deregulated labour relations are also on the rise in the old industrialized countries, to the extent that these forms of work can no longer be viewed as relics or exceptions from what became standard notions of employment. The concept of work began to open up: while the organized labour movement, oriented towards past achievements, lamented the loss of jobs through rationalization and outsourcing and demanded more 'work' through state-led job creation, an ongoing discussion since the 1980s sought to theorize how work could be freed from its economistic corset, recognized in its diversity, and distributed fairly.

NARRATING 'WORK' AGAINST THE GRAIN: THE FEMINIST PERSPECTIVE

Unpaid labour – whether domestic and subsistence work or social and political activity – played no role in the work discourse of industrializing European countries, installing in the minds of proponents and critics alike the notion that only activities which created products for sale on the market could be considered value-creating work. Although the transition was relatively smooth and older notions of work persisted in its wake, the eighteenth century can nevertheless be identified as a key historical break. One hundred years earlier, a separation between productive and reproductive or paid and unpaid work, or between work for one's own use and work for sale on the market, simply would not have made sense. In the context of the household economies of feudal estates, peasant farms and artisanal crafts, all of these activities were united under one roof, delegated according to status, gender and age, into a form often termed *das ganze Haus* in German social science.[18] In smaller households without land (or smallholders and so on), temporary or even permanent wage labour outside the home was taken on to supplement family income. All of this was considered work. Household members formed a life, work and care collective, structured around a status hierarchy. This orientation towards subsistence was not conducive to the economic growth demanded by the mercantilist rulers and capitalist entrepreneurs of the eighteenth century, who in turn managed to break apart the household unit in its various spheres by pressing forward and obtaining legal exemptions for their actions, all with the support and backing of state authorities. As a result, work was detached from one's place of residence, wage labour was removed from social security in a general sense, and market- and trade-oriented activities were decoupled from anything that fostered self-sufficiency and reproduction. The latter was transferred from the economic sphere ('outside the home') into the family ('domestic'), denied its working character, naturalized, and gendered, assigned to women due to their sex.[19] This conflation of the female gender with care work in the family, formulated in the context of a family ideology, imposed upon women sole responsibility for the entire household. Women's work in the family was no longer considered work. The gainfully employed male individual was deemed the 'breadwinner', while women's wage labour – still crucial to the survival of many families – was denigrated as 'extra income' and paid accordingly less.[20]

Work would henceforth be understood as a targeted, market-oriented, remunerated activity, excluding occasional and needs-based, non-remunerated activities. A sharp distinction was drawn between work and non-work – one that did not correspond with the overlaps and combinations of labour relations and working conditions in most people's lives. This distinction was gendered insofar as unpaid household and family work was considered inherently female. Thus regions where subsistence work continued to play a central role for the survival of entire countries were included in the gender stereotype, despite both women's and men's active involvement in unpaid work there. In the 1980s, some feminist authors pioneered the somewhat cumbersome 'housewife-ization' to describe this transfer, seeking to draw attention to the fact that, according to the housewife model, unpaid work, regardless of where it was carried out, was excluded from recognition and approval as a value-creating, worthy economic contribution, while simultaneously being utilized in terms of support and care for gainfully employed workers.[21]

NARRATING 'WORK' AGAINST THE GRAIN:
THE GLOBAL-HISTORY PERSPECTIVE

This particular discussion around a new, less productivist and employment-oriented understanding of work concentrates on the old, Western industrialized countries, where the narrowing down of work as gainful employment began its universalizing rise in the nineteenth century. In the emerging markets of the 'Third World', which witnessed a massive expansion of wage labour relations through the relocation of industrial mass production over the closing third of the twentieth century, an increasingly proletarian self-image has emerged which fights to improve working conditions within wage labour relations. While many in the old centres tend to indulge in the conceptual certainty that the transition to a global, post-industrial, knowledge-based society constitutes a universal reality generating new identities beyond (gainful) employment, the erstwhile Eurocentric conception of work is actually experiencing a major comeback in the newly industrialized countries.

The growing economic weight and self-confidence of non-European industrialized countries has stimulated curiosity in discovering their own economic and cultural traditions, which in turn connects to global history's scholarly mission to observe and study all regions and cultures equally, beyond Eurocentric biases. In this sense, the history of work as a concept must also be considered outside antiquity and the Judaeo-Christian tradition, although this perspective was globally determinant in the form of European expansion and ultimately adopted by pro-modernization elites across the non-European world. Global historical insights on the history of work are increasingly emerging in anthropology, global economic and social history, and the history of religion.

Insight into regional belief systems and practices can be gained from the various narrative traditions of indigenous peoples: knowledge of the respective cultures and languages obtained by regional cultural studies and social anthropologists are the only avenue for Western observers to observe or understand these traditions. Western colonial attributions formed by local elites and Western scholars have overshadowed and reshaped local memories, standing in the way of unprejudiced, unbiased understanding. Post-colonial approaches seek to theoretically deconstruct these attributions – also referred to as orientalization or orientalism[22] – and are reflected in discourse around 'developmental deficits'.

Anthropological field research can provide valuable clues for reconstructing indigenous traditions. Although their sheer diversity places them outside the scope of this book, they demonstrate that indigenous languages knew no generalized concept of work. Instead, specific names were developed for activities like hunting, farming, fishing or preparing food, as well as for the products of these activities and social practices and religious rituals, often in conjunction with the status accorded to an activity in the social hierarchy or family, or according to phases in one's life cycle. No generalized term separated gainful and market-oriented activities from others necessary for survival or subsumed them under an abstract concept of work.[23] Where a concept of work did in fact exist beyond specific tasks, it referred to the most difficult and harshest survival activities.[24] A general, market-oriented concept of work only appeared with colonial rule, or in the course of catch-up modernization efforts based on the Western model. The term was often inherited from the colonial language, either used as such, adopted or retranslated as a loan word into the native language. A generalized, Western-style conception of work allowed for the subsumption of various activities into one abstract category. On the other hand, this generalization of gainful, market-oriented activities entirely excluded from the definition of work everything that did not fit. The reciprocal, the immediate and the gratuitous were pushed out of the economic sphere, devalued and banned from economic statistics so that their continued existence went unnoticed, and could be absorbed by the dominant modes of production and perception.

This process of devaluation was not confined to indigenous, non-European cultures. It occurred during the transition from pre-industrial agrarian society to industrial capitalism in European societies as well, but was marginalized and largely forgotten by the pro-market-economy mainstream. The knowledge gained from post-colonial and anthropological counterreadings of colonial history provides an essential instrument for reconstructing these displaced European traditions.

Global history, which in the face of rapid globalization began to reject national-historical explanations in the 1980s, does not limit itself to contemporary problems. It began a renewed analysis and examination of human history from a new perspective, committed to avoiding the mistakes of Old World history, which largely took inherent European superiority and leadership as its point of analytical departure. In terms of work, all Eurocentric assumptions of wage labour's linear establishment over the course of capitalist transformation and modernization of working conditions and labour relations had to be abandoned: slavery, forced labour and subsistence work proved to be fundamental constants – these were not abolished through incorporation into the global capitalist economy, but rather persisted or combined with other forms of paid employment. Global economic and social history,[25] world-systems analysis,[26] studies of formalization and informalization,[27] of commodity and supply chains,[28] global migration[29] – all of these and many others are specifically dedicated to various forms and combinations of forms of work over the course of cyclical changes and regional reconfigurations within global capitalism. The International Institute of Social History (IISH) in Amsterdam, whose publishing and research programme has focused on global labour history since the year 2000, emerged as a particularly fertile centre for study and education,[30] developing into a network of global research initiatives on the history of work under research directors Jan Lucassen and Marcel van der Linden.

The inertia of the Eurocentric master narrative and its concepts, however, cannot be overcome through new social-scientific approaches alone. As with Christianity and Judaism, Hinduism, Buddhism, Confucianism and Islam also provide ethical foundations upon which people assess their various everyday tasks, ascribe them meaning and fit them into their lives. Throughout history, local belief systems have been influenced in different ways by overlaps of religious proselytization and foreign colonial rule, so that, in practice, hybrids and syncretisms are more the rule than the exception. Although our investigation is guided by the same fundamental questions determining the Eurocentric master narrative, we also remain open to the obstinacy (*Eigensinn*) of other cultures and seek to listen to points of view which may in turn offer new insights into European social relations as well. That such a comparative and interactive approach will take changes in tasks, technologies and economic sectors into account, as well as shifts in status and caste relations regarding social identities, can only be hinted at here.[31] Necessary prerequisites for this undertaking are sociological and historical studies of religion that comparatively analyse the changing concepts and attitudes towards work. In a next step, these must be placed in relation to colonial interventions and deformations, but also formation through European world views and oppositional countertendencies. Only then can the socio-economic transformations of the world of work be explored in the context of global economic and social history, freed from the conceptual and ideological ballast imposed upon the concept of work and the role of work for the meaning of life in the ancient world, Judaism and Christianity.

2.

Work Discourses

For most people, work is a daily reality. But work is more than that – work is also the subject of countless moral and political projections: why we work, how we work, how much we work, who works on what, and who does not work at all. Work constitutes a central discursive field, confronting individuals with diverse demands, and different sociopolitical concepts with one another. Work discourses have accompanied humanity throughout history, present in all religions, philosophies and ideologies.

In the world of sociopolitical concepts, notions of work as the basis of self-actualization stand diametrically opposed to notions of freeing humanity from the compulsion to work (as far as possible, of course). Upon closer inspection, however, these only *appear* as opposites, for in many cases critique of work and praise of work are merely two ways of addressing both the dual nature and divergent experiences thereof in everyday life. Therefore, the most common discourses can be attributed to a third variant, one that strives to change our human and social praxis, transforming the toil and burden of work into creativity and satisfaction. In the following, we look at each of the three ways of viewing work – overcoming, idealization and transformation – and provide examples from different epochs and contexts.

OVERCOMING WORK

If, as in the ancient Greek view, work is a burden, then clearly free citizens must avoid contact with it. The privileging of the *vita contemplativa* over the *vita activa* in the monasteries and nunneries of various religious communities grants freedom from laborious work for only a select few, however. It is far from a sociopolitical utopia, as laborious work can never be overcome, only displaced onto another group of people, who – due to their nature as women, barbarians, strangers, slaves of the *polis* or lay-people – are not subject to the same standards. This form of overcoming work through displacement runs through human history to the present day, but the specific action of making others work for oneself is restricted to individuals in specific contexts, and is accordingly excluded from the following analysis of work discourses.

Overcoming work for all generally manifests in one of two forms – 'wanting to have everything' versus 'not needing anything' – thus linking work to human needs in a fundamental way. 'Wanting to have everything' without working lies at the heart of all utopian dreams. These visions of paradise are inspired by religious themes, where fruit hangs ripe for the picking and roast pigeons fly straight into the mouths of the sloth-ful. Because they have nothing to do with contemporary life, they are transposed into the afterlife or to distant continents. Nevertheless, fairy tales and reports of trips to lands of milk and honey nourish hopes that chance, happiness, a handsome prince or a lucky number at the lottery might yet grant a personal paradise in one's lifetime.

The antithesis of this vision of milk and honey is the ascetic notion that paradise is not the land of abundance, but rather of frugality. Through ritual practices such as meditation, fasting or dancing, one pursues a state in which liberation from work is achieved through freedom from human needs and desires. In this light, it is more understandable why Arcadia, a rough karst landscape in the Peloponnese, became a byword for the carefree life.

The hedonistic utopia where laziness is the highest virtue and dili-gence the worst vice runs through history as a distinct literary genre,[1] which calls for paradise in the here and now in defiance of the church's moralistic appeals to work and the emergence of social discipline through labour during the industrial age. A notable protagonist of this current was Paul Lafargue, Karl Marx's son-in-law, whose *The Right to Be Lazy* (1883) formulated a critique of how Marx defined the human essence through work. Instead of the right to work as demanded in the *Com-munist Manifesto* (1848), Lafargue argued for a law that 'wisely regulated and limited [work] to a maximum of three hours a day', praising idleness with the lines: 'Oh Laziness, mother of the arts and noble virtues, be thou the balm of human anguish!'[2] Lafargue tied his call for a radical reduc-tion of working time to the maxim 'work and frugality', thus in close proximity to the ascetic version of utopia that removed suffering from work by restricting human needs.

Lafargue is often depicted as an opponent of Marx's theory of human actualization through labour. It is worth keeping in mind, however, that Lafargue in fact defended Marxist positions against utopian socialists and anarchists in the First International.[3] Marx's comments on work were highly contradictory over the course of his life, and can be associated not only with the emancipation of labour itself, but also with liberation from the compulsion to work in general. Thus, his vision of a communist society was perhaps not so far from his son-in-law's more utopian ideas after all.

While Lafargue's appeal went largely unheard in the nineteenth century, anti-consumerism played a central role in the new social movements of the twentieth century, as various alternative movements in the developed industrial countries which rejected the disciplinary nature of work and consumer society in the 1970s related to Lafargue's spurning of consumption, questioning the need for the level of gainful employment typical of that period. The Tunix Congress (from the German *tu' nichts*, or 'do nothing'), organized by the German Sponti movement together with other alternative groups at the Technical University of Berlin in January 1978, endowed the right to be lazy with a theoretical foundation. American pop singer Janis Joplin gave musical expression to the zeitgeist with her song 'Me and Bobby McGee' (1970), which posthumously rose to the top of the charts, proclaiming, 'Freedom's just another word for nothing left to lose.' The anti-work and anti-consumerist attitudes prevalent among the hippies and dropouts of the 1970s and 1980s forged a link between the ascetic and hedonistic outlooks in response to the rampant consumerism and orientation towards bolstering workers' purchasing power characteristic of the labour movement at that time. The environmental movement emerging shortly thereafter argued that 'less' consumption meant 'more' quality of life, and called for an alternative to capitalist society's growth imperative. The idea that two or three hours of daily work were sufficient to ensure survival rested on anthropologists' findings concerning 'the good life' as conceived by traditional indigenous societies. The thinking went as follows: if we cease to perform work that creates value for the capitalists and pay taxes for social projects we deem unnecessary, nothing will stand in the way of radically reducing working time.[4] The employment-oriented conception of work and the prices of raw materials and consumer goods available in developed industrial countries due to the unequal global division of labour, however, remained unquestioned. Criticisms from the Third World solidarity movement linked the critique of consumerism with criticism of global structures of exploitation, exposing the three-hour model as highly Eurocentric. The political objective of reducing working times could no longer be upheld once unpaid and underpaid caring and volunteering work beyond employment in industrialized countries was taken into account. As a battle cry against the amount of time spent working in paid employment, however, it retained a certain political explosiveness beyond Social-Democratic and Communist models for some time. In terms of real political significance, on the other hand, it had practically no impact.

IN PRAISE OF WORK

Anthems praising labour have been sung by all kinds of ideological and spiritual currents. In the Jewish, Christian and Islamic faiths, this cursed punishment could be transformed into a blessing from God, who turned love of work into a commandment: *ora et labora*. Tension arose from the fact that the clergy and nobility failed to comply with the call they directed towards the rest of society, prompting religious reform movements to advocate general industriousness. Calvinism was probably the most radical expression of this linkage between salvation and industriousness.

The professional ethos of the guilds also contributed to craftsmen's positive identification with their work as cities began to blossom in the Middle Ages. Artisans and merchants were allowed to participate in city politics based on their occupational status, in turn fostering a moral revaluation of work. The conception of work favoured by artisanry shifted its focus towards productive manufacturing, seen as the source of social order and value creation in the mercantilist state of the seventeenth and eighteenth centuries.

An understanding of productive work rooted in a triangular constellation of man–tool–nature thus emerged, in which fulfilment and satisfaction were seen as processes in which humans used their skills and actions with tools to shape raw materials prepared by nature, drawing their self-image and personal affirmation from this exchange. In the 1970s, feminists criticized the head–hand–builder model – cemented as an anthropological constant in the popular conception of humanity during the Enlightenment – for not taking women's care work into account.[5]

The positive conception of fulfilment through work, which had a pronounced effect on ideas in the ages of craftsmanship, manufacturing and industry, was characterized by specific work processes usually occupied by men. Apologists for the capitalist market economy saw actualization realized in every form of employment measured by its value creation, while showing little concern for the satisfaction of the individual worker. Ultimately, they argued, the woe and toil of laborious work would be mitigated by more sophisticated divisions of labour and mechanization.

Critics who insisted on discussing labour exploitation and structural income inequality between workers and capitalists clung to these same notions of fulfilment, but saw private ownership of the means of production; compulsion for workers to externalize (i.e. sell) their labour power; downward pressures on speed, time and wages; and a lack of influence on work processes and products as obstacles to actualization for all wage labourers. They sought to change working conditions, and thus bring to bear individual self-actualization in the process of manipulating nature with their heads, hands and tools.

At this point, work discourses based on the praise of work merged with transformational discourses seeking to enable this kind of fulfilment through work by changing the social order itself.

Karl Marx's 1844 *Economic and Philosophical Manuscripts* was a pioneering text in terms of praising work, arguing that it determined the very nature of human beings: 'the *whole of what is called world history* is nothing more than the creation of man through human labour'.[6] His concept of alienation begins with the externalization of labour power, which prevents workers from achieving actualization in the work process under conditions of wage labour carried out for a capitalist. His communist utopia was a social order facilitating individual self-actualization through work, polemicizing expressly against the idea that 'freedom and happiness' presupposed emancipation from the need to work.[7] When juxtaposing the 'realm of necessity' with the 'realm of freedom', he did not have an existence free of work in mind, but instead stressed the need for 'time for the full development of the individual, which, as the greatest productive power, itself, influences the productive power of labour'.[8] 'Necessity' and 'freedom' were thus interrelated, in that freedom is found in necessity, while necessity, in turn, is found in freedom.

That said, Marx's texts also permit a different reading:

> For as soon as the division of labour comes into being, each man has a particular, exclusive sphere of activity, which is forced upon him and from which he cannot escape. He is a hunter, a fisherman, a shepherd, or a critical critic, and must remain so if he does not want to lose his means of livelihood; whereas in communist society, where nobody has one exclusive sphere of activity but each can become accomplished in any branch he wishes, society regulates the general production and thus makes it possible for me to do one thing today and another tomorrow, to hunt in the morning, fish in the afternoon, rear cattle in the evening, criticise after dinner, just as I have a mind, without ever becoming hunter, fisherman, shepherd or critic.[9]

The third volume of *Capital* (posthumously published by Friedrich Engels in 1894) seems to contradict the theory of self-actualization through work informing the *Economic and Philosophical Manuscripts*: 'The realm of freedom really begins only where labour determined by necessity and external expediency ends; it lies by its very nature beyond the sphere of material production proper.'[10]

Ultimately, this question will probably never be resolved, as Marx was a wide-ranging author open to multiple interpretations. From an anthropological perspective, he understood human labour as an essential component of the human essence, and viewed the alienation inherent in capitalist property relations as an obstacle to actualization. A socialist society, by contrast, ought to create the appropriate conditions for it to develop fully. Here, Marx endorsed industrial society's general faith in historical progress, as his realm of necessity built on the achievements of the productive forces amassed under developed capitalism, described as 'one of the civilizing aspects of capital'.[11] Marx assumed that socialized machinery would provide 'the social process of production in general', on the basis of which self-determined activity could develop, in only several hours. Regardless of one's perspective – man or woman, worker or capitalist – the manifold forms of laborious and time-consuming care activities which require constant dedication were simply ignored in these considerations.

Another variant of praise for work emerged in forced-labour institutions, where the *ora et labora* of medieval monasteries was transformed from a path to salvation into an instrument of social discipline in the interests of state and capital. This perspective can be found in the eighteenth-century workhouses, the deportations of prisoners to labour camps, and, later on, the penal work camps of the Soviet Union and the People's Republic of China. A further perversion of this praise is evident in the slogan the Nazis welded above the gates of their concentration camps: *Arbeit macht frei* ('Work will set you free'). In this sense, the extermination of entire populations through work exposes the glorification in expending labour in the process of capital accumulation from its most cynical side.

THE TRANSFORMATION OF WORK

The transformation of work, which seeks to remodel toilsome effort into creativity and alienation into self-actualization, began in the second half of the nineteenth century with social reforms, organized labour and women's movements. Although objectives and methods differed depending on sociopolitical orientation, many concepts oscillated between notions of self-determined work requiring emancipation from capitalist constraints, and liberation from work in general. The means and measures for implementing such objectives varied across a range of more or less far-reaching reforms to existing conditions, all the way to revolutionary transformation.

Steps towards actualization through work are associated with technology, education, property ownership and women's liberation. These emancipatory concepts are counterposed by ideas that rethink the nature of work and progress in a more fundamental way.

Technological advance has played a role in the modern conception of work from the outset. The necessary intellectual framework was forged in the philosophy of the Enlightenment, the material basis in the Scientific Revolution of the seventeenth century. Technologies (*artes*) were to substantially lighten the overall workload. The conviction that technology would free humanity from laborious, mind-numbing toil united liberals and socialists, while conservative utopias often contrasted the factory system with fantasies of renewed forms of artisanry as had existed in the guild hierarchies. While liberals regarded technology as a form of emancipation within the capitalist system, socialist critics pointed to the character of the 'capitalist machinery', which intensified exploitation, control, and dependence. Technology would only unlock its liberating character when relations of power and property ceased to hinder the development of human creativity.

A second way of transforming painstaking work into creative activity was tied to education. The eighteenth-century workhouse was based on skills training with the goal of inculcating people with the values of industriousness, diligence and orderliness. Nineteenth-century education reformers, however, relied on inclination, interest and talent, rather than training and coercion. More basic knowledge, mastery of techniques and improved skill would refine labour and foster dignity among people carrying out their work. The combination of work and education was not limited to the bourgeois concept of education. As a proletarian cultural ideal, it worked its way into the workers' educational societies of the nineteenth century. For Johann Gottlob Fichte, technological progress and education were the most powerful liberators: 'thus are the forces of Nature confronted by the greatest possible amount of the cultivated, ordered and combined powers of Reason.'[12]

Discourse concerning education and technology took a drastically different turn when linked to changes in ownership, as in socialist utopias of various stripes. These were based on older utopias like those of Thomas More or Tommaso Campanella, who replaced property with work as the basis of social participation and belonging. Work was considered a duty to the collective and expected of all members of society. In the eighteenth century, Jean-Jacques Rousseau and Etienne-Gabriel Morelly were pioneers of basing the social order on principles of equality, while early socialists such as Gracchus Babeuf, Saint-Simon and Charles Fourier translated these philosophical approaches into political programmes.[13] Human existence was to be based on work alone, as opposed to status or possessions. Although work was still considered a burden, equal distribution among all members of society coupled with equal benefit from its returns could also make work a source of joy. While Fourier and other early socialists tended to emphasize the free nature of socialization in socialist collectives and work communes, Saint-Simon pioneered an industrially guided socialism in which control over nature through technology and industry were placed front and centre. Marx's arguments also relied on the development of the forces of production through large industry, and thus saw industrial capitalism as paving the way for a socialist society. He left no doubt, however, that the emancipation of labour could never be achieved under conditions of private property and alienated labour.

Social-Democratic pragmatists availed themselves of the praise of work via the socialist theoreticians, but without making the ideal of work subject to the condition of social transformation: the result was a restrained glorification of labour in large capitalist industry, which became the basis for German Social Democracy's understanding of labour since its 1875 Gotha Programme. Without criticizing exploitation and alienation, the demand for a 'right to work' can only be understood as an acceptance of prevailing labour relations.

> *Federal Anthem of the General*
> *German Workers' Association*
> Man of labour, wake up!
> And acknowledge your power!
> All wheels stand still
> If your strong arm wants it.
> Your oppressors blanch,
> If you, tired of your load,
> Put the plough in the corner.
> When you call out, enough!
> Break the double yoke in two!
> Break the plight of slavery!
> Break the slavery of need!
> Bread is freedom, freedom bread![14]

> *Song of Labour*
> Sing the song of the high bride,
> Who was already married to man,
> Before he was even human.
> What is his on this earth,
> Sprang from this faithful covenant.
> Up with labour!
> Up with labour!
> And as Galileo once exclaimed,

As the world slept in error:
And yet it moves!
So call out: Labour prevails,
Labour, it moves the world!
Up with labour!
Up with labour![15]

Women often encountered difficulties situating themselves in liberal, Marxist and socialist work discourses.[16] Questions like primary responsibility for the family, unpaid housework, requiring a husband's consent to accept employment, and exclusion from higher education and qualified occupations – as well as their relegation to low-paying segments of the labour market, were not adequately addressed in socialist social criticism – and were in fact taken for granted, almost as the result of a natural predisposition. Female employment was even opposed by the organized labour movement as a form of low-wage competition. In the second half of the nineteenth century, the emerging women's movements focused on fighting for the right to education, access to employment and equal pay. By demanding equal rights, they almost inevitably accepted the definition of work as developed from the male perspective,[17] bringing them into conflict with the other side of their identity as wives and mothers. This resulted in a division between the liberal and social-democratic women's movements, which generally promoted equal rights for women in working life, and conservative currents which accepted women's domestic role and strived for the respect and appreciation of unpaid women's work and inclusion in social life from this position. Uniting these two objectives was left to women's movements in the second half of the twentieth century.

In the 1970s, second-wave feminists elevated unpaid work performed by women in the household and family to a central concern. Reducing work to gainful employment as conceived within the practices of male productive industry was no longer tenable. That said, perspectives on how to deal with housework in the future were extremely varied: overcoming, praise and transformation would again emerge as characteristic attitudes within housework discourse. The increasing commodification of housework, i.e. the transformation of unpaid family care work into professional services, fuelled hopes that domestic and family work would someday disappear. This hope, however, conceptualized the future of work in the generalization of wage labour. It goes without saying that such ideas could only arise in developed industrial societies either with the purchasing power to pay for care services, or where the public sector and social security systems provided health and care services to begin with. This professionalization of care work was often associated with technological solutions, envisioning machines replacing hands, feet and wombs in society's maternity wards, hospitals, boarding houses, canteens and more. One example of this kind of thinking is American feminist Shulamith Firestone's *The Dialectic of Sex: The Case for Feminist Revolution*, which reflects this faith in progress in its dreams of freeing women from childbearing and professionalizing human reproduction by relying on test-tube babies.[18] This particular utopia, commonplace in reproductive medicine to this day, ultimately seeks to eliminate the very need for domestic and family work as such.

Other currents of the women's movement, however, followed a radically different path, declaring the home and subsistence work performed by mothers and housewives the foundation of their sociopolitical perspective. These feminists proposed basing the entire economy on the principles of care, reciprocity and long-term sustainability characteristic of this sphere,[19] and rejected efforts to mechanize or rationalize care work in the interests of women's liberation.[20] Whether paid or unpaid, these discussions around care work fostered a conception of work which elevated the creation, care for and preservation of human life as the epitome of actualization. This model offered a conceptual alternative to the head–hand–builder model's instrumentalizing notions of alienation of human activity from nature in order to control it, opting rather for a form of work that can be seen as a natural metabolic process. Nevertheless, many women neglected to join in the praise of housework, fearing that this may block the path to independent earnings or employment in occupational work.

The well-known demand for 'wages for housework', raised in the early 1970s by the radical women's movement, in fact consisted of little more than the pragmatic proposal to transform housework into paid employment, but proved neither popular nor practical enough to be realized.[21] The demand was criticized for essentially treating all women as solely responsible for housework, as well as for potentially serving as a step towards further bureaucratic control over women and their bodies. 'Wages for housework' thus soon faded as a political battle cry, but was, to a certain extent, implemented in the Western European welfare states in the 1970s in the form of state-subsidized maternity leave, early childhood education and other care services, as well as the decision in some countries to count child-rearing years towards women's pensions. In most countries around the world, however, a similar level of attention to female or male reproductive, educational and care work in state-run social security systems is practically unthinkable. Although 'wages for housework' would return as a political demand in the 1990s, the low-paid care work based on the privatization and commercialization of domestic services which ultimately emerged fell quite short of its feminist inventors' intentions.[22]

The most widespread attitude when it comes to transforming domestic and family work from a burden into an accepted, satisfying activity is the demand for relative equality among family members in the household division of labour. Men's involvement in child-rearing and paternal leave are naturally a prerequisite to this arrangement. In this way, family work becomes compatible with gainful employment through the aid of professional assistance, outsourcing to institutions or simplifying housework through technical appliances. Ideally, time will then be freed up for personal education and volunteer activities. How successful one is in combining mixed models in which working life is divided between work, housework, volunteering, and personal activity, of course, depends on how much time is occupied by gainful employment.

3.

Work and Language

Human language offers a wide variety of terms for life-sustaining and income-generating activities, including both specific designations for specific tasks and general designations subsuming a host of activities under a common notion of work. While concrete designations can be compiled into an exhaustive list and thus do not exclude unnamed activities as such, general designations convey inclusion and exclusion, based on a conception that identifies certain activities as 'work' and excludes others. Both forms are subject to change over time. Changes in specific designations reflect changes in techniques and tasks: activities, techniques and technologies no longer used or practised disappear from language, or shift completely to refer to their metaphorical meanings. A good example of this is 'defalcation', a nearly extinct medieval term referring to the curve of a sickle which is now a legal-term for embezzlement. Other examples include agricultural activities that grew into common expressions: ploughing, sowing or reaping. New terms are sometimes coined or given new meaning, such as the telephone or programming, or are added upon and given new properties (email, browse, surf).

Words are often borrowed from foreign languages, such as Russian's use of the German *Stempel* for stamp and *Buchhalter* for bookkeeper, the adoption of *mail(en)* into German as a verb to send an email, or the ubiquitous adoption of 'forward' or 'browser' by other languages. Indeed, email in particular is a global concept overtaking and repressing regional terms, even challenging the British penchant for 'post', referring to the thing sent over the institution doing so – while the Royal Mail delivers the post in the UK, the US Postal Service delivers the mail across the pond. The American notion of the word is now being tacitly reintroduced into the UK through the adoption of 'email'. Because the transfer is a reflection of an advance in competency, the newer English-language adoptions rarely exhibit similar transfers. Old English was greatly refined with

French terms, particularly in the domain of food preparation. English relies on Germanic roots to describe the animals themselves, such as chicken/chick (*Kücken*), hen (*Huhn*), cow (*Kuh*), swine (*Schwein*), but required loanwords to denote advances in culinary techniques imported by the Normans, giving English the French *poulet* (chicken) for poultry, *boeuf* for beef, and *porc* for pork. Other terms survived technical changes over time: plough still refers to the action in context, as does sow, but so do weaving, knitting, chiselling, drilling, breastfeeding, childbearing, swaddling, and so on. This occurs even when techniques and technologies evolve – as they have in the case of the '*labour of birthe*', where new techniques have allowed it to be referred to as 'delivery' since the 1570s. Broad changes to the meaning of words reflect, above all, shifts in the meaning of work and labour – what becomes associated with work or labour at certain time periods? What sort of differentiation and evaluation can be identified within them? And which terms are taken up and further developed by language?

Once a term becomes enshrined in a language, it can no longer be removed – although it can, of course, be forgotten. Its meaning may change, but it lives on in older writings and is transmitted through traditional stories, proverbs and idioms. Language is thus a multi-layered phenomenon with many overlapping, coexisting, and competing strata of terms and meanings which are used and understood, even when those who use them are unaware of their etymology and history.

When comparing languages, we find both similarities and differences. All languages have words for most concrete activities, while it is often the case that terms for seafaring, boatbuilding and fishing are less differentiated in inland regions than in coastal areas, or that terms for digging pits, tunnels, blasting, retrieving and processing ores are much less diverse. However, language areas usually extend beyond the confines of economic spaces, and words travel the world through trade and migration, often resulting in broad agreement across the vocabularies of larger language families. Similarities are also found among general terms, although cultural and political claims and meanings resonate more strongly here than with concrete tasks, as they do not refer to concrete activity but rather are based on categorization and evaluation. Moreover, equivalent words in other languages do not necessarily carry the same meaning. Comparative linguistics can thus contribute a great deal to decoding concepts of work in distinct cultural environments.

This chapter begins by outlining the two major categories of arduous labour and toil (*pónos*) and its realization in work (*érgon*), the foundations of which can be traced to ancient Greek and have since spread, by way of Latin, to all Indo-European languages (*labor–opus*). Over time, these have endured as central concepts, repeatedly incorporated into the world views of successive religious, cultural, philosophical and scientific currents. Here, we lay out the broad correspondences between these terms, as well as the shades of difference that can be observed among conceptions of work in various European languages. The next step deals with the variety of activities regarded as work, discussed with reference to the *Oxford English Dictionary* and the *Deutsches Wörterbuch*, published by the Brothers Grimm in 1854. Observing historical writing demonstrates that prior to work's establishment as paid employment in the nineteenth century, the lexical field of work consisted of much broader associations than after the shift to economism. Much of what once was assumed to be work was later excluded from the category as it became increasingly focused on gainful employment. That said, the diversity of terms for work is partially preserved in some regional dialects. A lexical correlation table expresses the wide-ranging lexical field with which work activities are described in various European languages (see appendix on p. 227). Finally, the Chinese example shows that the categories of work emerging in the European context cannot be directly transferred to other cultures.

Pónos–labor is rooted in suffering, signifying the effort, the agony, and humanity's compulsion to sustain and reproduce life. The origin of *laborare* is thought to lie within the swaying of slaves under their heavy

Overview: Greek and Latin Roots of Work Categorizations in Select European Languages

	Toilsome work	Creative work
Greek	*pónos*	*érgon*
Latin	*labor, molestia*	*opus*
English	*labour*	*work*
German	*Arbeit*	*Werk*
French	*labeur, travail*	*œuvre*
Spanish	*trabajo*	*obra*
Italian	*lavoro*	*opera*
Russian	*rabota, trud*	*proizvedenie, trud*
Polish	*robota, praca*	*dzieło*
Serbian	*rad*	*posao*

loads.[1] This is reflected in the English *labour*, in the German *Arbeit* and in the Slavic *rabota*. In German, labour was long used in the passive case to denote suffering. The meaning of the French *labourer* is limited to working the land, while *labeur* refers to hard, toilsome labour; the term we might most closely recognize as work comes, however, from an instrument of torture that was used to punish slaves, the *tripalium*, a three-pronged stake that gave rise to the French *travail* and the Spanish *trabajo*.

Productive, creative activities – the opposite of toilsome, agonizing labour (*labor*) – are grouped under the generic concept of *érgon–opus* in a second category. Critical to the notion of *érgon–opus* was that activity had a productive or creative character and resulted in a final product with which artists or craftsmen could identify, thus requiring either technical knowledge (*techné*) or creative artistic skills (*poiesis*). Mental and intellectual work also belonged to the creative activities. *Érgon–opus* stood for qualified, honourable work, for pleasure, joy, freedom and achievement in the work and of the work itself. It also gave us today's work, *Werk*, *œuvre*, and *obra*.

At this point, it ought to be noted that the distinction had nothing to do with whether an activity was performed for the market or the household, nor whether it was remunerated.

A third category of activities in Athenian democracy was the actions of individuals in the public sphere, which constituted political *praxis* as such. Praxis was subsumed neither under toilsome effort nor under joyful, creative work, but rather was seen as the intended, natural purpose of free citizens. The disdain for strenuous activity and material production so central to classical Greek beliefs leaves its mark on work to this very day, surviving, for instance, in hopes of reducing physical toil and material production through modern machinery as the foundation of a work-free, self-determined and active existence.[2]

All forms of employment were grouped under what frustratingly translates as 'leisure' (*scholé*, *otium*), the highest form of human purpose, embodied by the *vita contemplativa*. In opposition to economic or political business (*negotium*, *vita activa*), *vita contemplativa* referred to the pursuit of serenity and peace. The concept includes the notion of free time, but ultimately means much more: the Greek *scholé* gives English the word 'school', hinting at what is required for the pursuit of learning. Freedom from activity gives us leisure, from the same root as the French *loisir* – freedom, capacity, permission (to do something) – but is a great deal more than free time, which entered the language around the era of industrialization to differentiate from working time. It thus makes for a muddled translation considering today's use. The German *Muße* is a more direct translation of *otium*, and is the basis for our use of leisure henceforth.

While the Greek *polis* knew only contempt for profane human survival, Christianity ensured a positive view of toilsome labour in the Latin language, understood as a service to God. *Labor* was relieved of its disdainful connotations, but remained firmly on the dark side of life, primarily associated with necessity, emergency, monotony, estrangement and alienation. Work's fundamentally dual nature as laid down in language and structures of thought would survive even as early modern states and private enterprise, in the interests of capital valorization and economic output, stripped work of its toilsome nature and redefined it as a neutral factor of production ensuring growth and happiness. It is also here that the lexical distinction between effort and work also began to blur. Concepts of 'toilsome labour' penetrated spheres originally reserved for 'productive work' and vice versa. However, the experiences of suffering and exploitation inherent in language and social practice retained work's dual nature, later rediscovered and detached from Christian reasoning by critical philosophy and socialist theory.

The old dichotomy of *labor–opus* became a category of social analysis and critique at the outset of the nineteenth century. Humanity's estrangement, alienation, fulfilment and actualization through active creation were formulated by Hegel as dialectical categories, and later taken up by Marx as guidelines for overcoming capitalist property relations and class society as a whole. *Labor* and *opus* therefore stand not only for two different contexts in the exertion of human labour power, but also for two different contexts of appropriation: while the English *labour* – stemming again from *laborare* – refers to alienated waged labour for a capitalist entrepreneur who uses the labour to generate surplus value and appropriate it as profit, *work* in this context raises the possibility of self-determined activity beyond the compulsion to sell one's labour power to capital. Marxist terminology, explicated by Friedrich Engels as editor of the English translation of *Capital*, volume 1 (1890), accordingly differentiates work as labour which generates a product's use value from labour connected to exchange value.[3] Adam Smith and other British economists also use this dual conceptuality to distinguish between exchange value and use value. In fact, Marxist analysis only applies this difference to capitalist relations of production in an abstract sense, whereas, in practice, each marketable commodity unites use value and exchange value, so that both work and labour are exerted in its production.

Some languages fail to discern clearly between the self-determined and externally determined sides of work, often blurring them. Such is the case in French, where the word *œuvre*, derived from *opus*, refers to a physical or virtual result of *travail* (from *tripalium*); there is little or no difference between *travailleur/travailleuse* and *ouvrier/ouvrière* – just as *worker* and *labourer* are more or less synonymous in everyday English. German also lost the ability to clearly distinguish between toilsome labour and productive work with the rise of the word *Arbeit* and its verb form *arbeiten* over the creative act of producing a *Werk* and its rarely used verb form, *werken*. English opted for *work* as the general term, which now refers to both result-oriented and strenuous aspects of the work–labour duality, and has marginalized labour in contemporary speech. In the Slavic languages, *rab* and *rabota* are both associated with the work of servants and slaves, and share the same root as *Arbeit*. *Trud* (Russian, Serbian) and *praca* (Polish), on the other hand, mean heavy, painstaking work, while also including volunteer work and job satisfaction. These words are used to describe modern wage labour and relations of employment, while *rabota/robota* dominates in everyday speech. The Slavic languages transformed the root *arb* into *rab/rob* – *rabota* refers to servitude and forced labour; *rob* to villein, serf or servant; *roba* to maid as well as prostitute; *robalko* to boy and child servant. Both come from the Latin *labor* and *labos*, the root word for toilsome, lowly work in the Romance languages.

A direct correspondence with productive, creative, skilled craft work stemming from *opus* cannot be as clearly traced in the Slavic languages as in the Romance languages, English and German. This may be because crafts practised in the towns of Eastern Europe were introduced by masters and skilled workers from the West, who brought with them German, English and French words for their work and products. These often appeared as loanwords in the Slavic languages, such as the Russian *Spinnhaus* (spinnery) or *Arbeitshaus* (workhouse), closed-off poorhouses and labour colonies for poor workers built in the eighteenth century along Western lines. Other terms were needed to describe productive, artisanal production processes and crafts.

WORK AND LABOUR IN ENGLISH AND GERMAN DICTIONARIES

Allow us to look closer at the definitions of 'work, to work' and 'labour, to labour' with the help of two historical etymological dictionaries: the *Oxford English Dictionary* (1857–2016), and the *Deutsches Wörterbuch* compiled by Jacob and Wilhelm Grimm (1854–1960). The *Oxford English Dictionary* was initiated in 1857 as the *New English Dictionary on Historical Principles* by the London Philological Society at the behest of Richard Chenevix Trench, Dean of Westminster Abbey, and has appeared regularly since 1884. The first twelve-volume edition was published in 1928. The second, twenty-volume edition was published in 1989, and has been available online since 2010.[4]

The Brothers Grimm began working on the *Deutsches Wörterbuch* in 1837. The first volume, which included an entry for *Arbeit*, appeared in 1854. Entries for *Werk* and words formed in composition with it were not penned by the brothers themselves, but only appeared between 1958 and 1960 along with other words from the second half of the alphabet, as part of ten uncompleted volumes published by the Arbeitsstelle Deutsches Wörterbuch in East Berlin. These cleaved to the original dictionary's structure, but incorporated more recent literature and linguistic developments. Comparable works are the *Dictionnaire de l'Académie française* (since 1694, currently in its ninth edition) and the *Diccionario de autoridades*, issued by the Real Academia Española (1726–39). All of these reference works begin definitions of words with their etymological background, as is their stated purpose, before explaining the various areas of use with historical and literary examples.

In tracing the evolution of language use, we uncover the flattening that the concept of work has been subjected to in the modern period, but also reveal the conceptual resistance inherent therein, whereby older terms survive with their meanings intact over long periods of time. Upon closer inspection, German and English exhibit divergent terminological developments: in English, the subsumption of multiple meanings under one term can be traced back to the Latin *érgon–opus*, whereas German tended toward *pónos–labor*. Moreover, the words *work* and *labour* both remain common in English, whereas in German the use of *Arbeit* proliferated while *Werk* receded over the nineteenth century.

All Old Germanic languages knew the words *arbja*, *arbed*, *arbaid* and *arbeid*, appearing as a noun with masculine, feminine and neutral declinations and as a verb with both passive and active, transitive and intransitive forms. The Slavic *rob, rab* and *rabota* also share the same root. While the Anglo-Saxon *earfode, earfede* disappeared, its place in English was taken by *work*.[5]

The *Oxford English Dictionary* lists the following uses for *work*: 'act, deed, action, labor, result or product of labor, structure, edifice, fortification, workmanship, literary composition, frequently used to translate classical Latin *opus*, which has a similar semantic meaning'.[6] The key definitions given for the use of *labour* are similar to its classical Latin etymon *labor*: 'work, toil, industry, task, result or product of work, struggle, hardship, physical pain, distress, pain of childbirth'. *Labour* derives from the Anglo-Norman and Old French *labur, labor, labeur*.

Although overlapping, the dual terms *work* and *labour* both survived and have signified a variety of meanings rooted in different world views across different historical periods. It is practically impossible to draw a clear-cut distinction between the two, whether in terms of remuneration and non-remuneration or of creation of use and exchange value.

The Grimms' *Deutsches Wörterbuch* lists the following meanings for *Werk, werken*:

creative activity (*Wirken* [acting upon, affecting]),
the product of creative activity,
the to-be-processed as well as the processed material,
the acting agent, which includes both the active persons (*Werker* [worker],
Gewerken [trade], *Handwerk* [craft] as an individual and as a community)
as well as the instruments (*Werkzeug* [tools]),
the operations facility (*Werkstatt* [workshop]).[7]

The German *Werk(en)* clearly stems from the *érgon–opus* tradition, while *Arbeit, arbeiten*, on the other hand, not only unifies the dual meanings, but also emphasizes the changed use of the term.[8] Although German and English took different tracks along the classical dichotomy, it may be useful to assess the English language's transformation as well. Both languages reflect the merging of a vocabulary that accommodates a conflicting interpretation of what work *is* and what work *could* or *should* be. This is accomplished with a vocabulary that reduces work, or labour, to gainful employment (for the worker) and surplus accumulation (for the employer). Other meanings survive in dialects and specific contexts.

When the Brothers Grimm began their dictionary in 1837, the term *Arbeit* was already in the middle of this reinterpretation process. The entry reflects the difficulties posed by the term's shifting usage, which the authors acknowledged and documented in order to provide a more systematic explanation. The Brothers go beyond the explanations given by the *Oxford English Dictionary* and instead address the change in meaning explicitly, making the entry itself a documentation of its time. It reflects the term's use in both its original meaning of 'toil' and 'burden' and its extended meaning as something active and creative, the production of a work. No reduction of work to gainful employment can be observed here. Grimm and Grimm describe six areas in which the term *Arbeit* applies:

1 the original 'toilsome labour of the farmhand in the fields for a daily wage';
2 'altogether, all is called *arbeit* which is done by the so-called *handwerker* (craftsmen), which, as evidenced by the name itself, originally would have been called *werk*';
3 *Kopfarbeit*, intellectual labour;
4 figurative application, in which no specific work is produced;
5 'the idea of labour is linked to individual conditions characterized by sustained effort or natural activity';
6 'the abstraction of great toil and effort, derived from heavy servile labour'.

It is worth noting that, in German, *opus* merges into *labor* around the beginning of the nineteenth century, relieving the tension between *Arbeit* and *Werk*.

Werk continued to embody its original meaning in braiding and weaving techniques for trellises, containers and textiles, masonry tools, artisanal products, and buildings, through to works of art, science and statecraft, as well as figurative meanings like God's work, the work of the Devil, or a *Werk der Natur* ('work of nature'). Effect, product and result are also integral to the term. Although we also find examples of the term *Werk* extending into the area of strenuous activity, much more common are instances where *Arbeit* repressed the application of *Werk* in New High German, which is no longer common only in the negative sense of 'effort, toilsome-ness' but has become a positive designation for craftsmanship and mental activity, and can now also refer to the result of this activity. The word *Arbeit* rising in importance especially in everyday vernacular, however, has not repressed *Werk* in all language landscapes to the same degree.[9]

In contemporary German, the notion of *Werk* as 'euphemistic label for coitus' has disappeared.[10] The French *corvée* was used to denote the same, and specifically referred to prostitution until at least the early 1900s.[11] In English, the expression 'working woman' is still widely understood to denote a sex worker. Confusion can arise around the fact that *Werk* can also mean pain, something originally reserved for *Arbeit*: for instance, menstruation can be described by stating *sie hat ihre werke* ('she is having her works').[12] Compound terms demonstrate how the concept of *Werk* survived *Arbeit*'s onslaught by receding into the background, in words like *Handwerk* (craft), *Tagwerk* (daily chores), *Feuerwerk* (fireworks), *Schmelzwerk* (smelter), *Werkmann* (workman), *Werkstatt* (workshop), and so on.

Quite the opposite is true in English, as the *OED* points out. While *labour* designates hardship, pain and toil, *work* is more all-encompassing and contains a double meaning – one synonymous with labour, the other referring to the piece of work in the sense of *opus* as in the Romance languages. In this respect, the distinction between *labour* and *work* remains more significant than in German, and both terms have survived on relatively equal footing. Building compounds is also rather common in English, e.g. workbench, workbox, workmate, workhand, workhour, workhouse, workforce, or labour force, labour market, labour class, labour law, and so on, allowing one to express subtle differences and nuances beyond a static, binary logic.

There is no definitive explanation for why *work* and *labour* developed differently in English and German. Richard Biernacki cites the divergent mentalities framing workers' notions of work and labour under capital-ism, arguing that while British workers felt they sold the products of their labour to their employer, and therefore referred to their activity as 'work', German workers perceived themselves as selling their 'labour power'.[13] The respective meanings of *work* and *labour* developed accord-ing to political, economic and cultural circumstances. However, it would be oversimplifying to explain the dominance of labour over work by the persistence of guilds in industrial production and feudal labour relations in agriculture in German states, as Biernacki suggests. Marx, whose first language was German, most certainly employed the meaning of *work* common among German workers, stimulating Engels to comment on the term's usage when editing the English translation of *Capital*, volume 1 (1890).

Both dictionaries devote special emphasis to the labour performed by women in childbirth. The *Oxford English Dictionary* lists multiple usages of *labour*, including 'the process of childbirth from the onset of uterine contractions to delivery of the fetus and placenta':

> God spede yow, and Owre Ladye hyre to hyre plesure, wyth as easye labore to overkom that she is abowt as euyre had any lady or gentyoll-woman saff Owre Lady heer-selffe (1472)
>
> some woemen ar as yet not used unto the labouringe of childe (1598)
>
> in the tyme of the byrthe & labour bounde to the Leage, it bryngeth for the chaylde wythout payne (1580)
>
> The Queens in Labor They say in great Extremity, and fear'd Shee'l with the Labour, end (1623)
>
> They hold a Piss-pot over the Womens Heads whilst in Labour, thinking it to promote hasty delivery (1744)
>
> Although water can't take away the pain it can help you to relax, making labour easier (2004)[14]

The Grimms' dictionary also documents the use of *labour* to express the work of giving birth:

> *thaʒ wib, thanne siu gibirit then kneht, iu ni gihugit thera arbeiti* (... wife, when she gives birth to the child, thinks no more of the labour of birth) (1549)
>
> *die frau liegt in arbeit, in kindsnöthen: ein fraw, die in kindsarbeit ligt* (the woman lies in labour, in child hardship; a woman who lies in child-labour) (1445–1510)
>
> *gleichwie ein hochschwangerer leib, der die herbe zeit erkannt, die ihm zu derber arbeit ruft, schmachtet in der wehmut band* (just as the pregnant body, which apprehends the harsh time that calls it to labour, languishes in melancholy) (1698)
>
> *einer zum Kind arbeitenden frauen einer haselnutz grosz bibergail in bier zu trinken geben* (give a hazelnut-worth of castoreum in a beer to a woman labouring to child) (1716)

schwangere weiber, wenn sie zur geburt arbeiten (pregnant wives, when they labour to birth) (1716)[15]

The labour of childbirth is, of course, treated in these texts as part of a notion of suffering that cannot be separated from effort and activity, corresponding to an image of women propagating birth and child-rearing as women's natural characteristics. Nevertheless, the sustained toil and pain that birthing women endure appears as a natural process which, like the movements of nature, were also described as *Arbeit*, e.g. earthquakes described as mountains that 'labour and deliver'.[16] This analogy should not necessarily be understood as a devaluation of a woman's child-birthing labour to an expression of her corporeality, but rather is included here to illustrate the broad spectrum of applications for *Arbeit* as painful suffering. To convey a sense of pain, *Arbeit* was often used in passive verbal constructions, although this perspective would disappear from the term in the nineteenth century.

Today, it is practically impossible to find conceptions of labour associated with giving birth in the German language, and only feminist theory has reopened the language to perceiving the process of childbirth as labour. In English, on the other hand, 'labouring, to be in labour, to go into labour' is still used to express the physical strain and suffering linked to childbirth.

Both the German and the English dictionaries list a series of further words that overlap with concepts of *arbeiten* and *labour*, and *werken* and *work*. Noteworthy instances include *schaffen*[17] and, from the same root, *schöpfen*,[18] meaning 'to create'. Regional dialects, colloquialisms, slang and group-specific jargon also provide a wide range of terms revealing language's stubbornness in the face of attempts to homogenize and codify words by economic and political institutions, such as referring to work as slogging away, drudgery, busting a hump and the daily grind, or describing a job as the railroad, the chain-gang, the mines, to dig in, to chip away. Language development is also influenced by the blending of indigenous terms with the languages of immigrants and migrant labourers: *schlep*, for example, has its origins in the German word for carrying a heavy load, and was introduced to English via Yiddish.

Conversely, colloquial language also contains numerous ways to express circumventing toilsome wage labour and dodging pressure at work from the perspective of the worker, such as skiving, slacking off, dragging one's feet, bunking off, shamming, shirking or playing hooky. In German, the fantastic expression *blau machen* (to make blue), stemming from woad dye production which we will encounter later, refers to the time workers spent waiting for dye to oxidize. A similar example from the employer's perspective, by contrast, is the racially-charged acronym known for its role in an unfortunate joke by Hillary Clinton during the 2016 presidential campaign: CPT, or 'coloured people's time', which refers to workplace lateness.

WORK AND LABOUR IN CHINESE

Can our analysis of the lexical field be extended to non-European languages? And if so, how? The near impossibility of such an undertaking speaks to the challenges confronting scholars who strive to compile a global history worthy of the name. Although a global linguistic overview is beyond the scope of this book, it seems appropriate to take a look at developments in the Chinese language, where in fact two terms for work are common.[19]

Dagong refers to employment or short-term jobs for a capitalist entrepreneur who employs wage labourers to realize surplus value; hiring and wages are determined by the market and subject to little or no state regulation, and the employment relationship can be ended by either side at any time. These precarious circumstances have fostered a trend towards frequent job hopping (*tiao cao*) among Chinese workers. The second term, *gongren*, was commonly used to denote workers during the Maoist period, but first emerged in the nineteenth century and is still applied to workers in state-run factories today. *Gongren* worked in state enterprises known for lifelong employment and stable pensions, where wages made up only a part of a worker's income. These workers embodied the new socialist subject ideal type, who, together with the peasants of the people's commune, constituted the social base of Maoist socialism. Being *gongren* meant freedom from alienation and belonging to the socialist proletariat (*wuchan jieji*, literally 'no-property-class').

Almost all Chinese terms for work under capitalist or socialist conditions are in fact loanwords from Japanese. Although this comparison could lead one to draw parallels between *dagong* and wage labour or *rabota*, and between *gongren* and work or *trud*, drawing exact parallels

between Chinese and European labour relations proves more complicated. In order to grasp the meanings and tensions between *dagong* and
gongren, we must first sketch out the specific, historical sets of labour
relations in which they emerged: *gongren* was institutionalized during
the Maoist era – forced onto Chinese workers from above as their new,
mandatory identity – and has gradually diminished in importance since
the outset of 'reform and opening up' in 1978.[20] *Dagong* and *gongren*
are not fixed categories, but rather emerge and change in interaction
with socio-economic and political conditions, and must be contextual-
ized within other types and understandings of work historically. Class
position and class relations were deeply politicized questions in Maoist
China:[21] on the one hand, class struggle was championed as an active
instrument of the self-transformation of society, while, on the other,
social origins and occupation determined one's class position. Every
citizen of the People's Republic of China was assigned a class position by the state, which was documented in their *hukou*, or household
registration. Work was thus tightly integrated into the social structure, urban–rural relationship and political strategy of Mao's socialist
transformation.

The present situation only makes sense when placed in historical context. Traditional Chinese society distinguished between good,
respectable citizens (*liangmin*) and worthless people (*jianmin*). Servants
(*yongren*), for which there were more than forty distinct terms, belonged
to the latter category, subject to a different set of laws, forced to adopt
the name of their employer, and barred from taking the civil service
examination.[23] Although servants' highly dependent status was formally
abolished at the end of the nineteenth century, the system persisted well
into Sun Yat-sen's republic. Only with the establishment of the People's
Republic (1949–) would domestic servants become paid wage labourers,
employed in the homes of high-ranking party cadres where they were
referred to as 'aunty' (*ayi*) or 'protective mother' (*baomu*) like the nannies
of the old imperial court, often enjoying a great deal of independence in
managing the household.

The overwhelming majority of the population had comprised peasants, farmers and farmhands since time immemorial. Because the gentry
was centrally controlled, nobles were free but paid taxes collected by
state officials. Peasant households had access to both agricultural and
commercial means, combining subsistence farming with production for

Shifting Work Characters and Labels in Modern China[22]

Until 1900	Officials (examination) (*shi*), landowners (*dizhu*)	Free peasants/farmers (not serfs) (*nong/nongmin*)	Writers, craftsmen, merchants, etc.		'Worthless' (*jianmin*): serfs (*nu*), handmaids (*yongren*), beggars, etc.
1900–49 (Communist takeover)	Officials (*gongwuyuan*), landowners (*dizhu*)	Free peasants/farmers (*nong/nongmin*)	Intellectuals, middle-class professionals	Wage labourers, factory workers (*gongren*)	Despite abolition of the caste system, servants remain lowly regarded (*yongren*)
1949–78 (Maoism)	Party cadres, officials (*ganbu*)	Farmers in the people's communes	Intellectuals	Socialist workers (*gongren*), proletariat (*wuchan jieji*), workers in labour camps (*laojiao renyuan*), contract workers (*mingong*)	Service-sector workers (*fuwuyuan*)
1978– ('reform and opening up', particularly since mid-1980s)	Party cadres, officials (*ganbu*)	Private farmers in the household responsibility system (1983–)	Intellectuals, middle-class professionals	State-run factory workers, on the decline (*gongren*), wage labourers (city residents with *hukou*, peasant labourers or *mingong*), migrants (*dagongmei*, *dagongzai*)	Service-sector workers (*fuwuyuan*)

the market. In the nineteenth century, over half of peasant households were involved in cotton production, which made its way to the market through a putting-out system (*baomaizhuzhi*) in which agents collected finished products on behalf of large merchants, in turn organized into merchant guilds (*gongsuo, hang, bang*). Unlike cotton production, silk was produced in central facilities – although most of the labour was performed by weavers in their own workshops. What could arguably be described as an early version of the modern proletariat began to emerge here in the eighteenth century.[24] As the end of the nineteenth century brought with it the rise of the first mechanized cotton and silk factories, personal relationships played a large role in recruitment and control over workers. The search for a predominately young female workforce was incumbent upon older women, the so-called 'Number One' responsible for protecting and supervising the girls in the factory and dormitories. Sisterhoods (*jiemeihui*) formed in opposition to dependency on supervisors, particularly among better-off workers in the silk industry, to protect and support one another. They articulated their demands through collective action, sent remittances back to their families at home, and made themselves visible as confident consumers in urban life. As textile production was completely incorporated into the factory system in the People's Republic, the Communist Party sought to coopt and organize them into 'red sisterhoods'.[25]

Chinese Communists viewed the peasant population as the vanguard of the revolution, which in turn enjoyed a high degree of prestige in the socialist society. Retaining household self-sufficiency was touted as one of the goals of the people's commune, ruling out the possibility of socializing housework.

The collectivization of the food supply was limited to the 'Great Leap Forward' of 1958–61, when communal kitchens and public cafeterias were established in the rural people's communes. These were based on Western models of collectivist utopias, as well as socialistic concepts like the socialization of housework, rational planning and women's liberation from patriarchal constraints.[26] In a sense, every rural settlement unit was organized as a large household in which all production and reproduction was to be carried out collectively. This experiment failed, and the disastrous famine of 1959–60 triggered a turn to family households within the people's communes. Many subsistence tasks nevertheless remained the responsibility of public institutions, workplaces, schools and childcare facilities.

Along with the communalization of the peasantry, another product of the revolution was the rise of industrial workers (*gongren*) in state-run enterprises. Factory workers had been concentrated in several branches and were largely employed by foreign capitalists in the late nineteenth century and the first half of the twentieth. The heavy, toilsome labour exploited under capitalism was reinterpreted as socially valuable work under the Maoist model, codified in the term *gongren*. Belonging to the proletariat (*wuchan jieji*) was now a source of pride. The number of *gongren* in the cities was regulated through the typically lifelong assignment of individuals to specific workplaces. Relocating to the city required the appropriate household registration record (*hukou*), which granted access to residency, housing and social services. Along with urban industrial workers, there were also service-sector wage labourers, for whom the term *fuwuyuan* was coined (from *fuwu*, 'to serve the people'), replacing the submissive service class known as the *yongren*. The socialist system was thus characterized by new labour relations and working conditions as well as a renewed self-confidence in the value of work, as reflected in changing language.

The Communist Party–controlled, state-run introduction of capitalist privatization linking up the economy with global commodity chains, and with it the repealing of state direction of the labour force in the 1980s, brought an end to the egalitarian and self-sufficiency-oriented Maoist planned economy. The people's communes were dissolved in 1983. Peasants were discharged into the private agricultural sector, where most could not survive, and were transformed into surplus labour (*shengyu laodongli*), which now served as a reserve army of peasant labour (*mingong*) for the booming industries of the special economic zones and coastal cities serving Western clients. Restrictions on urban migration were lifted while the *hukou* system was not, trapping migrant labourers in a precarious state with no job guarantees, let alone the right to start a family, buy a house or access medical care and schooling for their children. Patronizingly referred to as *dagongmei* ('labour sisters') and *dagongzai* ('labour sons'), they are dependent in a dual sense: on their employers, who hire them for extremely low wages and generally without a contract or social benefits, and on the state, whose restrictive residency policies turn them into second-class citizens. Many are employed as temporary workers (*laowu gong*) or as so-called interns under very precarious conditions.

Surpassing 200 million by 2010, these peasants and migrant labourers are now referred to as a 'floating population' (*liudong renkou*) and considered uneducated, uncouth, uprooted, dangerous and volatile, subject to constant supervision and harassment by authorities and employers alike.[27] These workers are not taking their predicament lying down, however, and have drawn attention with numerous protest actions in recent years. The sector's initial lawlessness has given way to gradual regulation since the turn of the millennium, establishing contracts, minimum wages, social insurance and arbitration bodies to reduce conflict potential and realize the Communist Party's goal of a 'harmonious society'. That said, officials generally refrain from using the term 'working class'. On the one hand, doing so would underscore the party's break with Maoist class ideology, while on the other, the rulers are keen to avoid the formation of a confident, combative labour movement.[28] Instead, the Communist Party has made a concerted effort to shift its recruitment strategies towards the emerging bourgeoisie and urban middle classes.

The second vanguard of Chinese Communism, the class of state-run industrial workers (*gongren*), still enjoy a higher degree of job security and labour rights than their colleagues in the private sector – to the extent that they still exist in the first place. Their ranks were decimated in the 1990s. Massive protests failed to halt the decline, despite the fact that state-run industry still constitutes a major component of the Chinese economy, with state monopolies controlling most of its strategic sectors. Many former state employees entered the free labour market after losing their jobs and thus became competition for the country's millions of internal migrants. Others joined a shift towards self-employed small-business creation, which also experienced a boom. This social upheaval, partially planned through deregulation, led to intense social polarization. The number of paid domestic servants (*fuwuyuan*), limited to a small minority in Mao's time, exploded among middle- and upper-class families, surpassing the 10 million mark in 2004.[29] Most of these workers also come from rural areas. Studies reveal the high degree to which they depend on their employers: one housemaid reported that 'in the city, migrants are the servants (*yongren*) of the urbanites', belying her subordinate status with her word choice – *yongren*, the common label for servants in China's imperial period.

4.

Categories of Analysis

A look at different types of work in terms of variation across time, space and socio-economic contexts reveals a practically limitless diversity of work forms and characters. The following chapter sets aside considerations of temporal, spatial and contextual specificity in order to construct a working typological overview of work and establish a categorical classification model sufficient to cover all possible types thereof. This model will allow us to compare different cases and contexts in order to arrive at mutual understandings of key concepts – although it should be noted that these analytical terms do not necessarily correspond to the self-conceptions of the workers who perform them.

This model's practical use is to precisely capture and order individual cases and types of work, as well as the kinds of worker performing them. The theoretical backgrounds and debates surrounding these categories can only be touched upon here. In closing, we discuss the various occupational grey areas straddling the threshold between work and non-work.

Types of work will first be defined according to the framework or social context in which they are performed, or the beneficiary of their products – who uses it, sells it, or realizes it (as subsistence, reciprocity, tribute or for the market). Beyond its specific context, work can be systematized into a multitude of categories connected to status in the work process or in society, to the form of employment and payment, to legal regulation, to social security or to forms of collective representation.

WORK FRAMEWORKS

Subsistence work

Subsistence stands for work carried out to meet immediate individual, household or family needs. Accordingly, it creates use values rather than exchange values and occurs, in principle, in the absence of money or markets, and therefore cannot be regulated by institutions developed for the money and market economy. Subsistence work is subject to the applicable rules of households and families.

Work for the collective or community

Collective and community or communal work consists of activities members perform to help one another or the community as a whole. Such activities generally correspond to the rules of maintaining social relationships and reciprocity. Collective and community work can be paid or unpaid; in some cases, the collective can participate in the market directly by offering its labour for sale.

Work as tribute to a political sovereign or state

This category encompasses surplus product that a person, household or community offers to a political body. Tribute is paid either in kind, as physical labour, or in monetary form, while the volume, type, recipient and purpose of such tribute is determined by political will, mediated by the political constitution and power relations of a given social formation. Tributary forms of pre-capitalist and pre-democratic societies have been democratically legitimized by modern states in the form of taxation. While some taxes continue to be collected directly from individual citizens (taxes on consumer goods, for instance), taxes related to operating costs, wages, income and wealth generally apply to both capital and labour, and thus tend to be more a function of the market.

Work to be sold on the market

Work for sale on the market aims to generate revenue or profits in the form of money realized as an exchange value for commodities sold. The status of the person working, their type of occupation, as well as their working conditions and labour relations vary and include both self-employed and wage labourers, free and unfree, both voluntary and forced labour. While the vendor of a product is primarily concerned with exchange value, the consumer only cares about use value. A specialized form emerges when not the product of labour but rather labour power itself is sold (or rented) to an entrepreneur on the market. This is referred to as commodified labour. The person selling their labour power, i.e. working for someone else, earns a wage, while the entrepreneur uses their purchased labour to profit from the value created in the work process. The worker's wage is used to reproduce or regenerate their labour power, while the difference between wage costs subtracted from the new value resulting from production is what is called 'surplus value' in Marxist terminology. Capital accumulation occurring through the exploitation of wage labour is different from profit, which is garnered within the margin resulting from selling products on the market. Most people, families and households can be – and usually are – involved in multiple contexts and types of work.

CONCEPTUALLY PAIRED CATEGORIES OF LABOUR RELATIONS

Independent (with or without employees)/dependent

'Independent' describes individuals who run one or more businesses as an owner. Some employ additional workers, while others run the entire operation themselves – this is known as 'self-employment'. The German language uses the same term, *selbstständig*, literally 'self-reliant', both for self-employment in the sense of a modern-day freelancer and for being able to support oneself – revealing a dual meaning that the English translation of 'independent' does not manage to capture. The category is applied primarily to market-related gainful employment, but can also apply to labour relations where tribute is paid to a feudal lord of some kind. Even in situations of subsistence work and non-market forms of communal work, it still makes sense to differentiate between the leading member of the household, who owns and directs household affairs, and other members dependent upon that person. The category thus applies despite the fact that they are not dependent members of the workforce in the strict sense.

Dependents are members of the workforce who offer their labour power to the self-dependent entrepreneur for a wage. This does not necessarily entail freedom or free movement for such persons – as wage labourers, they are dependent upon their wage, while gains from their work are accrued by the entrepreneur as value creation and added value. Wage labour, free or unfree, is not a unique feature of capitalism, but was common in ancient, feudal and tribute-based societies as well. Dependence on one's wage is all the greater the less other means of survival from independent work are available to the individual concerned.

Although the peasant farmer couple fall into the category of independent work as far as the whole household is concerned, the housewife is additionally subject to the housefather's patriarchal power. Together they manage the dependent family and non-family household members in their work for subsistence purposes, for the community, for the feudal lord and for market sale. Beyond that, each may perform additional paid, independent or dependent activity either in the home (e.g. home-based work) or outside it (e.g. wage labour).

This categorization can also be transferred to family-run commercial operations employing apprentices, journeymen and servants, in which the master leads the market- and expense-related components of the enterprise, while the housewife organizes subsistence activities. In contrast to the peasant farm, a gender-specific division of labour is more pronounced in the small industrial family business, which relegates acquisition to the husband and dependent apprentices and journeymen who belong to a specific profession and thus to a professional association or guild. The management of the household is clearly subordinate to professional work, but is an integral part of the family enterprise, with its own independent sphere of influence dominated by the housewife and her assistants. Should she participate in artisanal production activities, this further strengthens her authority in the family enterprise and on the market, as well as in the tradecrafts' forms of collective representation – a public affair. Both independent and dependent craftsmen participate in subsistence activities as active members of the household unit.

Free/unfree

This categorical pairing is generally applicable in status- and estate-based, i.e. feudal, societies, although it is often difficult to reconstruct a clear picture of the nuances and transitional forms within this category. In a feudal or tribute-based society, for example, an independent entrepreneur in agriculture, trade or services can only be seen as partially free, insofar as he must pay duties and payments (tribute) to a feudal authority. A subjugated entrepreneur (or couple) can operate more or less freely in terms of managing the multifaceted aspects of their enterprise, despite this wider relationship of servitude or bondage. Those labouring as serv-ants, assistants, apprentices or journeymen (whether under patriarchal or matriarchal yoke) are considered unfree – all the more so if they are also subjugated to a feudal lord.

A certain degree of unfreedom (so to speak) can be found anywhere religion, often in connection with ethnicity, is used to exclude entire social groups from certain spheres of activity and relegate them to others instead. The Indian caste system, which assigns people to a social status or 'caste' by birth, does so in a language couched in claims to honesty and purity. In the *dhimma* system found in the Arab world, non-Muslim 'Peoples of the Book' (Jews, Christians, Sabians, Zoroastrians) were called *dhimmi* and granted special protections. *Dhimmi* enjoyed the right to exercise their religion freely, but paid higher taxes and were excluded from government or military service, thus predestining them to work in trade and crafts.[1] Inhabitants of the Ottoman Empire were similarly grouped along religions lines into so-called *millets* (nations). Muslims and Jews coexisted alongside Greek Orthodox and Armenian Apostolic *millets*, each with their own structures of self-governance and special courts. With the exception of Christian boys conscripted into the Ottoman army as janissaries, sometimes even rising to powerful posi-tions, Christians were barred from public service and thus often focused their energies on commerce and early industry. In doing so they became intermediaries between the Ottoman and Christian European powers, which in turn began asserting extra-territorial protective claims over the Ottoman Christians as the empire became increasingly integrated into the capitalist world market from the eighteenth century onward.

Honourable/dishonourable (dishonest, unclean)

This status- and estate-based distinction assigns individual status groups, castes, denominations or groups of people to specific, permitted spheres of activity or work. This applied to jobs like the medieval knacker, who carted off animal carcasses for rendering, or the executioner in pre-industrial Europe – both of which were considered dishonourable although their activities were recognized as socially necessary labour. Knackers' homes were generally located outside village settlements. Grain millers and tanners also reeked of impurity, and their houses often attracted the poor or people looking for odd jobs and itinerant work, carrying out activities on the fringes of legality (smuggling, theft, and so on). Considered even more dishonourable were the so-called 'gypsies' – unlike the kind of dishonour associated with certain types of work, however, this categorization was of a purely ethnic nature and thus could not be escaped. Gypsies either belonged to a parallel society tied to peasant households which depended on their labour, or lived as wandering merchants, tradesmen or servants (as horse traders, blacksmiths, performing metal work or basketry and various repairs, as fortune-tellers and so on). Other groups known as the *Yenish*, *Travellers* or *Voyageurs* fulfilled the same tasks, but unlike gypsies were considered dishonourable due not to ethnic but rather social distinctions related to their nomadic lifestyle and the specific nature of their work.[2] Nevertheless, they were often subsumed under the broader term of 'gypsy'.

Further examples of inclusion and exclusion through work can be found among the Jews (in majority Christian and Muslim societies) and untouchables like the *hijras* in the Indian caste system. Until their legal emancipation was established in the nineteenth century, Jews were forbidden from owning land or working in the artisanal crafts due to their religion. To the extent that their presence was tolerated at all, they were excluded from local structures of community governance and guilds. Their autonomous communities, spatially separated from the majority populations into Jewish districts called *mellahs* outside city walls, were under direct protection of the local sovereign or sultan. In exchange, the ruler demanded from them certain monetary services forbidden by the Bible or the Quran. This opened up the possibility for a small minority of Jews in Christian and Muslim societies to move up in society as merchants and bankers, while the majority continued to perform small-scale and itinerant merchant activities. Although some Jews accrued wealth and influence by performing these activities, wider society still perceived them as dishonourable.

A comparable phenomenon persists to this day in India, despite the institution of an official ban on such practices in 1950. The effective exclusion of untouchables from all prestigious activities forces them to secure their survival through socially necessary but disdained kinds of work considered unclean and dishonourable. They thus perform tasks like rendering animal carcasses, disposing of rubbish and working as porters or street performers. Hinduism regulates the link between hierarchy and certain spheres of activity once common in status-based feudal societies through the caste system. Believers are placed into castes based on their ancestral lineage and bound by endogamy and commensality (dietary restrictions and obligations to eat and drink among themselves) for their entire lives. While *Brahmins* may join the priesthood, teach in universities or serve in government, *Kshatriyas* are considered nobles and soldiers. *Vaishya* are landowners and merchants, while *Shudras* are expected to work as farmers, artisans and servants. The lowest social group are the *Dalit* – the untouchables, or *harijan* (Children of God), as Gandhi used to call them in order to overcome their degradation. These primary castes are further differentiated into hundreds of subgroups, reflecting how the social hierarchy is constructed in terms of purity and honour. Accordingly, the kinds of activity reserved for each respective caste are also linked to honour and dishonour. According to Hinduism's understanding of reincarnation, overcoming one's inherited social status is only possible in the next life.[3]

The so-called *hijras* constitute a separate subgroup due to their transgender identity. They are also perceived as 'impure' and belong to the lowest rung of the social hierarchy, but are both despised and feared for the healing and divinatory abilities they are believed to possess. They use these abilities to preside over births, marriages, dance ceremonies and temple services, for which they are paid in money and basic goods.[4]

Voluntary/forced (under political coercion)

This tandem becomes operative in modern bourgeois constitutional societies. 'Voluntary' refers to an individual's free decision to enter into a particular set of labour relations, while political coercion can suspend this freedom. Political coercion is often associated with polities lacking basic forms of bourgeois legality: these societies are built on limitations to personal freedom and freedom of movement, such as serfdom, which subject the population to forced labour (unfree). However, it can also emerge within bourgeois, constitutional states, namely when the voluntary nature of work is suspended for all, or, more frequently, for specific groups of the population. This applies, for example, to the use of slaves by colonial empires and settler colonies. The category also applies to states which subject citizens to forced labour without a fair trial for political, religious or ethnic reasons (workhouses and labour camps of all kinds).

Even the institutions of marriage, family and household grant the husband, the head of the family, or the leader of the household the right to exercise force over dependent individuals whose freedom to choose their workplace or occupation is limited and who are obligated to perform labour against their will. Although basic human and legal rights restricting the use of force within marriages and family life have been implemented in some states, the compulsion to perform certain kinds of work under familial coercion has failed to disappear in either legal or factual terms (servitude, care, sex). However, this constitutes a specific, patriarchal form that cannot be subsumed under political coercion as such.

Paid/unpaid

Whether work is of a paid or unpaid nature constitutes a central line of division in the categorization of work forms. This dichotomy is justified in some sense, given that unpaid subsistence work and paid labour represent the two extremes of the remuneration axis. That said, the same activities can often manifest as both paid and unpaid work depending on context, while levels of payment also vary enormously. Within the family, care work is by and large unpaid. Paid care work either belongs to the low-wage sector or, if training and formalized qualifications are involved, becomes the purview of top-earning professionals. Work falls into the realm of unpaid labour when individuals are forced to work without remuneration, or when entrepreneurs fail to pay wages owed in cases of bankruptcy or wage theft.

Surviving without a monetary income became practically impossible following the dissolution of small-scale, subsistence-oriented ways of life. People who work without pay are thus often compelled to take up additional paid work or rely on family members to gain access to money; in other cases, they may depend on public or private welfare relief. Completely substituting family care by relying on professional care workers is impossible for most wage labourers and self-employed people. Remunerated and non-remunerated work thus appear in an inseparable symbiosis of varying compositions, both in family contexts and for individuals who divide their energies between multiple tasks in their single households.

Forms of payment include income from both independent and dependent work (both of the employer and their employees). According to the Marxist definition, an entrepreneur only profits (beyond their own wage) from the surplus value created by relying on the labour of employees. Remuneration for work performed by dependent workers ranges from hourly wages (payment according to time worked), to piece-work wages (payment according to amount produced) and mixed forms (hourly wages paired with production bonuses or discounts), all the way to sharecropping, in which the worker retains a share of the sales price. If shares are only paid when an actual sale is concluded, this should be considered a form of commission on a self-employed basis.

Paid work does not necessarily have to be performed voluntarily in order to be considered paid. Even the serfs of feudal England and other status-based societies, or the slaves and servants employed in the mines and plantations of colonial economies, were sometimes allowed to pursue independent remunerated activities. In some cases, they were even paid for the work imposed upon them by force.

Contractual or regulated by law/unregulated (formal/informal)

The categorical pairing of contractual/non-contractual differentiates between labour relations based on a formal contract and those determined by some form of obligation-based reciprocity, power relation or feudal domination (tribute-based conditions/relations). In the ideal type, contracts are produced in written form, but can also emerge as verbal agreements.

Employment agreements specifying performance and payment for waged work extend far back into human history: clay tablets of ancient Middle Eastern cultures, for instance, recount how the builders who erected the palaces and temples of old were paid for their labour. Nevertheless, waged work generally constituted a rare exception, while reciprocal and tributary labour relations remained deeply embedded into most human lifeworlds throughout history. The growth in non-domestic, paid employment brought about by the rise of industrial capitalism saw the contract become the most widespread form of agreement in the buying and selling of labour.[5] The contractual character of modern wage labour entails, first, that a person is assigned to a labour relation based on supply and demand; once a contract is agreed upon, labour power itself becomes a commodity. Second, it transforms the social relation resulting from social inequality (capital owners versus those limited to their own labour) into a condition in which unequal partners enter a contractual bond in a state of formal equality.

The existing power imbalance is disguised by the contract form, which simultaneously guarantees that infringing upon said contract will result in legal consequences. Nevertheless, every contract hinges upon the existing legal order as protection against such infringement. Before civil codes were widely introduced, labour issues were dealt with by occupation- and sector-specific mining and maritime courts, or by the guilds themselves. Town or city residents could turn to municipal courts, community members to the local judge; peasants were subject to their lord's estate and servant codes.

The general form of bourgeois legality that developed in the industrializing states at the beginning of the nineteenth century initially neglected to limit what services could be contractually agreed upon between entrepreneurs and workers. Anything was allowed, to the point where long working hours and lack of secure or sanitary conditions in capitalism's early factories physically exhausted workers so quickly that legal protections were deemed necessary. The social and economic legislation that emerged from labour movement demands and business owners' growing need for increased performance and qualifications from their workers – together with numerous social conflicts and struggles, of course – gradually formed what we think of today as labour law. These laws regulated minimum wages, working hours, job safety and social benefits. Through legislation, institutional arrangements concerning workplace inspections and state employment policies were established, which led to workers' dependency on their employers being relaxed in the twentieth century as workers' rights were strengthened. The emergence of labour unions further bolstered their position, facilitating collective action and negotiation. Unions were also enshrined in the legal structures of many societies, acknowledging them as partners in collective bargaining and the drafting of labour laws.

The legal regulation of labour relations in the twentieth century was almost entirely limited to the developed industrial countries, and only remained in effect as long as the economic conjuncture would allow it. That said, it still managed to inspire workers in developing countries. The International Labour Organization (ILO) strives for global formalization, enforcement and monitoring of minimum labour standards. Those adopted by ILO bodies, however, rarely correspond to the achievements won by previous generations of workers in the West.[6] Should profits lag in the industrialized countries, employers' associations can often push through relaxations or restrictions on labour and social laws. Many also manage to reduce labour costs by circumventing existing regulations, such as by transferring work orders to self-employed, temporary or short-term contractors not subject to collective-bargaining agreements, or to countries with lower wages and laxer regulations.

The existence of strong labour movement organizations in the West, as well as the relatively generous labour legislation in what was referred to as 'actually existing socialism' in the East, resulted in competition between social systems and thus posed certain barriers to the dismantling of labour laws. The neo-liberal turn of the 1980s, however, prepared the ground for widespread degradation of social and labour laws, and contract work and new labour relations outside existing collective-bargaining agreements are now on the rise. Unprotected or specifically deregulated labour relations are called 'precarious', while the overall tendency is often referred to as 'deregulation' or 'informalization'. However, these terms are only accurate to the extent that they refer to older legal and contractual forms. Once these laws have been replaced by new legal and institutional arrangements, they will become the new form(ality) and thus begin to constitute the new regulatory system as such.[7]

In historical terms, the contractual allocation of labour power characteristic of industrial capitalism can be only understood as formalization if previous systems of control, in which relations of employment were based on family or social obligations, are regarded as functioning without contracts of any kind. This view fails to hold water, however, as concrete agreements and sanctions of various forms existed in these social formations, and simply lost their meaning as regulated wage labour increasingly became the norm. The transition from personal, trust-based relationships to contractual legal relations has only improved workers' social position in a superficial manner. A major criticism is that the equality achieved between contractual partners became confused with social equality in the popular mind. The same observation applies to gender equality. Thus the coercive relations resulting from the overwhelming majority's exclusion from the means of production – the very conditions forcing workers to enter a contract of employment (seemingly) voluntarily in the first place – are obscured. This appearance of voluntariness is also the obstacle preventing so many workers from perceiving their own alienation from their labour power, and the transformation of the use values they create into exchange values for their employer, as unjust.

Socially secure/socially insecure

This dichotomy is closely related to legal and contractual regulations. The urbanization, migration and proletarianization characteristic of the nineteenth century eroded traditional systems of social security, and thus made institutions responsible for social security (social insurance, or what is known as 'social security' in the US) increasingly necessary to assist wage workers and their families in cases of illness, accident, disability, unemployment, pregnancy, birth, care and ageing. Nevertheless, these arrangements only applied to a small segment of the labour force in industrializing states, and to a fraction of the cases described. Most social issues remained problems to be addressed by individual families or the municipal poor house. Building on the older workers' self-help institutions such as medieval guilds or the miners' insurance associations of the early modern period, voluntary collective funds were established in the nineteenth century to help bridge the gap in emergency situations, funded by entrepreneurs and industrial workers alike. In Germany, individual services like health care in the case of injury or illness have been directly tied to employment contracts under statutory insurance obligations since the end of the nineteenth century. Later on came new municipal and state welfare agencies, access to which was independent of employment contracts. The strongest industrialized states stood at the pinnacle of this development, particularly when it came to the indispensable sections of the organized industrial working class, i.e. the skilled, permanent workforce, which were also the most able to advance their demands. This forged a link between wage labour and social security that would become the model for other regions and groups of workers. As regulated employment expanded over the course of the twentieth century, it would come to include further spheres of social welfare. The expansion of social services was not by any means an automatic occurrence, but rather required constant negotiation regarding services and eligibility between the needy, employers' associations and state authorities. The high standards achieved by established workers spurred on the struggles of subaltern working classes and inspired visions of a universally secured proletarian existence. In reality, no such harmonization occurred: even as access to services expanded in the industrialized states, differences in levels of social security grew with the mobilization of wage labour in other parts of the world and among other segments of the population, preventing wage rises from being accompanied by increased access to social services.[8]

Moreover, despite professionalization of some types of work associated with birth, child-rearing, nursing and elderly care in the developed welfare states, most tasks remained in the domain of the individual family, where members were available to perform this work for free. A form of indirect compensation occurs in instances where the breadwinner's wage is sufficient to support all members of the family: here, the family acts as a collective unit not only of reproduction and subsistence, but of consumption as well. If neither wages nor social insurance and public welfare prove sufficient, the burden and responsibility of survival fall to family households, which must compensate for insufficient wage income and social services with their own unpaid care work.

Labour relations in which employees and their families are not offered social insurance or state-run social services are considered 'unsecured' or 'precarious', yet describing this situation as such belies a belief that security is tied to social insurance benefits and government social policy. This perspective overlooks the reality that familial, paternalistic or solidary ties and obligations are also sources of security, and in turn ignores the fact that these older systems are activated in developed capitalism to ensure the survival of working-class families outside core classes and regions.

Organized/unorganized

Organization refers to worker self-organization in the broad sense. In principle, this can encompass both independent and dependent, as well as paid and unpaid, workers – although we include neither employers' associations nor company unions in this category. Guilds possessed a dual character, functioning purely as entrepreneurial organizations on the one hand, while also providing the legal framework and setting for organizations of wage-dependent journeymen and apprentices on the other. Miners and sailors also formed their own associations early on with the intent of articulating their political and social concerns in opposition to those of their employers. The veritable pinnacle of the organized labour movement, however, comprised labour parties and trade unions. While parties focus on pressuring the political system to enact worker-friendly legislation, unions function as workers' collective representatives in their struggle against the bosses. Unions faced and continue to face considerable opposition in taking on this role: only in the second half of the nineteenth century were trade unions able to represent workers beyond the level of individual companies, and accepted as a legal model for the integration of workers' interests into capitalist industrial society.

The line between political and trade union work becomes increasingly blurred to the extent that unions manage to assert control over entire branches of industry and establish larger trade union federations. In some cases, trade unions and workers' associations take active part in the legislative process – this kind of institutionalization of trade union power reflects the degree of influence workers' interests carry in a respective state. At the same time, these processes also tend to alienate union leaderships from their base, and facilitate a deprioritization of local demands and protest actions at the workplace level. In situations where unions prove unable to fulfil their assigned function in the political system, workers must rely on their own readiness to take strike action in order to push through demands.

As associations under private civil law, trade unions can decide who they accept into their ranks. Although conceived as a form of collective representation for all wage-dependent workers, the trade union crystallized as the paramount organizational body for the steadily employed native workers of large-scale industry. Farmworkers, day labourers, servants, seasonal workers and migrants found that their interests were given significantly less attention, and in turn often neglected to join the powerful industrial unions. Consequently, they typically belonged to the broad masses of unorganized workers. On the one hand, their relegation to the organizational fringes resulted from the fact that their working and living conditions failed to produce a proletarian self-understanding nor, accordingly, aspirations towards collective representation. On the other hand, however, precarious and irregular workers were explicitly marginalized by the trade unions as potential threats, as their willingness to work for lower wages undermined the bargaining power of organized workers. Their protests were often seen as unruly and disorganized. In some cases, subaltern workers such as farm or domestic workers formed their own unions.

Trade union strength grew with the emergence of large-scale industry, which depended on workers' knowledge, skills and willingness to cooperate and assume co-responsibility in the workplace. Accordingly, companies guaranteed the primary workforce a privileged position vis-à-vis their more precarious counterparts, as reflected in trade union participation in the political system. In the 1970s, many industries began to outsource certain tasks to cheaper, unorganized workforces in new social milieus and regions of the world on a large scale, undermining social and spatial cohesion on the shop floor and placing additional pressure on trade unions. Unions often defended the rights they had fought for and acquired by opposing migrant workers and the workforces of countries with lower wage levels, regarding them as international competitors brought in to eat away at 'normal labour relations' in the core. An internationalization of trade union work along the commodity chains of globalization was supposed to counteract this fragmentation, but its success has remained negligible thus far, as strengthening workers on the lower rungs of the commodity chain stands in the way of minimizing costs. Corporate globalization strategies also undermine trade unions in the industrialized countries, forcing them to tread a thin line between defending the privileges of what is seen as a shrinking core workforce, and attracting precarious workers they had long ignored. This was made more complicated as unions lost their official influence and social partnerships were dismantled over the course of the neo-liberal turn of the 1980s and 1990s, often supported by Social-Democratic parties. This has cost them many of the tools necessary to effectively represent their members' interests. Losses in terms of both membership and influence have led to the growing marginalization of many unions.

The fragmentation of working conditions and labour relations driven forward by new technologies, questionable work contracts, outsourcing and relocations – resulting in a loss of spatial and social cohesion between shop floor activities and political and trade union organization – also leads to individualization and isolation. Several attempts to restructure workers' power beyond the old, established organizations have emerged in response. The May Day movement is one of these responses, whose gatherings of precarious workers in large Western cities hark back to the First of May traditions of previous generations, while reviving ritualized union celebrations by mobilizing a broad and colourful spectrum of social movements. Despite expressing solidarity with precarious workers the world over, the limited nature of these events shows how difficult it is to foster these connections in practice.

GREY AREAS AT THE INTERSECTION OF WORK AND NON-WORK

Makeshift work

Makeshift work describes a form of livelihood in which various forms of paid activity are carried out in conjunction with subsistence work and efforts to acquire income from other sources such as charity, donations, benefits in kind and subsistence allowances from private individuals or public institutions. This type of income transfer often relies on exchanges in the form of cultural performances (e.g. playing music) or services (errands, general assistance, repair work, public services). Makeshift livelihoods become necessary when one's gainful or subsistence base is insufficient to sustain a family, forcing workers to explore any and all possibilities of securing basic needs. Context demonstrates that these activities are connected to work for those forced to engage in them. Outsiders are often unwilling to view activities like begging or busking as work; the same is true of openly demonstrating one's need or handicap, or performing small conveniences in exchange for charity or in unpaid exchange. Instead, activities of these sorts are considered 'idleness' or an expression of a person's 'laziness', and banished into the category of non-work. This form of non-work, however, is obviously different from leisure in the sense of *otium* or other socially accepted forms of freedom from work such as childhood, old age or disability, which are not associated with comparable negative connotations.

Shadow work

The term 'shadow work' was coined by Ivan Illich in connection with new findings in women's studies at the end of the 1970s. Illich included in this category all those activities needed to survive on a monetary income in a modern market society. By this, he did not mean use-value-creating subsistence activities – the material basis of which was steadily eroding in industrial society – but rather activities like shopping, queuing, waiting, comparing prices, and visits to the bank, court or other state authorities and welfare bodies. This 'drudgery in industrial society' is the flip side of work and of its necessary corollary, surviving on a monetary income, and is carried out predominantly (albeit not exclusively) by women. Commonly, neither the people engaged in these activities nor observers perceive this as work as such. Shadow work creates neither use value nor exchange value and thus appears to belong to a different category of human activity. Illich, however, located these activities squarely within the sphere of securing one's survival and thus linked them intimately with paid labour.

Feminists criticized Illich for denying that this (feminine) survival work possessed value-creating character. In doing so, however, they overlooked the fact that shadow work does not belong in the category of subsistence work, as it is in fact an expression of market-related activities and a kind of activity necessary for commodities to be acquired and consumed in the first place.[9]

Shadow work has undergone unprecedented expansion in recent years due to digitalization and the rise of seemingly constant availability facilitated by mobile phones and Internet connectivity. Administrative tasks and services once performed by paid staff are shifted onto the customer (self-service and online sales, the digital shopping cart which needs no cashier). This transfer is connected to countless hours of shadow work for the consumers themselves, yet produces no use value to speak of. What it does for the company, however, is to realize considerable savings in terms of human resources and other expenses. Around the clock digital accessibility and availability can be seen as a creeping expansion of working time, which has now settled comfortably into the grey area of what an employee's or contractor's obligations are, an accompanying feature of one's actual working conditions and labour relations. Although this is often described as 'flexibility', it has a major impact in terms of cost savings and control factors.

One noteworthy manifestation of shadow work is *blat*, a Soviet-era invention describing the system of informal agreements practised in the USSR and other state socialist societies in order to compensate for deficits, restrictions to access and imbalances in the supply of goods and services. The Russian phrase *po blatu* means obtaining that which was officially unobtainable, like scarce or rationed foods, particular medications or a hospital bed, or even access to higher education, an apartment, or a vacation home, in a way that was not permitted, i.e. through patronage or personal connections.[10] It could also mean acquiring some products more quickly or more easily than otherwise possible. Payment was usually not cash but the prospect of receiving a favour in return, placing both giver and taker in a long-term reciprocal relationship. Maintaining the relationships and networks associated with such favours required a personal investment of one's time, contacts and knowledge. *Blat* is thus often used to illustrate the importance of social capital in Pierre Bourdieu's understanding of the concept. Although Illich neglected to investigate the role of shadow work in centrally planned economies, it is clear that the term is more suited to the character of such activity than any attempt to expand our conception of capital might be. It is clear that *blat* neither created value nor served solely to secure basic needs, unlike domestic self-sufficiency, private markets or the personal vegetable gardening economies common in Eastern Bloc countries. Despite this fact, *blat* was certainly part of the system of distributing scarce commodities in a planned economy.

Blat stands for a type of relationship network which was widespread but not officially tolerated by authorities, and which in some cases actually crossed over into illegality. The level of ostracization, criminalization, informality and clandestinity that *blat* encountered makes it difficult for contemporary scholars to study its actual range and extent or the self-perceptions of its practitioners in retrospect.[11]

Unpaid/invaluable

Distinguishing between paid and unpaid work is fairly straightforward. But can all forms of unpaid work theoretically be turned into paid work as well?

The category of 'invaluable' raises a twofold question: first, can every form of unpaid work be transformed into paid work? And second, is such a transformation always desirable? After all, converting reciprocal work into commodified work concerns more than whether or not a state has sufficient purchasing power to replace all household and subsistence activities with market products.

The transformation of self-sufficiency activities into paid wage labour in a household, family or (agrarian) subsistence context is an inevitable result of the separation of people from the land and their means of subsistence, as engendered by urbanization and industrialization. Aspects of everything from home construction, food production and preparation, child-rearing, nursing and even affection and sex travelled from the sphere of unpaid work into that of the consumer economy. Commodifying the satisfaction of needs stemming from subsistence and reproduction often serves as an engine to propel economies past stagnant revenues and profits by creating new perceived needs and corresponding products. There are limits, however, to what is affordable: in industrialized countries, certain parts of the workforce, as well as the socially vulnerable, only benefit from these effects to a limited extent; furthermore, global inequality means that, in developing countries, only a wealthy minority can afford such remunerated social services. The effect of wage differentials between global cores and peripheries is such that people from low-wage regions migrate to wealthier countries to engage in commodified care work. This extraction of unpaid family and professional caregivers from low-income regions is called 'care drain'.[12]

This category also addresses the character of social relationships and whether transforming domestic, reciprocal labour into paid work in fact stands in opposition to the very character of the activity itself. The idea that education, medicine, social work or personal care ought to be provided by institutions and professionals financed by the public sector, social insurance and private demand is almost taken for granted in modern society, and generally perceived as 'progress'. The fact that this situation is anything but inevitable only gets our attention when access to these services is restricted by privatization. Critics branded this professionalization the tyranny of experts, a form of control and standardization, as well as a way to disenfranchise people and undermine their independence.[13]

This is particularly true for the spheres of love, care and nursing, where personal attention, sacrifice, reliability and reciprocity are essential elements. Yet professional staff are often incapable of providing precisely these elements. After all, should the (often immigrant) nurse happen to bring these capabilities to her work in a hospital, elderly home or client's private household, she most likelvvvy would not find time for her family back home.

It is thus becoming increasingly evident that leaving certain domestic reproduction and care activities out of the market and protecting them from commodification may be socially desirable. Existing work (time) regimes and career plans, however, greatly limit most families' room to manoeuvre: as the nuclear family is often overwhelmed in many respects, protecting such spheres of invaluable work would require social solutions. Some of these could be new forms of living and cohabitation, or support and care arrangements practised among groups of people or an entire community. Furthermore, new ways of distributing gainful subsistence and care work must ensure that enough time remains for invaluable work to be done in the house, family or cohabitation group (flat share, commune). Such an achievement must also guarantee financial support for unpaid workers, and ensure that women are not disproportionately burdened. One prerequisite for such an arrangement would be increased social appreciation of invaluable work more generally.

ACROSS REGIONS AND CATEGORIES

Gender – marital status – origin/ethnicity/nationality

Gender, marital status and age are conditions which stem from a combination of biological factors, perceived affiliations and social attributions. They are changeable and exhibit vast differences across cultures and regions. Male/female, single/married, young/old are more than just additional tandem terms for defining differences in labour relations, but are rather existential conditions appearing in all vertical reference frames and horizontal categories. Their existence demands that we investigate the roles of gender, life cycle and age in terms of allocation and attribution in every sphere of work we discuss.

A similar dynamic is at play in the differentiation between native populations and foreigners, later translated into citizenship in the course of modern state building. The overlapping of gender, social condition (class), skin colour and ethnic belonging (race), as well as origin (otherness) manifests differently for every person (intersectionality). On the labour market, this translates into hierarchical gradations regarding access to or exclusion from certain activities and labour relations, and their perceived value and remuneration.

Work and non-work

Grasping what exactly work is can perhaps best be accomplished by looking at what is *not* work. Just like defining work, defining non-work proves to be multifaceted, and many aspects remain disputed. We will thus distinguish between leisure, free time, volunteer activities, exemptions from work and unemployability, as well as various subsistence and makeshift activities which the gainfully oriented perspective often excludes from its definition of work.

Rest and leisure

Rest and leisure belong to a conception of work including a broad spectrum of diverse activities performed throughout the day, the work year and the course of one's life. Rituals and ceremonies are counted among essential everyday activities in traditional societies. Whether sombre or ecstatic, ritual in these societies is not separated from other aspects of daily life. Gods and goddesses are omnipresent and assist believers in daily activity. In the conceptual world of the great monotheistic religions, the cycle of days, weeks, years and life as a whole are filled with times and moments in which work is forbidden. This is derived from the idea that 'the Creator' rested for a day after finishing His work of creation. Religious law defines specific days and times of day to honour this act, often in connection with places of prayer, rituals of worship or pilgrimages. Rest mainly refers to those moments of reflection in which people turn to God, prayer or contemplation. Monks, nuns or dervishes are people for whom the contemplative service of their religion is something to which they often devote their entire lives. Rather than take up an occupation or trade, they choose devotion to God as their calling. It thus becomes clear that rest is far from idleness, which is condemned in most religions.

Leisure, however, describes moments of relaxation, repose from work, or short breaks alternated with work or between phases of work. In English, the word arose in Middle English from the Old French term *leiser* (to be permitted), a derivation from the Latin *licēre*. The German word *Muße* originally signified free space or room to manoeuvre. It shifted to the temporal domain as 'free time of any sort "(distant from affairs or conducting business)"' as well as 'the opportunity to do something'.[14] Leisure entails rest but also socializing and maintaining relationships and networks. That said, doing something that contributed to survival while undertaking another specific activity was not ruled out, as with rest in the religious sense. Women often knitted or embroidered together in the evening after finishing their work in the household and fields, and still do today in some places. In earlier times, they often sang. Before the rise of spinning factories, they spun wool or, in cold regions, processed feathers for use as insulation (i.e. separating the soft vane from the stem). For men, connecting leisure and sociable subsistence work is rarer – whittling or woodcarving is an example, albeit only if done to pass the time.

More often they spent their time outside work in sporting contests, typically embedded in seasonal customs, or visited the local tavern.

In many Western Roman Catholic societies, rest, contemplation and leisure were tolerated and considered socially acceptable. The rise of Protestantism, however, led to their stigmatization as idleness. In Orthodox Christianity, by contrast, the value of contemplation was considered unassailable. This apparent correlation led Max Weber to situate the spirit of capitalism in Protestantism.[15] In Weber's native tongue, the difference between leisure (*Muße*), being idle (*müßig sein*), and idleness (*Müßiggang*) had been rather negligible.[16] But as the workshops and factories of the eighteenth and nineteenth centuries increasingly required labour to operate punctually and regularly, workers were forced to change their behaviour and rid themselves of their attachments to leisure time, transforming it into diligence and industriousness (*industria*). This went hand in hand with the decline of contemplative orders across the lands of the former Western Roman Empire, as idleness became increasingly equated with laziness, slovenliness and sloth.

Free time

Free time results from a conceptual world in which work is conceived as gainful employment performed within a specific time frame and, ideally, remunerated with monetary means to secure commodities necessary for survival. Anything else is considered free time. Various activities required for reproduction are not included in free time, however, such that individual phases of free time can be longer or shorter according to subsistence obligations. Forms of living where work and leisure intermingle are strangers to the concept of free time, which itself, along with spare time, is a fairly new concept altogether. The expression succeeded 'leisure' but simultaneously signifies a change in meaning.

Free time is temporally separate from gainful employment, as well as from subsistence and housework. Free time does not mesh with work, i.e. there is no sequence between or overlay of working and leisure times, but is rather altogether separate. It is seen as an achievement that can be used for rest or play without regard for social obligations. It may be filled with activities like hobby crafting, tinkering or gardening, provided that these contribute not to one's survival but rather to pleasure and play. The idea of indulging in a hobby grew over time, as seen in the German adoption of the English term 'hobbyhorse', translated as *Steckenpferd*: 'a stick that boys put between their legs to cavort around upon as the heart desires, to enjoy, one's soul full of childly desire'.[17] In German, this entailed anything that invited a light-hearted romp: 'hobby, inclination, occupied idleness', while the English term went on to signify (over)indulgence in an activity or topic. In the context of travelling and vacation, free time is also spatially divorced from one's living and work space. Hospital stays or spending time at home due to an illness, in turn recuperating one's capacity to work, on the other hand, are considered neither free time nor indulgence.

Volunteering

The concept of volunteer work exists within an overlapping space of free time and unpaid but socially respected work. It generally refers to political work in municipalities, political parties and citizen initiatives or professional organizations, as well as social work in aid, care and disaster relief institutions. It also encompasses activities performed for non-profit associations and clubs that fulfil cultural, scientific or civil educational duties (museums, galleries, lectures, sport, traditional culture, historical preservation, environmental conservation). In the broadest sense, these volunteer community activities are expressions of what is often called 'civil society'. In terms of our categorical typology, this falls into the category of 'work for the collective or community'.

Volunteer activity is characterized by the fact that it is performed for free. If the same activities are carried out by a paid professional, it becomes a form of employment or paid labour. Often volunteer work in clubs, associations and parties is organized and directed by such professionals, while most individual members work for free. If work done in a volunteer capacity is somehow remunerated, independent work transforms into dependent employment.

Which tasks are performed by volunteers and what is kept in the hands of professionals is subject to vast temporal and spatial differences. The citizens of Athenian democracy were compensated for their participation in political meetings and decision making, making it a paid activity in some sense.[18] The physical labour necessary to ensure the livelihoods of free citizens, however, was performed by house slaves and women under coercion – without payment.

Work services imposed on certain age groups, such as military and civilian service performed on behalf of the state, could also be categorized under volunteer activity. It remains debatable whether or not such services can be seen as forced labour, as would clearly be the case under a dictatorship. In other circumstances, it could be viewed as an obligation, as part and parcel of the social contract.

Exemptions from work

Various groups of people are exempt from work in every society. When certain people do not have to work, it is often rooted in wealth and status. Such privileges gave nobles the right to land ownership, for example, along with the ability to tax their subjects and force them to work so that they did not have to. The same effect occurs when someone can afford to live off inheritances, capital or interest dividends. That said, life as a rentier is not necessarily completely free of work: organizing one's estate, its operations and finances is tied to all kinds of work, albeit usually associated with a standard of living much higher than normal gainful employment could ever provide.

Second, social practices free certain groups from paid – and, in certain circumstances, unpaid – work due to their age, gender, health or other factors. In the modern era, these exemptions from work face increased regulation and legal codification. Living expenses are shouldered by family, spouses, public institutions or social insurance. The more various activities of life, work and the household merge or intermingle, the less each individual can be free of work altogether. Rather, each is drawn towards work that matches their abilities: easy tasks are performed by the young, the old and infirm. Young mothers tend towards childcare and work around or near the home. Youth and young adults may take jobs requiring courage and risk taking, or seasonal employment. Tasks requiring a wealth of experience are reserved for the middle-aged, and only the sick and disabled remain largely exempt from work altogether. Furthermore, the rules for who is exempt from what work become more defined and binding, along with the tendency for work to detach from the family household and take on a character of gainful employment outside the home. After an early industrial period when factory workers were completely used up and worn out, Western industrial societies began to exclude first children, then teenagers, pregnant women and young mothers from the obligation to perform non-domestic labour over the course of the nineteenth century. Early old-age insurance was the first step towards introducing retirement pensions. Except for civil servants, pension insurance was only introduced after the First World War.

These people were not automatically freed from housework. Women remained, regardless of whether they were employed or not, committed to leading the family households as daughters, wives and mothers. They generally received assistance from both female and male family members, but fully employed men – as the family breadwinners – were exempt from helping out in the household by definition.

Who exactly is exempt from work varies wildly. Historically, the developed industrial states were the first to grant non-working time for education, maternity, recreation and a secure retirement to the proletarianized workforce, thanks to innovations in labour and social law. In terms of social policy, these states were surpassed in the second half of the twentieth century by the state socialist industrial nations, which could cite higher levels of social and gender equality and greater worker protections despite lower standards of living.[19] Education lasted longer on average and retirement ages were lower than in the West. The labour and social legislation of socialist states put pressure on Western governments to make concessions to unions and labour parties during the years of system rivalry.

Developing countries never had the financial potential to guarantee their wage-dependent citizens secure, work-free time. Minimum standards adopted by the International Labour Organization (ILO) and other United Nations organizations are quite meagre and often simply ignored. Even in the states of the global North, time away from work has not grown: its zenith was reached in the 1970s and has since experienced an ongoing regression with the consolidation of neo-liberal thinking in the West and the collapse of the Eastern Bloc, which eliminated state socialist achievements. At the same time, flexibilization of working time has resulted in a softening of existing standards of work exemption as well as job security. On the one hand, this has produced an enormous rise in pressure on employees, for whom work-free time has seemed to melt away in recent decades. The darker flip side of this freedom from work can be seen in the growth of structural unemployment. The rise in retirement ages around the world is justified by citing rising life expectancy, while rising productivity and unemployment in old age are ignored.

Work prohibitions – bans, blacklists, and so on – can be seen as yet another non-voluntary form of freedom from work. Those affected are not entirely exempted from work, however, but rather excluded from certain spheres of activity. Laws to protect women and children not only shield them from toilsome labour, but also serve to relieve male adults from unwelcome competition on the job market. The same is true of work prohibitions that exclude members of specific ethnic or religious groups from certain professions and thus force them into other areas of activity, as with Jews in Christian societies, or Christians and Jews in Muslim societies, as discussed earlier. Bans from public service are usually imposed on political dissidents. Here, exemption from work is linked to social exclusion.

Controversial and contested

A narrow definition of work as paid employment pushes unpaid household and subsistence work into the realm of non-work, yet hardly anyone would actively refer to domestic work as non-work. The question of whether a housewife works, however, is generally answered in the negative – even by women themselves. Housework is thus as controversial as it is contested. Strategies to address this predicament are highly divergent, ranging from overcoming (through professionalization of housework), to payment (wages for housework), to social revaluation (through moral recognition, mandatory distribution among the adult members of the household, or social insurance contributions).

In order to view domestic and subsistence work as socially necessary work, we must first recognize all paid and unpaid activities, independent of worker's age or gender, as work: going through the *labour* of giving birth and raising children, providing food and care for family members, producing and repairing clothing, home construction, food preparation and preservation, transport and assistance, community aid, services, and much more. But mere recognition runs the risk that the question of securing one's basic needs may be obscured in the discussion.

Several concepts under the term 'mixed work' deal with how personal working time can be assigned equal parts of domestic and gainful work, volunteering and personal education during one's lifetime – in many ways, these concepts hark back to the utopias of early socialist and communist projects.[20] One's livelihood would be secured despite drastically reduced time spent working to earn money in order to engage in one's other, non-paid activities. Personal combinations of the various spheres of work would vary according to age. The concept's crucial factor is that income gaps between gainful activities must be as narrow as possible. It is contested whether every man and woman would be obliged to take on each and every sort of task, as envisaged in most designs for utopian societies. Viewed the other way around, this would also mean that every man and woman would be entitled to this versatility and also to gainful employment.

The Universal Declaration of Human Rights, adopted by the United Nations General Assembly in Paris in December of 1948, was rather vague and non-binding on the subject. It was not until 1976 that the Universal Declaration gained formal legal status. Political and civil public spheres, as well as survival and acquisition, were treated therein as separate domains, therefore falling short of bolstering this desire to merge the various aspects of human self-determination and actualization. The International Covenant on Civil and Political Rights covers individual liberty, while the International Covenant on Economic, Social and Cultural Rights encompasses the rights to work, education, food and water. Arguments regarding the right to work at the UN are carried out on the basis of a conception of work reduced to paid labour or employment.

An alternative conception of the right to paid work is a guaranteed basic income for all, regardless of one's occupational status. It is intended to ensure access to basic survival needs through a minimum income, which can then be supplemented through paid activities. Drafts of such unconditional basic income schemes do not require recipients to take on paid activities or employment, nor do they envisage a right to paid work.

All such visions and debates and the public discussions and disputes associated with them are phenomena of post-industrial societies. They hardly make sense in the context of labour struggles raging in the newly industrialized countries of the southern hemisphere; indeed, they stand quite uncomprehending and helpless in the face of global inequality.

5.

Divisions of Labour: The Simultaneity and Combination of (Different) Labour Relations

We must assume that the frames of reference for work and associated labour relations do not reflect a simple transition from reciprocal to market forms. Rather, each historical time period is characterized by a unique combination of frames and forms of work. These connections can be further delineated into local and interregional distinctions, depending on their geographic scope.

LOCAL CONNECTIONS

From the household perspective, it is quite normal to divide members' working time and capacity into work for subsistence, the community, the political sovereign and the market. Distribution ensures that unpaid domestic work and contributions to the community are performed alongside tribute or taxes paid to landlords and states, as well as work for the production of commodity goods. The household division of labour allows for each member to spend most of their time on an individual focus, usually according to gender, age, abilities and skills.

Because every household member is somehow involved (even if the household only consists of one person), the household perspective is crucial to understanding broader connections within the world of work.[1] In this case, we exclude completely self-sufficient households as subsistence households without any relation to the market. That said, producing for one's own consumption is usually insufficient to cover all needs, compelling the household to accrue some kind of monetary income by producing for the market or pursuing wage labour. Moreover, practically every household offers its extra labour power to fulfil communal duties or produce surplus to pay a political sovereign. While tribute and other feudal customs fall under conditions of servitude with the benefits going to the sovereign directly, taxes are generated indirectly through consumption, revenue, income or wages. Extra-domestic income flows back into the household in the form of the worker's income, where it can be used for consumer spending. Additionally, individual members of the household may receive state aid financed with tax revenues.

Subsistence and community work play little role in the microeconomic calculations of businesses and entrepreneurs. Hiring workers is a market-level concern, where a form of rent is paid for the labour power on offer in the form of wages. Whatever additional value an employer manages to extract from the expended labour power is what Karl Marx called 'surplus value'.[2] The employer profits because the wage labour purchased in contractual form produces values worth more than the wages paid out to workers. The employer also pays taxes, which constitute the means to cover public spending; at the same time, companies benefit from public spending themselves, both through specific funding measures and generally in the form of infrastructure and a legal system that supports entrepreneurial activity.

Organization and technology represent instruments of profit maximization in the face of competition: dividing work into manageable tasks and assigning it across the differently suited, educated and paid sections of the workforce plays a major role here. The use of machines, meanwhile, can increase productivity at each step of the work process as well as coordinate the individual steps more efficiently. As a result, a given company's operational division of labour will exhibit a highly varied distribution of pay, job security and education across its workforce – in terms of wages and other forms of remuneration, working hours and duration, prospects for advancement, safety and social security.

Each wage labourer employed in the workforce serves as a link to the subsistence work performed in his or her household. Their wage income must be made available to all members of the household, even if they are not wage labourers themselves or contribute only partially via extra-domestic income, as they depend on said income both to secure long-term needs and to satisfy short-term consumption. This connection, however, also has an outflow effect: work performed by other household members flows outward to the company through the employed member, in the sense that housework regenerates the worker's labour power, while value drains out of the household to the employer of the household member in relation to their earnings. This drain can be seen as a 'transfer value of unpaid work'. When added to the 'surplus value from paid labour', these make up the sum value appropriated by the employer through contracting the workforce.[3]

If the worker earns enough money to support a family (the idea of the *family wage* arose with the concept of the male breadwinner in the nineteenth century), this can be seen as indirect remuneration for unpaid work taking place in the family household. This family wage simultaneously feeds family budgets, which in turn drives up demand and boosts commodity sales. Workers unable to support a family with their earnings, however, can only take part in consumption to a limited extent. In order to compensate for low wages, more family members are forced to seek employment or rely increasingly on unpaid activities performed within the household. Thus each wage labourer also activates a greater share of unpaid work, meaning that the volume of transferred value grows.

In the relationship between members of a household and employers, public redistribution schemes play a role in funding aid for needy households through taxes and social insurance funds. Depending on which particular redistribution framework has been negotiated or won in struggle and legally agreed upon, conditional wage losses and costs are compensated in cases of maternity, unemployment, education, illness or old age among household members. The effect is twofold: these forms of compensation reduce the need to compensate low wages with household work, while strengthening the workforce in general and thus (also) benefiting employers. A multi-layered macroeconomic perspective also comes into play, which can take on domestic, state, or even bi- or multi-state dimensions. According to the level of social, tax and economic policy, households, individual wage earners and companies are all tied into a system of public support, taxation and redistribution. These measures are pivotal in determining the composition of the social benefits that households can expect from paid and unpaid transfers and/or welfare.

INTERREGIONAL CONNECTIONS

Interregional connections occur when households and companies span multiple locations or production sites incorporated into interregional divisions of labour and multi-regional networks. Our study differentiates between the household and the company perspective here as well, although both are subject to the regulations of state, international and supranational institutions.

From the household perspective, interregional connections are created through migration. When individual family members manage to find extra-domestic employment away from their homes for shorter or longer periods of time, the result is a regional network that functions along the same lines as it would locally. Family members leave (or are sent away) to take up paid work in order to send back remittances to support those staying behind. Conversely, the household in the country of origin offers a social anchor for the worker, who can rely on their support in trying times and even return to them if necessary. Characteristic of these interregional combinations of paid and unpaid activities are the various differences in kinds of job available, as well as wage and price gaps between the migrants' countries of origin and their destinations. Family members choose or are chosen to stay or go according to personal situation, age, family status and personal suitability, as well as propensity and motivation.[4] Wage and price differentials compel many migrant workforces to resign themselves to lower wages, fewer social services and less job security. Nevertheless, they can save money to provide for their families back home by living cheaply and consuming less. Another motivation for frugality is that many wish to bring their families over, or save money to use as capital after returning home. The family thus provides more than simply refuge for reproduction, but rather includes self-employed or employed workers who can benefit from the extra income sent back by migrants, stabilizing and ameliorating their situation. This in turn also stabilizes the ability and willingness to send more workers to emigrate, and eventually take them back if they must return.

Interregional connections are not exclusively the products of family or household ties, as the contacts that emerge between regions also represent structures of opportunity which build the bridges and information channels that facilitate further migration. The direction and character of migration are shaped by differentials in supply and demand between countries of origin and destination. Personal motivations to leave one's home country generally correspond to these uneven regional structures. Migrants' chosen destination, as well as a given country's willingness to accept political refugees, align with historical connections and responsibilities stemming from those connections, along with the opportunities posed by inviting a qualified workforce with lowered work expectations than the citizens of the target country. Migration is thus always tied to a loss for countries of origin, even when the individual migrant experiences migration as personal advancement or escapes political persecution. Destination countries then benefit from a migrant workforce, particularly when it fulfils local demand and contributes to lowering wage costs while externalizing social costs onto the countries of origin. This is especially the case when migrants maintain strong ties to their families at home and see their work mainly as a contribution to supporting their family or building up capital with which to return later on. Because they often evaluate their income in relation to purchasing power and consumption levels at home, migrants are more willing to work for lower wages and fewer social rights. General insecurity in terms of residency permits adds to this perspective, driving them to view family networks as their primary social safety net.

For companies, on the other hand, interregional connections between different labour relations express themselves in two ways: unequal exchange and interregional commodity chains.

In abstract terms, unequal exchange means that products are exchanged which represent different amounts of realized working time.[5] This can occur for various reasons: in the case of raw materials and finished commodities, goods can differ in terms of the amount of processing necessary, which delivers a higher degree of value added to the industrial producer. Inequality can also stem from differing levels of technology and logistics, which ensure better-equipped manufacturers advantages in productivity. Differences in labour costs are also a relevant factor: wage and price gaps between regions make imports from low-wage areas quite cheap, while export goods from high-wage regions become more expensive. That low-wage earners nevertheless manage to survive comes from their ability to combine several sources of income – individually and in the context of family networks – while supplementing this income with housework and subsistence work. Should family strife or a lack of access to their means of subsistence impede this process, then the exhaustion of

Value transfer	
Surplus value from paid work	**Surplus product/rent/tribute**
From free paid labour	Product of personal dependence on a
From unfree paid labour	landlord (servitude)
	Charges for use of land, buildings or privileges (entitlement of which was often based on feudal allocation)
Realization through employment of a wage labourer (free or unfree)	Realization through rent payments in the form of work, products or monetary tribute/taxation, or through pillaging

Transfer value from unpaid work

Realization through:

familial combination of paid, underpaid and unpaid work

combination of different working conditions and rent income in the context of commodity chains or migration

complementary and renewal sources undermines the very basis for this unequal exchange.

Both products and various types of work are traded in this unequal exchange. The forms are distinguished by their payment (or non-payment) and the level thereof, as well as levels of technological development. The exchange thus consists of a value transfer from producers of raw goods to those of finished goods – from low-tech regions to high-tech regions, from low-wage regions with high supplemental subsistence to high-wage regions with less demand for subsistence in the population's material survival. Differences in taxation and environmental and social laws also play a role in price gaps.

While the shifting of costs and profits in unequal exchange is based on existing regional differences, interregional commodity chains are the product of active corporate policies, arising when individual production steps are divided across different locations so that qualifications, wages, subsidies, taxes and political conditions at production sites can be combined in a way that cuts costs for the company.[6] Different amounts of paid and unpaid surplus work are activated in family households at each of the locations, and fed into the commodity chain through the employed member of the family. Global commodity chains can exist within companies or between formally independent enterprises. Some arrangements are organized at company headquarters, while others are set up by contractors, dealers or brand owners – these are known as producer- or buyer-dominated commodity chains. In both cases, those responsible for organizing these chains have the capability not only to combine different types of paid labour relations, but also to activate or tap into unpaid work activities at a more or less existential level to varying degrees.

Unequal exchange and interregional commodity chains are a prerequisite for incorporating transfer values from paid and unpaid work – which, in principle, can be incurred anywhere in the course of capitalist exploitation – into the unequal interregional division of labour. The same applies to migrant labour, which emerges from the decision to migrate, which is in turn made within the family context. Migrants then search for the best possible job offered by the interregional price gap, where they are predestined to undermine the labour laws and contractual practices of their new place of employment due to a combination of vulnerability in terms of residency, social and political discrimination, obligations to send back remittances, and the desire to ultimately return home themselves. They thus contribute to accelerating the dualization of the labour market. In other words, native labour movements often perceive migrants as competition; however, they themselves deepen labour market divisions by denying them union and political representation, regardless of whether this is done intentionally or not.

The circulation of capital, commodities and workforces is bound up in a macroeconomic context structured around the political conditions imposed by national laws, international treaties and agreements. For migrants, this means immigration laws, residency rules or labour market and employment policies concerning foreign workers. The effects of trade on the various parties can be influenced by customs and monetary policy. For interregional commodity chains, critical factors include (a lack of) controls on capital movements, most-favoured-nation status, and rules of origin. Through these means, it is possible to influence market mechanisms in the interests of individual actors.

Governments are confronted with myriad conflicting interests in both domestic and foreign policy. Migration policy, for example, is not merely a question of whether, how much, and what kind of emigration and immigration is best for the state, but rather raises issues like who covers the costs of raising children and training workers? And who pays for their social security? The instrument of citizenship allows for costs to be at least partially transferred to non-naturalized workers' countries of origin. Many states use similar restrictions on residency in large cities as control mechanisms for internal migration. Keeping migrants in a legally precarious state of residency forces them to work harder, maintains low wages and transfers social reproduction costs back to their regions of origin and family households.

The distribution of profit in international trade is influenced through pricing, taxation, customs, currency policy and investment protection agreements. Tariffs and barriers to trade can help protect the internal market from imports by preventing outflows of purchasing power and trade benefits of unequal exchange to the countries providing foreign imports. Economic policies of these sorts, along with other measures, can facilitate industrialization aimed at substituting the now overly expensive imports with a country's domestic production, which in turn bolsters employment and value creation in the former importing region. Conversely, while devaluation of a national currency may reduce the price of goods produced for export, the increase in export volume makes up for it in greater overall revenues.

Interregional commodity chains are only possible with the free movement of capital. Restrictions on the export of capital serve to promote investment and jobs domestically by preventing domestic capital from utilizing cheaper locations or production sites. Companies bypass such restrictions however they can, such as by establishing new branches abroad, while at the same striving to create national, international and supra-national frameworks and institutions to prohibit governments from interfering with capital movements. Multinationals thus not only secure the free movement of commodities and capital by establishing free-trade zones (EC/EU, NAFTA, ASEAN, and so on) and agreements (GATS, TRIPS, and so on) regulated by international financial institutions (IMF, WTO), they also conclude bilateral agreements with individual states to protect their assets, income and profit transfers against political intervention. Social and environmental regulations are considered forms of such political intervention, along with corporate taxation and expropriation via nationalization. The International Center for Investment Disputes, headquartered at the World Bank, is an international court of arbitration established in 1965 to adjudicate in such cases. It only hears suits by investors against states, however, and not the other way around. In 70 per cent of cases, its verdict falls in favour of the plaintiff.[7]

Free movement of capital is thus clearly in the interests of multinational investors and organizers of commodity chains, but stands diametrically opposed to regional economic development and integration. Local industry and labour movement organizations often praise the perceived benefits of importing cheap goods and components from the global commodity chains, as it generates additional profits for their employers and grows workers' purchasing power. However, this perceived advantage ultimately stems from international investors' freedom to exploit cheap labour costs and an increased mobilization of under- and unpaid workforces at the low ends of commodity chains, allowing workers at the higher end to enjoy cheap goods and high levels of consumption.

6.

Historical Cross-Sections

This chapter is broken down into six historical cross-sections marked by years, each of which represents a broad spectrum of coexisting labour relations. Capturing the sheer diversity of work forces us to rely on summaries and abstractions in many cases. This section focuses on the simultaneity of different forms of work, asking, how are various conditions and relations of work and labour combined? When do they coincide? And to what degree do these combinations mutually complement or benefit one another, or represent a value transfer advantaging one side over the other?

The representative years chosen are 1250, 1500, 1700, 1800, 1900 and today. Obviously, long-term social and economic changes cannot be neatly aligned to specific dates. The cross-sections thus serve as signposts for the striking changes in the way work has been perceived and organized throughout history, and the ways in which different conditions and relations combine. They delineate developments which occurred in the epochs lying between them and which, of course, continue to evolve. This necessitates a closer look at each period to identify important consequences for the next conjuncture. Both ruptures between and continuations of periods take different forms in different regions of the world. The six cross-sections will be analysed from an interactive historical perspective that takes the participation of actors in various regions of the world into account.

The individual sections begin with the general characteristics of the world economy at the time, as well as the political forces controlling interregional relations. Three ties between labour relations will subsequently be considered: local labour relations, interregional links and large-scale connections. The introduction is followed by a focus on the local level: the region in which the author and readers of the original German edition of this book find themselves, the German and Austrian countries, which once spread deep into South, eastern Central and South-Eastern Europe through eastward colonization by the Holy Roman Empire, Prussia, the German Empire and the Habsburg Monarchy – followed, finally, by the Third Reich's war of conquest, which brought it as far as the Soviet Union. Italy and southern France also belong to this Central Europe. The differences between and within these states characterized by small-scale regional diversity can only be illustrated here in passing examples. Select cases of local conditions and relations will be compared with other forms from regions around the world. Interregional connections between individuals, households and companies will be explored, always proceeding from the Central European regions onto a European and greater intercontinental level in two follow-up steps.

As all forms of work are included (reciprocal, tributary, commodified), reproduction and care work will, of course, be considered – whether as unpaid housework, provided by charities, provided by institutions with professional care personnel within the framework of public poor relief or private social services, or financed through social insurance.

To understand the connections between working conditions and relations, we must also look at inequalities between the regions concerned. Each region's role in trade, commodity chains and migration networks reflects its position within the international division of labour. These aspects thus offer a backdrop for a closer investigation of unequal labour relations. First, we find the households of which everyone is an integral part. Their roles and individual prospects for action are determined by gender, age and ethnicity. Companies and corporate bodies are active agents connecting regions with different labour markets through procurement, sales, commodity chains and relocation. Last but not least, political conditions and government intervention are also crucial factors shaping the actions of individuals, households and businesses.

The guiding approach of this book, namely assessing work from a global perspective by understanding interregional connections and contexts, cannot claim to represent the entire world in a complete fashion. It does, however, span the globe in so far as the source region (Central Europe) managed to influence the individual affairs of trade, business and migration in other regions, and thereby contribute to attaining the mutual effects and interactions between the labour relations of those far-flung places. Taking Central Europe as an analytical point of departure for exploring global entanglements may seem unusual for an

English-language publication. Admittedly, this regional approach corresponds to the author's own area of expertise. Moreover, it allows us to introduce parts of Europe into a global perspective which are otherwise often neglected. Selecting Central Europe as the region of reference for analysing medium- and long-range combinations of labour relations allows us to differentiate within Europe and break up the alleged uniformity of European development that usually serves as the basis for generalizing the Western European experience. However, Western Europe continues to play a role in this study through its interrelations with Central and Eastern Europe. Moreover, global entanglements between the European and non-European world include examples of Western European colonial and commercial activities, which often paved the way and set the standards for Central European economic and political actors.

1250

Characteristics

The European town began to take shape around 1250. The first towns were founded at the outset of the thirteenth century, followed by a wave reaching its peak between 1250 and 1300.[1] The European town was an expression of the new division of labour between urban space and rural surroundings, and laid the legal foundations for eligible citizens to specialize in an independent craft. Trade and distribution were reserved for merchants, while both social groups formed the town councils. Town charters authorized municipal organs to dictate rules for producers, retailers and consumers at urban markets, applying both to locals and to those travelling through. Guilds were associations of commercial producers whose rules regulated access to industry, the quality of products, training and working conditions. Here, a division of labour emerged in terms of specialization, contributing to an understanding of work based on practicable skills and knowledge within a profession. Markets were tied into relations of varying scope: peasants offered foodstuffs for sale, while local artisans supplied daily necessities to the surrounding urban population. Export products were distributed at medium-range markets and fairs, where merchants peddled specialities from other, more distant, regions.[2]

What appeared as an innovation for Western and Central Europe at the time and spread to Eastern Europe over the following two centuries in fact enjoyed a much older tradition in West Asia, that is, from Constantinople across the Black Sea to Egypt and Persia. The continuity of the ancient cities of the eastern Mediterranean continued uninterrupted, even experiencing a renewed boom in the wake of the Islamization of West Asia. The same is largely true for China. Chinese, Arabian and Persian cities were enormous: Baghdad was a city of one million by 1250; Basra, Cairo and Delhi between 200,000 and 600,000; Hangzhou, the capital of South China, had 650,000 inhabitants, with some estimates ranging up to several million. The largest cities in Europe at that time were Venice, Milan, Genoa, Naples and Paris, with 80,000 to 100,000 inhabitants each. North of the Alps, Cologne, Bruges and Ghent each counted around 50,000 inhabitants. Kiev was the largest Eastern European city with 30,000–40,000, followed by Novgorod's population of 10,000–12,000. Most European towns only counted a few hundred to a few thousand, but all in all were rather dense.[3] Distinguishing towns and cities from other settlements, however, was not size but legal status. These figures correspond to the relations of power in the world economy, in which Asian regions occupied the leading positions. The Indian Ocean connected both North and East Africa into these relations of exchange, while Europe stood on the periphery.

The centralized form of rule dominant in East and West Asia differed from the political self-government found in Western cities. The economic affairs of the trading cities on the Indian Ocean, on the coasts of South East Asia and along the Silk Road were clearly distinguished from political administration.[4] Conversely, the Asian ruling houses ensured high demand for luxury goods, which brought forth a high level of technical expertise in both private and state-owned workshops.[5] Here as well, the qualified work of trained craftsmen stood apart from common household and agricultural work. On the Indian subcontinent as well as in the South and East Asian empires, specialized export industries supplied goods to Africa and Europe by sea and the continental Silk Road.

Intense exchange strengthened West, South and East Asian trade networks in the thirteenth century, mostly devoted to prestige goods. The engine of this intensification was the Mongol expansion between 1206 and 1287 – originating from the Mongolian core – which broke over all of Central Asia and China, Iran, the Caucasus, Anatolia and the central Russian principalities in several waves.[6] This process brought all trade routes from China to the Black Sea and the Mediterranean, collectively known as the Silk Road, under one controlling power – only India remained independent under the Sultanate of Delhi. Following the death of the Mongol Empire's legendary founder Genghis Khan in 1227, Mongol territory was divided up among his four sons. Although they fought amongst themselves from time to time, his sons and their descendants consolidated the Mongol conquests under the leadership of one Great Khan. After the end of Mongol rule in China and Persia, an outsider known to history as Timur managed to reunite what was left of the empire in 1370. His successors would give the cities of Herat and Samarkand their unique character in the fifteenth century.[7]

Janet Abu-Lughod provides a useful depiction of how the three large trading zones of Asia, the Middle East and Europe comprised eight overlapping subsystems, which merged into a unified world-system between 1250 and 1350.[8] The Eurasian world-system was characterized by a relative balance between its primary regions, thereby differing significantly from the later concentration of political and economic power in North-Western Europe – which Abu-Lughod, Fernand Braudel and Immanuel Wallerstein identify as emerging in the sixteenth century, while Andre Gunder Frank und Kenneth Pomeranz locate it in the nineteenth century. The world-system of 1250 was multi-centric and formed through connections between adjacent centres of trade which then spilled over into the next subsystem.

The legacy of the *Pax Mongolica* was decidedly mixed: in the historiographies of conquered territories, Mongol invasion was usually linked to the devastation of entire landscapes, destruction of towns, decimation of irrigation systems and huge losses for the native population. Global history, for its part, tends to highlight the integrating effects of 'warrior globalization' as a positive step forward for global trade relations. Mongol rulers built a centralized administration tailored to managing military operations and implemented a uniform code (*Yassa*) for elites. The various regional trade networks under Mongol control were both intensified and chained together more tightly in a process referred to by Abu-Lughod as the premodern Eurasian world-system.[9] This interlinking of pre-existing networks extended beyond actual Mongol territory, running through Venice and Genoa to the leading Western European cores in northern France, Flanders and Burgundy. The trade fairs of the

Champagne region linked the Eurasian connection paths to Bruges, where the trade networks of the Atlantic Ocean and the Mediterranean, North and Baltic Seas finally met.[10]

From a Western and Central European perspective, trade with Asia flourished as a result of Mongol consolidation, which also fostered urbanization, commercialization and the development of specialized craft, and helped Latin Europe to strengthen its position on the Western edge of the Eurasian system. Latin Europe also met the Mongols' territorial ambitions with its own military expansion into Byzantium/ Constantinople and West Asia through the Crusades (led by the French, the English and the Holy Roman Empire). Inroads were also cut into North-Eastern Europe by the Teutonic Order's Prussian Crusades and by German colonial settlements in the East. These were enabled by Hungarian and Polish military weakness, worn down by Mongol encroachment into Silesia and Hungary and along the Adriatic in 1242.

The story is quite different in places where Mongol expansion entailed the destruction of existing political, social and economic structures. The Russian principalities, which had consolidated into the East Slavic Kingdom of Kievan Rus', were brought under Mongol rule between 1237 and 1240. Towns were pillaged and set ablaze, Russian artisans kidnapped and hauled off to the Mongol court.[11] Baghdad, the capital of the Abbasid Empire and seat of the Caliphate, was razed in 1258.[12] Mesopotamian and Persian cities faced a long, slow recovery from the destruction. In China, the Mongol ruler Kublai Khan ascended the throne of the Chinese emperor and reunited China's divided north and south in 1271 under the Yuan Dynasty (until its eventual fall in 1368). However, Mongol rulers demonstrated a great willingness to adapt to the cultures of the areas they controlled during this period, incorporating their languages and religions after consolidating regional power. Mongol rule in China underwent a veritable sinization; Mongol rulers in Persia, the Ilkhanate, adopted the Persian language, which became a lingua franca spoken well into China.[13] People from all parts of the Mongol Empire as well as Europe were employed as experts and advisers. Trade contacts flourished, and renowned travellers like Marco Polo and Ibn Battuta wrote accounts of Chinese technologies and administrative developments.[14] Back in the Kievan Rus' under the Kipchak (the Golden Horde), however, the khans refused to adopt both the Old Slavonic language and Orthodox Christianity, instead converting to Islam in 1313.

Nomadic horsemen had long watched over transport along the Central Asian trade routes. Rural peasants provided the travelling caravans with food and horses, monetary tribute and potential new recruits. This tribute-based clientele system was the bedrock of Mongol imperial expansion in the thirteenth century, allowing them to subjugate whole populations and states throughout China and Russia to their raids and territorial advances. Securing that which had already been conquered was relatively unimportant, as the Mongol economy was based largely on territorial conquest and pillaging. Whatever managed to survive this devastation was appropriated by Mongol rulers in the form of tribute or, in the case of people, as slaves. The Mongols did not aspire to build up their own system of accumulation, focusing almost exclusively on appropriation and transfer of resources. Specialists from Baghdad or Russian artisans were kidnapped in order to place their knowledge and skills in the service of Mongol courts; slaves constituted an important trade good. Only with the complete seizure of political power in the conquered territories would local reconstruction and economic development become a priority.

Local conditions and labour relations

The majority of people in Western and Central Europe lived in villages and hamlets. For rural households forced to pay tribute to a local lord, the yield of their work was divided into products consumed at home and those produced for the market. Various levies were also common, paid in kind, in monetary form, or as work (*corvée, robot*) to the owner of the land, the noble lord. Peasants working as serfs on manorial estates took their orders from estate stewards, sometimes called *vogts* or *drotts* (*Meier* in German). On the side, most engaged in subsistence farming on the land apportioned to them by the feudal arrangement, known as fiefs. In this sense, peasants' land-usage rights entitled them to an indirect form of ownership, and they largely determined the course of work on their respective fiefs themselves. A wide variety of work was generally performed in this context, as peasant work did not just mean agriculture and livestock, but also included the production of essential goods, building and maintaining housing, and providing sustenance for the household's family members, lodgers and servants. Male household members were generally placed under the authority of the housefather, or patriarch, female members under the lady, the housewife. Paternal authority and community politics were matters for the male head of the family. Work was distributed among the household members according to status, skill and capacity. Although work allocation and provisioning were mostly of a habitual nature according to age, sex and marital as well as social status, changing demands could occasionally or even continuously affect the distribution of work. The household economy as a unified life and work form is characterized by a strong sense of community, which expects specific obligations from each individual as well as a large degree of flexibility and willingness to adapt.[15]

The commercial households of urban artisans followed a similar principle. Craftsmen in small towns often owned a bit of farmland which provided them with both food and livestock. Their household was an undivided whole incorporating both agricultural and commercial production for the market in addition to domestic consumption. These were joined by journeymen and apprentices and even day labourers, who were all involved in commercial production and often lived or at least ate in the household. The distinction between men's work and women's work was clearer than in the rural household, with responsibility for crafts belonging to the patriarch and housekeeping to the housewife. That said, women participated in the former as well, and male members also performed a number of subsistence activities. The idea that commercial activity was exclusively a man's domain could be challenged in cases where a widow oversaw the craft trade following her husband's death. Generally speaking, however, women in handicraft remained an exception limited to a few sectors, differing from region to region. On the other hand, women dominated small-scale retail.[16] Artisanry enjoyed a special status in the spectrum of necessary activities, albeit one not rooted in the market so much as in the professional specialization required, which ensured proper guild training and high-quality standards. Guilds and brotherhoods of journeymen connected their members with non-domestic commercial activities and public life. This development detached gainful, paid employment from the household, despite the fact that these activities were all performed under one roof.

Apprentices and journeymen, itinerant artisans, day labourers and servants all belonged to their employer's household as long as they lived and worked there. Yet the fluctuating durations of their stay which hindered their integration into family life, their exclusion from any form of inheritance, and the fact that they were paid for their work made them ultimately a form of wage labourer. Sometimes, if circumstances allowed, they returned with their wage labour earnings to the family household they were from, or even founded their own. This fluctuating composition also emphasizes the flexibility of domestic work and living arrangements.

Lacking a house of one's own meant submitting to the authority of a household leader or resigning oneself to a life of odd jobs and begging. In an agrarian society with an ossified status hierarchy, flat specialization and a high degree of self-sufficiency, itinerant workers or travellers performed the work that no one else could or wanted to, whether because it was deemed dirty and dishonourable or because a work-intensive project required more workers or expertise and experience than was locally available. Surviving records describe groups of mostly young single men who took on heavy earthworks and construction, and were described as dangerous in the testimonies of local observers. Itinerant worker groups often comprised family groups of men, women and children, for which a wide variety of regional names existed: *Yenish, Tinker, Irish Travellers, Voyageurs, Viajeros* and so on. These families would perform certain tasks in exchange for food, lodging and money. Often they spent several months in a single village performing construction and repair work for local peasants and lords. Metalwork, from blacksmithing to repairs and recycling scrap metals, was one traveller speciality. Men were often well versed in dealing with horses, while women specialized in basket weaving, harvesting and fortune-telling – but were also responsible for managing their family household, which travelled along with the family due to the itinerant nature of their work.[17]

Among these groups of travellers were the Roma, commonly referred to as 'Gypsies' (*Zigeuner, Bohémiens, Cigani, Cikan, Tsiganes, Zingari, Gitanos* and so on), who first came to Europe from India in the twelfth and thirteenth centuries, taking on a similar social role. Although they were despised by most settled communities for reasons of ethnic and cultural difference, this rarely prevented residents from employing Roma for a number of tasks necessary to village life. Although the term 'Gypsy' was initially used pejoratively by settled residents, it would become a self-designation over time. For local travellers, these new arrivals from India represented a form of competition. Settled populations, however, made no distinctions in their disdainful attitude towards both the Gypsies and other travellers. Gypsies lived in larger clans or extended families (*fatja*). The household (*familija*) was composed of several generations, who lived in the same house or in close proximity. Women were subordinate to men, while increasingly revered with age for their alleged healing powers and visions. The oldest son derived his own high status from his role as her protector.[18]

Dishonourable professions such as the executioner or hangman, or the skinner and knacker who rendered dead animals on the outskirts of town, played additional outsider roles in the villages. Lying outside villages, their houses can thus be viewed, similarly to various contractors and other travelling craftsmen, as rural agricultural economies.

Belonging to a household entailed access to basic means of sustenance. Itinerant craftsmen and servants, students and monks were often temporarily incorporated into household communities. In situations where a person was cut off from their source of sustenance, as was often the case for warriors, adventurers, the impoverished and vagabonds, other means of survival came into play: mercenary work, odd jobs, temporary work and begging, and (if they had access to weaponry) thievery, forced tribute collection, and piracy. Under certain circumstances, these forms of acquisition also fed back into a household unit.

Strangers were only granted temporary protection by the household. When they were no longer welcome, their means of support were revoked and they were expelled. Enemies were denied any protection whatsoever; they could be attacked, robbed, killed or enslaved. Their resources and even their person represented potential goods to be taken by the conqueror, as anything of value in their possession went to the winner. This included any lands captured, along with their inhabitants.

The social structure of rural, commercial and itinerant households and the ways in which they organized their labour exhibited a wide range of special forms of work at the local level. Unlike the feudal structure of Western and Central Europe, tribute-based forms of rule were common in Eastern and South-Eastern Europe as a legacy of its Byzantine traditions. The eastward colonization of German settlers in the thirteenth century, driven by demographic pressures from a growing population and demand from Eastern European rulers for professional craftsmen and artisans, brought with it family structures, agricultural systems and legal concepts developed in the Holy Roman Empire.[19] However, these traditions and rights remained confined to the German towns and settlements – as was also the case for the Magyars in Transylvania and Hungary. Local peasants and propertyless rural lower classes remained excluded from these privileges, or were merely permitted a subordinate existence as small peasants, labourers or serfs. Russia also witnessed a phase of feudalization, during which hitherto free peasants (*smerd*) were compelled to deliver additional tithes and charges to noble landowners (*boyars*) endowed with lands (*votchina*) by the lord, who paid tribute to the sovereign. Rather than live as free farmers, *boyars* increasingly relied on the servitude of *kholops* or *sakups* (serfs), who formed a part of the manorial household (*chelyad*). In the process of this feudalization, a new term entered the language in order to designate a peasant: *krest'yanin* (Christian).[20]

Eastern, eastern Central, and South-Eastern European household and family forms differed from those in Western and Central Europe in a number of ways, particularly in the existence of larger, extended households in which several brothers lived with their wives and children, along with older generations. The typical marrying age was significantly lower here than in Western Europe.[21] Eastern Slavic peasant families and tri-generational southern Slavic households (*zadruga*), however, did resemble those of peasant households in Central and Western Europe in terms of the degree of close interaction and cooperation between family members. The village peasant community supported the households and strengthened them vis-à-vis the landowner; community members were entitled to use common forests and grazing lands. In Russia, increasing manorial taxation of peasant communities (*obshchina*) eventually transformed them into bodies of collective liability (*mir*) responsible for all payments to the local lord.[22]

One feature distinguishing Eastern from Central and Western Europe was its population density, which made peasants much harder to control by feudal lords. When foreign conquerors demanded tribute or local lords tried to collect duties and coerce work from the peasantry, the large, sparsely populated stretches of land offered refuge for those who refused. Accordingly, the Mongol invasion of Russia prompted an exodus of peasants into the deep forests of the north where they could clear a piece of land and farm in relative freedom, or they fled to neighbouring areas less affected by the expansion. The Russian peasantry's freedom of movement would only be restricted later on, when direct serfdom was introduced in the seventeenth century.[23]

Tributary relations were also characteristic of empires spanning across Eastern and Western Asia. This can be attributed to the unbroken continuity of political rule, which in the case of the Western Roman Empire ended with its disintegration in the fifth century. Moreover, natural geographical conditions also favoured centralized forms of power, which were able to provide elaborate irrigation infrastructure and only meddled in the everyday life of peasants when taxes and duties went unpaid. Rather than feudal lords entitled to labour and levies from their peasants in order to maintain their manorial economy, Asian empires relied on political governors, state officials and tax farmers (who leased tax-collection rights and thus 'farmed' taxes) operating on behalf of the central government. As subordinates of the sovereign, these representatives did not enjoy the autonomy afforded to feudal nobility and thus were much more susceptible to central control. The same was true for cities. Asian cities were highly complex, centralized settlements with a stratified population, within the confines of which free trade, commerce and science could unfold. Because they did not enjoy codified institutional rights of the sorts common in Western cities, many Western scholars have traditionally denied these Eastern settlements autonomy.[24] Chinese cities were modelled on the image of the capital city; the urban upper classes followed no specific special interests, but rather identified with the goals of the imperial central power whose values were represented by local officials. It appears as though interests between the imperial core and the cities were harmonized along the lines put forward by the philosophical ideology of Confucianism. The economic foundation of this arrangement was taxation, pumped from the rural regions into the cities. Only after the state had ensured greater population density through protective measures for its smallholder peasantry did it lay the groundwork for levies to finance urban growth. This discouraged merchant and artisan guilds as well as regional groups from positioning themselves in opposition to the central power.

An approach which takes the Asian model's divergence from the Western and Central European model of urban autonomy as the basis of its comparison runs the risk of evaluating these differences as deficits. It would, for instance, ignore Islamic traditions, which consigned legal decision making to the *ulema*, specialized religious scholars. Non-Muslim religious communities (*dhimmi*) were recognized and granted protection and limited autonomy – these would later constitute the *millets* of the Ottoman Empire. The Muslim clergy and its institutions acted largely independently of their secular rulers, and were recognized as legal and moral authorities.[25]

For Asian peasant households, the absence of mediating feudal powers meant greater economic flexibility, although they faced tax officials and governors who supplemented their salaries with undue charges. Daily life as a peasant in Asia was largely similar to that of one in Central Europe: activities were carried out for subsistence, trade, taxation and tribute, divided among household members in accordance with prevailing customs and habits. Rural underclasses worked for landowners or independent peasant farmers, or eked out a living on the fringes of society. Nomads practised an itinerant lifestyle, combining seasonal migration with annual return to specific areas, and often exchanged livestock for agricultural goods. Industrial production for personal consumption also played a central role in rural households, even for nomads. This stood in stark contrast to warrior and mounted nomads, who practised no business of their own but rather lived from plunder and tribute and demanded protection payments from settled populations. The Islamic *iqta* system, which paid military leaders in land instead of wages, represented a heavy burden for the peasantry, who then became subjugated to the military lords.[26]

The city's particular importance can only be understood in terms of its relationship with the surrounding rural area. In Western and Central Europe, the urban market formed a link between rural agricultural production and urban commerce. In China, Persia and Arabia, however, cities were only weakly interwoven with the rural surroundings. In China, the city functioned as a centre of administration, trade and luxury production, especially of silk fabrics for urban elites and export markets. The rural population played no role in commercial production, as peasant households were largely self-sustaining. In cotton production, they were even competitors – in fact, the low production costs found in the peasant family economy made an urban cotton industry untenable.[27] Rather than thrive off of exchange with the countryside, then, cities lived on taxation brought in by tax officials. We must not forget that urban households required various subsistence activities, depending on status, which often included the production of foodstuffs and clothing. Due to this separation between town and countryside, the degree of commercialization was much greater than in smaller Central European towns. The same applied to state officials, independent commercial producers and merchants, as well as their permanent or temporary wage-earning dependents. Japan, by contrast, developed a feudal system much closer to the Western European model.

Personal and domestic services for the wealthy were often performed by slaves, although who was considered a slave and under what circumstances varied across regions. Slavery was essentially based on prisoners of war whose labour was appropriated by their captors. Slaves were also captured in raids against people of other religions; the legal systems of the various regions offered them no protection, allowing unrestricted access to their person.[28] They were exploited for the hardest of labour and carried off to be enslaved in faraway places (as the Mongols had done).[29] But 'slave' was often also a synonym for domestic servants, who were integrated into the household and often even enjoyed a close relationship with their masters or mistresses. Additionally, a significant number of people lived from charity and begging. All major religious communities committed believers to voluntary donations for their own salvation.[30]

Slavery in the thirteenth century was by no means limited to Africa and the Asian empires: Christian Europe also forced their prisoners of war to the galleys as rowers, or exploited their labour for other hazardous and strenuous tasks. House slaves from Eastern Europe, Asia or Africa were often found on the wealthy estates. Italian colonial expansion into the eastern Mediterranean region and along the coasts of the Black Sea brought not only raw materials and foodstuffs to the Crimea, but additional house slaves as well.[31] There, the Genoese came into contact with the Mongols, who in turn kidnapped Christian slaves and took them to Western and Central Asia.

In the Islamic world, the recruitment of military slaves was practised to counteract the growing autonomy of local military elites. In Egypt, the Mamluks brought in from Eastern Europe and Central Asia solidified into a caste in their own right, overthrowing the ruling Ayyubids and seizing political power around 1250.[32]

Interregional connections

Western and Central European towns were tightly connected to the surrounding countryside through intense exchange. Villages brought not only foodstuffs but also raw materials and products like wool, dyes, wood and semi-finished goods (yarn, wooden items and basketry), produced in rural households. The relationship between town and country had the character of a commodity chain in which the village occupied the low end and the urban trades the high end. The town market functioned as an economic intermediary. Given the greater concentration of value in the towns, we can reasonably speak of a form of unequal exchange. For villagers, supplying the urban craft market represented a way to increase their monetary income; it also strengthened the independence of servants and other co-resident unfree household members, especially those who brought their own products to market of their own accord.

The larger the city and the greater its centralizing function within the region, the more differentiation could be seen in the commercial landscape overall. Textiles could be divided among linen weavers, wool weavers, heavy cotton weavers, silk weavers, ribbon makers and hosiery or coat makers – not to mention the various divisions of further material processing among seamstresses, tailors, upholsterers, and so on. This kind of specialization, however, did not consist of a commodity chain lining up the various divisions of labour. Rather, each business manufactured a finished product, even if this product was often the basic material for a neighbouring industry. Merchants exported exceptional goods or products only available in certain areas to other regions. Urban market regulations ensured that regional market developments did not disadvantage local merchants and consumers, compelling travelling merchants who might otherwise simply pass through to sell their goods at local markets. In Eastern and Central Europe, this was done through the laws of *Straßenzwang*, which obliged them to only use certain protected roads and trade routes, and *Niederlagszwang*, which required travelling merchants to offer their wares at marketplaces along the road. Larger towns had specialized marketplaces for specific groups of products: separate markets for hay, meats, grain, cloth. Rules dictated when and in what order consumers had access to goods (opening and closing times, periods for certain goods). Quality regulations and inspection protected buyers from inferior wares.

Market rules were accompanied by rules concerning the transport of goods: merchants were obliged to hire local carters and coachmen to take their wares to the next town.[33] Blacksmiths, wagon and wheel makers, inns and horse-changing stations each had a role to play in interregional trade. Such tasks often became the basis for German family names: Wagner, Fragner, Schmied. This interregional exchange resulted in small-scale value creation and supported a dense infrastructure and population. *Sam* or *Saum* (related to the word 'seam' in English) was the German word for how many sacks or baskets a single horse could carry. Customs checkpoints were set up by local rulers, in order to participate in interregional trade.[34]

Attempts to circumvent regulations, taxes and tolls led to various detours, such as along mountain passes, fostering the growth of infrastructure and services along these roads as well. The valleys of the rivers Eisack and Etsch (Italian: Valle Isarco and Val d'Adige) in South Tyrol were one such route between Italy and Central Europe. In Roman times, this same path had been served by the Via Claudio Augusta. The valley road could be circumvented by travelling along the right side of the bank between Bozen (Bolzano) and Brixen (Bressanone) to avoid the tolls and *Niederlagszwang* in Klausen (Chiusa), which lies between the two. Along this path, a whole second level of service infrastructure sprang up high above the valley, with inns, transport businesses and eventually even mining and settlements. The hamlet of Dreikirchen was built in the thirteenth century on the site of an older sacred spring. It gained interregional significance because the inn, mineral spring baths and churches drew not only merchants and miners, but also women seeking a cure for infertility.

The specialized industrial sites and markets of Central European towns exerted a pull of attraction on the surrounding rural areas, while larger cities had a similar effect on smaller towns. Immigration also played a role in this process, as permanent town and city residents acted alongside those passing through or staying for a time, who also played a major role: travelling merchants were subject to market regulations, artisans were subject to guild rules. In addition, of course, there were unorganized wage labourers. Villages maintained personal networks through these migrant servants and craftsmen (who often operated outside the guilds), as well as through resettlement following marriage or the founding of one's own household and/or business.

When neighbouring smaller regional units began to intertwine, broader connections grew and trade and migration soon spread. This mainly occurred between cities, however, while villagers remained focused on their rural household economies, on cooperation with adjacent neighbours and on local markets – rarely leaving their home village.

Despite a great degree of heterogeneity, a broad balance of wealth and income existed between the different areas. Nevertheless, a hierarchy would emerge among the regions due to variations in natural surroundings, resources, transport, population density, settlement size, and social and economic differentiation and specialization. This hierarchy existed between cities and towns of different orders, between fertile and infertile regions, mountain and forest regions, flat lands, river valleys and coastal regions. The income disparities between the more and less developed regions in the first half of the second millennium only reached 1:1.5 on a global scale.[35] Regional differences mattered relatively little, as priority was mostly given to small-scale trade – partly due to local transport restrictions and partly to customs duties and tolls, as well as market fees levied on foreign merchants, which altogether meant that local products enjoyed a noticeable price advantage.

Interregional trade routes passed through local areas but clustered around more important central nodes, generally supported by city networks. One central axis connected Venice to the Upper German cities of Augsburg and Nuremberg through the eastern Alpine passes. Another central axis ran from Genoa over the western Alpine passes towards the towns of northern France, Burgundy and Flanders.[36] These trade routes brought Western European industrial regions into contact with Eurasian trade networks. Commercial and financial expertise flowed into these routes, thereby strengthening their regional leadership in Europe. The Italian city states with their trade and financial institutions were important mediators in this process.[37]

The recapture of formerly Christian territories (*Reconquista*) by Catholic rulers beginning in the eleventh century prevented Spain from assuming a central role in connecting Africa and Western Asia through the Maghreb. The Emirate of Córdoba was cut down to a small principality with Granada as its seat during the *Reconquista* in the thirteenth century, obligated to pay tribute to the kings of Castile and León. Nevertheless, Córdoba remained a central European hub for the flow of badly needed gold from Africa.

The Lower German merchants along the Baltic coast set up the Lübeck-based Hanseatic League in the twelfth century, and were also connected to Mediterranean trade via Bruges.[38] Further Hanseatic trading posts were Novgorod, Bergen and London. With its more than 170 members, the Hanseatic League formed the trade link between Western commercial regions and the North-Eastern European regions incorporated through the Hanseatic towns of Danzig/Gdansk, Königsberg (today Kaliningrad), Riga, Reval/Tallinn, Dorpat/Tartu, and so on. The Baltic towns granted Lower German merchants access to the countryside with its skins, honey and beeswax, as well as wood and forest products essential to shipbuilding and other construction in Western cities. Manufactured goods flowed back in the other direction.[39] While merchants transferred resources out of the hinterland through market mechanisms, the German presence in the Baltic region also began to consolidate politically and territorially. The Teutonic Order founded an autonomous branch, the Livonian Federation, in the thirteenth century around present-day Estonia and Latvia with other Christian principalities. They were subordinate to the Pope but can actually be understood as a German colony, as bishops, friars, nobles, knights and burghers generally came from the Holy Roman Empire, while neither the peasantry nor the urban lower classes were of German origin. Feudal nobles appropriated the rural surplus through work service and direct payments. Salt, cloth, metalwares and wine were imported to North-Eastern Europe via the Hanseatic towns in exchange. The unequal nature of this trade connection is blatant – the ethnic difference between the German citizens, merchants and feudal lords on the one hand and their Slavic and Baltic subjects on the other reeks of colonialism.[40]

How people were linked together via trade routes was felt by the residents of the affected areas themselves only indirectly; not everyone could afford imported goods, nor were they really aware of how imports were processed. Nevertheless, the peasants producing and tradespeople manufacturing these products, as well as their consumers, were all affected by the new conditions and labour relations. Over time, these relations would expand to become decisive factors in the development of the regions involved. Moreover, the presence of merchants, travellers and immigrants made it quite evident for residents that their locality had become part of an interregional division of labour. Certain activities were necessarily associated with mobility. On the one hand, this could mean a need for sought-after specialists willing to migrate. Another possibility, however, was the forced transport of people against their will to work elsewhere. Travel and migration were not always the result of economic rationale, but could also be triggered by military, religious or ideological considerations.

Specialized tradespeople in building and mining, or dike, levee and pond construction, regularly found themselves in high demand. The movements of master builders, engineers and craftsmen were one of the major agents of knowledge and technology transfer at that time. Heavy earthworks were performed by day labourers, some of which were available locally, while others were recruited into travelling groups of workers who followed construction sites around Europe. Large construction projects were based on wage labour, due to the fact that the workforce needed was often greater than local populations could supply. In contrast, basic works and routine maintenance of buildings and infrastructure could be carried out by local peasant workers and skilled craftsmen.

While intra-European land routes were serviced by locals whose pack animals and wagons could carry goods only so far, the maritime and fishing professions required full-time itinerant workers. Sailors belonged to an interregionally active wage-labour force in high demand, travelling from the North and Baltic Seas to the Mediterranean and the Black Sea, as well as up and down the continent's large rivers.

The movement of mercenaries and soldiers corresponded to the locations of the wars they fought. They were accompanied into battle by other conscripts responsible for provisions and supplies, often tapping local resources through theft or seizure. Soldiers generally comprised two groups: some belonged to temporary groupings of noblemen serving their prince; others were professional mercenaries recruited by various armies in the event of war. Generally, these were long-standing commitments – the dream of a glorious return home little more than a distant and seldom-fulfilled one. Soldiers were not tied to a household. They received a wage for their work, as is reflected in the word itself: *soudeer*, from the Anglo-French word for wage, *soud* (a shilling), and related to Medieval Latin *soldarius*, 'one having pay'. Young men from the Swiss Alps had acquired such good reputations as soldiers that Pope Julius II requested they guard the Vatican in 1506, as the 'Swiss Guards' still do today.

The theatres of war littering the thirteenth century are too numerous to list here. Of the many border skirmishes and larger conquests of the period, the Christian Crusades into North-Eastern Europe as well as, most famously, the Byzantine and Arab worlds and even Islamic Spain, stand out. The Christian armies also put down social and heretical unrest within Europe itself, such as the Albigensian Crusade in southern France, or the wars of conversion against the Slavic peoples of the Holy Roman Empire's eastern frontiers over the course of German expansion.[41]

For soldiers, victory in war could mean a long, perilous return journey to their homeland, often involving detours of veritably Odyssean proportions. Prisoners of war were used at home by the victors for forced labour. On the other hand, defeat could mean slavery – Mongols, Tartars and Turks were keen to capture Christian slaves.

Apart from merchants, who often also served diplomatic missions, journeys were undertaken by the sons of the nobility in the form of so-called 'knight's journeys' (*Kavaliersreise*, which inspired the aristocratic Grand Tours of the seventeenth century). If necessary, these could take on a military character, like the Crusades of 1095–1291. Pilgrimages to Santiago, Rome or Jerusalem were also common. Some 200,000 people travelled to Rome when Pope Boniface VIII proclaimed the first 'jubilee year', a record number for the year 1300.[42] During the arduous journey to Jerusalem, boundaries between peaceful pilgrimage and military crusade were blurred. A large percentage of the pilgrims headed to Jerusalem were noblemen who went to the Holy Sepulchre to be knighted; these men felt committed to carry on the religious war even after the end of the Crusades. Beginning around 1200, a guild of professional pilgrims evolved, the *Palmeros*, also known as the *Sonnweger* in German. These men would accept payment in exchange for undertaking this journey, either for oneself or even deceased relatives.[43]

Venice attained a monopoly of sorts in the transport of people to Palestine during the Crusades. The city was home to professional agencies which turned pilgrimage into an excellently organized travel event as early as the thirteenth century: groups were offered a basic, two-week group trip with accommodation in the pilgrims' hospice, indulgences, knighthood at the Holy Sepulchre (for nobles), viewings, relics and souvenirs all offered on site, or an extended tour that went from Jerusalem through Mount Sinai to Cairo. Yet Venice was not the only city doing brisk business – in the Holy Land itself, a whole tourist infrastructure revolved around the biannual arrival of pilgrims from Venice. The pilgrimage was the single most significant impetus behind the emergence of the service sector. In Venice, pilgrims were outfitted with travel necessities and provisions, while even currency exchange was available. Various tour operators sent their agents to St Mark's Square to promote their ships, most of which could transport roughly two thousand passengers.

By the twelfth century, the Venetian Republic already employed its own pilgrimage officials, the *cattaveri*, and their subordinate *piazza-guidas*, who were sent to the square or the Rialto Bridge to help pilgrims negotiate contracts with shipowners, buy supplies and change money, and work as translators. In Jerusalem, the Franciscans were responsible for the smooth running of the tourist programme and for dealing with the Muslim authorities. For local tours and tours to Egypt, Muslim guides who spoke fluent Italian, *kalini*, were hired.[44] Shipping and transport across the Mediterranean, on the other hand, remained a Christian monopoly. These ships not only serviced Christian pilgrims, but also ferried Muslims from the Maghreb to Spain and Egypt.

The Islamic counterpart to the Christian pilgrimage was the *Hajj*, a mandatory rite for every Muslim to perform once in his or her lifetime. Here the pilgrimage also comes in two forms: the *Umrah*, to the Black Stone of the Kaaba in Mecca, or the great pilgrimage *Hajj*, which includes other important sites such as the tomb of Muhammad in Medina.[45] Pilgrims came from the Arabian peninsula, Central and Western Asia, northern India, Africa and Muslim Spain. These group also required tour operators and service providers. Charities and foundations were established for poor pilgrims. Desert guides led caravans of travellers on camelback; the number of participants in such a caravan could run up to 50,000 pilgrims with just as many animals. Visiting the holy places of Hinduism was likewise an important commitment in the life of believers.

A wider group of people who often travelled were students, navigating the networks of European universities as well as the Islamic *madrasahs* which maintained close ties to religious institutions. Monks, nuns and other devotees made up yet another mobile population. When moving among the monasteries of their orders they belonged, in a sense, to an interregional household which sustained them. While travelling, they generally lived off alms. Christians, Hindus, Buddhist monks and Muslim *sufis* all did the same.

Large-scale connections

As a discipline, global history expresses broad agreement that the Eurasian world of the Middle Ages under Mongol rule constituted a period of intense integration.[46] Africa was also incorporated into this early globalization via the Indian Ocean and the Mediterranean Sea, while the Americas and Australia, on the other hand, remained apart. The differentiation of social roles over the course of urbanization and extended horizons of trade and general possibility that grew out of this thirteenth-century integration (particularly in the cities) fostered the emergence of a new work ethic, which conjoined labour with commercial specialization, training standards and creativity. Craft is characterized by its holistic mode of production. Although there were no interregional connections between localities in the production chain, trade goods gradually shifted from luxury items for the elite to mass products available for a broader public.

The connection of individual world regions into overlapping circuits of tribute payment facilitated the emergence of multiple cores in the Eurasian world-system, between which a relative balance existed. The division of Mongol power across four areas reinforced this multi-centricity, while Western and Central Europe were connected to Eurasian integration through long-distance trade. The impulses emanating from the eastern Mediterranean were passed along by the Italian merchants of Venice and Genoa to northern France and Flanders. Marseille, which belonged to the Holy Roman Empire, was also an important port and stood in competition with Aigues-Mortes, commissioned by the French king in 1240. These axes made up the European core at the time.

Integration, of course, came at a price. The *Pax Mongolica* was based on a period of violence, looting and destruction that squeezed the conquered communities, regardless of losses, until the Mongols finally discovered a degree of self-interest in allowing their conquered subjects to recover economically. Although Mongol hegemony may have created peace – the prerequisite for exchange and cultural contact – this 'warrior globalization' ought not be viewed all too positively.

Europe received a degree of social 'fertilization' on its edges, where the Mediterranean and the Black Sea met Western and Central Asia. The Venetian and Genoese presence at these points of contact explains the strategic importance of the two cities in further transfer to the Iberian Peninsula and North-Western Europe. The connection to the Mongol-ruled world-system was realized not only in trade but also in armed conflict: against people of other 'hostile' faiths (these were primarily the Egyptian sultans and their subordinate rulers in Syria and Palestine) and in intra-Christian competition over said points of connection (the

Byzantine Empire). Constantinople would fall prey to Venetian pillaging during the Fourth Crusade (1204).

The impulses brought by Eurasian integration strengthened the Western European cores, and empowered them to expand into and connect with the zones on their own periphery, whether at the edges of the empires or at higher altitudes within. Urban influence stretched outward, accelerating eastward colonization in the German context. The Prussian and Slavic Crusades in Eastern Europe, led by the Holy Roman Empire, came on the heels of Eurasian integration – albeit indirectly.

European empires could remain peripherally integrated into the world-system as long as Mongol cohesion stayed in place. With the collapse of the Mongol lineages in the fourteenth century, Asian unity and thus its world-systemic centrality watched its foundations crumble. The plague also represented an important moment of disintegration, first emerging in 1320 in Mongol-controlled Central Asia or perhaps in southern China (its precise origin is unclear). Intensified trade and exchange would spread from China to Europe within a generation.[47] China's withdrawal from world trade and maritime engagement was another factor, a decision taken by the Ming Dynasty after the overthrow of the Mongol Yuan. Asia began to regionalize, which in turn put conditions in place for the rise of European power as a global actor.

1500

Characteristics

By 1500, the Mongol Empire had withered to a Central Asian principality ruled by Timur's successors from Samarkand. His death in 1405 had effectively brought the Mongol Empire to a close. Following their expulsion from Central Asia, the Timurid Empire took refuge in India, where it founded the Mughal Empire in the sixteenth century. When Janet Abu-Lughod describes the Eurasian world-system of *Pax Mongolica* as a multi-centred precursor to the European world-system built over the course of global European expansion,[48] she is only partly right. The emergence of relationships of global interaction under Western European leadership actually remained limited to the transatlantic world in the sixteenth century. Although Christopher Columbus and his cohorts set out to reach east India, they arrived instead in the Americas – two continents which, as a result, were subjected to horrific pillaging and colonial conquest.

Triggering Spain's overseas expansion was the end of the *Reconquista* (1492), and the expulsion of the Muslims (and Jews) from Spain. The tradition of war as a form of occupation and spiritual affirmation for young aristocrats found its continuation in the voyages of discovery, missionizing and conquest to the newly discovered Americas. These followed an older pattern of European advances against the Muslim presence in the Holy Land, around the Baltic Sea and into the eastern flank of the Russian state, which consolidated itself after the end of the Mongol invasions. Travels to the New World – which was very new indeed to the Europeans – took place under changed economic conditions. The economic cycle fostering population growth, urbanization and settlement expansion in the High Middle Ages had descended into the late medieval crisis of Western and Central Europe by the fifteenth century – leaving the nobility to fear for their feudal rents. The nobility increased the pressure on rural subjects and towns, who responded with passionate social protest movements, combining their forces to defend their old rights and freedoms. In the early sixteenth century, Protestantism reinforced the backlash against Catholic rulers tied to the Church. Sovereigns took advantage of this conflict by intervening on behalf of the aristocracy, but did so to consolidate their own direct power over their subjects. The power struggle between the aristocracy and the centralized state would remain the main theme of the centuries to come, for which solutions and compromises varied widely. While Western European landowners developed a form of commercial agriculture in which agricultural land leasing and wage labour rose in importance, eastern Central Europe – the kingdoms of Poland and Lithuania, Bohemia and Hungary – felt the pressures of increased demand from the West for basic grains and cereals. This resulted in the emergence of manorial estates operated by serfs who faced restrictions in geographical mobility; in other words, they became 'adscripts of the soil' (*adscriptus glebae*). The Central European feudal system, by contrast, retained the practice of peasants producing for themselves while offering their surplus in the form of money or tribute in kind.[49]

Early modern state formation was accompanied by both intra- and transcontinental expansion, allowing the emerging core areas to draw on the resources and labour forces of newly enclosed areas without extending the benefits of state development and resource accumulation. As a consequence, these regions underwent a process of peripheralization. An unequal division of labour shaped Western Europe's relationship with eastern Central and Eastern European suppliers of grain, forest products and shipbuilding materials, as it did with suppliers of silver, gold, sugar and cotton from South America, where production relied on the rapid exhaustion of the indigenous population and increasingly on slaves imported from Africa. One effect of this process was that the northern part of eastern Central Europe became closely connected to the North-Western European cores via the Baltic Sea route. Meanwhile, continental Eastern Europe felt the division of labour between core and periphery only marginally, and thus underwent regionalization as the European cores shifted westward.

While agricultural raw materials from the colonial economy increased the overall commercial base of European cities, American silver gave European traders the purchasing power to buy increasingly popular South and East Asian spices and commercial products. Persian, Arab and Jewish merchants were especially active dealers until the beginning of the sixteenth century, when the Portuguese, Dutch and English grew increasingly involved in the east India trade. In the Asian empires, they encountered wide-ranging relations and restraints.[50] In South and South East Asia, traders could develop independent relationships with local suppliers, although the Chinese rulers exercised strict state control over foreign trade. Each transaction was handled through government-authorized intermediaries (*hong*), who sent desired goods to the city of Guangzhou (Canton) where foreign merchants were assigned specific districts for their trading operations. The eastern Mediterranean, the Black Sea and the Arabian peninsula were consolidated under Ottoman rule in the fifteenth century. Tensions between the Sublime Porte and the Holy Roman Empire as well as Russia regularly ignited so-called 'Ottoman Wars' in South-Eastern Europe, which essentially cut off land routes between Western Europe and Asia as well as the Red Sea passage. This compelled Europeans to sail around Africa. The Ottoman Sultan eventually granted trade privileges to allied European powers in exchange for tribute and military subsidies; these 'Capitulations' placed foreign signatories at a great advantage over local traders. France was the first country to enter such a capitulation in 1536, choosing to ally with the Sublime Porte due to its rivalry with the Habsburgs.

The participation of European merchants in the east India trade changed nothing in the positions of the West, South, South East and East Asian regions as the workshops of the world. Development of relations was very much in the interests of local producers, as well as of their respective political rulers. These regions received in return silver, increasingly sourced from American mines in the wake of European expansion into Latin America. There is thus little reason to suspect that Asian countries and regions were subjected to European domination, as Abu-Lughod postulates with reference to Portuguese colonial advances in the Indian Ocean.[51] She overlooks the fact that the Portuguese colonial presence in Goa and the South East Asian islands could only have had a marginal influence on the great empires of South and East Asia.[52] This is not to say that European merchant shipping around the Horn of Africa and in the Indian Ocean was a peaceful endeavour – each ship was equipped with cannon, and prepared to respond with force should resistance arise. Yet because Indian and Chinese rulers' self-understanding remained largely continental in nature, they neglected to interfere with the European maritime powers, especially the Portuguese around 1500 as they established their naval bases, protection systems and control regimes. After the seven legendary naval expeditions of Zheng He (sometimes Cheng Ho) to the Arab world and East Africa (1405–33), a last high point of Chinese naval power, Chinese maritime activities in the Indian Ocean ceased entirely. China instead focused on its centralized trade system, based in Canton.

When Immanuel Wallerstein writes of the formation of a 'capitalist world-system' under European dominance at the beginning of the sixteenth century in the first volume of *The European World-System*,[53] he limits the scope of its effect to intra-European and Euro-Atlantic relations, thus excluding Asia, Africa, the continental and especially western parts of the Americas, and Russia. Wallerstein identifies these regions as 'external arenas' because they were not subordinate to European interests. André Gunder Frank develops another perspective in his book *ReOrient*,[54] seeing the continuity in Abu-Lughod's medieval Eurasian world-system as extending into the early modern period[55] and claiming that the dynamics of that world-system remained anchored in South and East Asia, thus interpreting colonialization as merely an attempt by Western Europeans to buy their way – with American silver – into a world economy still dominated by Asian 'small players'.[56]

These two approaches result in different ways of conceptualizing the simultaneity and interconnection between various labour relations in the regions involved in world trade. According to Wallerstein,[57] the expansion of Western Europe into North-Eastern Europe and the Americas around 1500 marked the outset of a functional division of labour encompassing all parts of the system, which is in turn the key to understanding the simultaneous emergence of wage labour, forced labour (*corvée*) and slavery. Labour relations in regions of the world not under Western hegemony cannot be explained in the context of the European-dominated transatlantic system, but rather must be examined, even when parallels emerge, from within the locally prevailing socio-economic and political conditions. This does not exclude a comparative approach, but refrains from explaining visible parallels through reference to a world-systemic context.

On the contrary, if one understands the world-system in 1500 (like Frank) as one that spanned the world but centred around South and East Asia, none of what Wallerstein locates in 'external arenas' – the decline of Mongol rule, the formation of subsequent dynasties, the commitment of European merchants to Asian trade – can be externalized. The labour relations of 1500 would then be part of an already existing global capitalism. In their book *The World System: Five Hundred Years or Five Thousand?*,[58] Frank and Gills locate the origin of a single global system characterized by unequal interregional divisions of labour in the Neolithic Revolution. This, of course, is hardly relevant to the world-system of 1500, but shows what sort of consequences can result from one's view of the relationship between a system's parts and the whole, which Frank takes as a given in 1500: whether on Sumatra or Ceylon, in Guangzhou (Canton), Halab (Aleppo), or Potosí, the goods produced locally for the world market introduced the labour realized within them into the labour relations of the European workshops where they were processed and the households in which they were consumed. Frank's attempt to date capital accumulation and transfer of value further back in history reflects widespread scepticism in the historical social sciences, which tend to relativize the modern era by situating capitalism's origin in previous epochs.[59]

One potential compromise between these two conceptions lies in the thesis of the two colonial styles.[60] Western European relations with the Americas and northern Europe in the early modern period were characterized by an unequal transnational division of labour in which labour relations and potentials for adding value in each area depended on a region's position within the global commodity chain, whereas trade between Europe and Asia was characterized by relative balance. Although a certain hierarchy of products exchanged can be observed in terms of quality, degree of processing and popularity, the Asian commercial regions excelled. Absent from Asian trade in 1500, however, was a functional division of labour splitting up individual regions along the commodity chain into sites of higher and lower wage levels and greater or lesser added value, as was characteristic of Euro-Atlantic relations.

Local conditions and labour relations

Local labour relations are characterized by the persistence of engrained structures, whereas climatic and demographic changes trigger crises at regular intervals, leading to catastrophes but also to adaptation and innovation in the organization of production and work. The old societies were thus in no way static and hostile to change, as modernity would later characterize them. The basis for our analysis of the labour relations prevalent around 1500 is the social types that existed in hierarchical agrarian societies centred around the household, which incorporated both subsistence self-sufficiency and market production, with a concentration of artisanal specialists in towns connected to long-distance trade networks. Regional changes, which would naturally exhibit a local dimension as well, will be depicted in the following within the context of their interregional relations, first at a continental level, then with regard to intercontinental networks.

Interregional connections

Agrarian relations began to undergo a process of differentiation around 1500, resulting in the emergence of new social and work character types across the European regions. The answer to the late medieval agrarian crisis was a transformation of European feudalism into a system of capitalist agriculture based on tenant farmers (Western Europe) and a seigneurial rent economy based on peasant labour and levies (Central Europe). In eastern Central Europe, where western Central European patterns were imposed upon the tributary economy and society over the course of German settlement expansion in the thirteenth and fourteenth centuries, Western feudal dynamics came to a standstill and peasants faced stricter dependency on noble landowners.[61] This differed from the forms of serfdom introduced in Russia because they could not be attributed to external demand.

Introducing a land-tenure system rather than direct feudal relations allowed the noble landowners of North-Western Europe to shift responsibility for risks and price fluctuations onto the tenants themselves – peasant farmers were in effect independent agricultural entrepreneurs with all the opportunities for social advancement that went along with it, but also risked financial ruin. Tenancy payments freed them from personal subjugation, as feudal *corvée* was replaced by capitalist rent paid to the landowner, while taxes were collected by the state. The landowners could use rent income from tenants for personal spending and/or as capital for investment in other branches, like trade or commercial production.

Transforming land into a commodity, however, first required that the rural population abandon claims and rights to common land use and the social security this granted. This separation of the small farmer and peasant population from the countryside through barriers became the notorious 'enclosures', erected at that time in England, Scotland and northern France.[62] Leasing land to tenants was only possible in the absence of any other rights to land. Peasant families were freed from feudal bonds. That is, released to fend for themselves. For those without money or recourse to land, this meant seeking work as wage labourers in agrarian enterprises or in the commercial and transport sectors. This proletarianization was frequently associated with relocation and resettlement, as many English agricultural capitalists now conducted extensive sheep grazing in the parcelled-off lands, replacing people with sheep in the truest sense of the word. Wool became an export good as well as raw material for the wool-processing industry, which found its own necessary workforce in the newly expelled peasants.

Farmers who were not expelled from the countryside could become agrarian entrepreneurs in their own right and, under favourable circumstances, hire agricultural workers of their own. Peasants who stayed in the countryside but had neither money nor land relied on familial subsistence work to survive. In the towns, subsistence farming was simply not an option. These local migrants were forced into wage labour or relied upon the social system. England is known not only for its population's relatively early proletarianization, but also for its Poor Laws.[63] The 1601 law provided for the destitute and members of the community left entirely to their own devices. It was designed as a form of compensation for when family networks failed; self-sufficiency was replaced by welfare payments. The Poor Laws only came into effect under strict conditions – one of them being birth within or belonging to a community – and thus were not able to hinder social protest movements. The fact that a peasant lifestyle and identity had already been extinguished resulted in these protests being carried out by the lower strata of the 'working class'[64] rather than in peasant uprisings.

Central Europe, on the other hand, evolved into a feudal rent economy based on seigneurial estates. Lords maintained their supreme ownership over the land, which was given over to the still-subjugated peasants to farm. In return, these were obliged to pay rents in the form of labour (*robot*), as well as tribute in kind or monetary payments – often to more than one lord, whose rights and demands could overlap with one another. One lord might demand flax and eggs, while the same peasants offered work to the other. The demographic collapse of the Late Middle Ages, which was due to the declining yields linked to lowered fertility in newly ploughed regions among other things, led to a drop in agricultural prices in the fifteenth century. Lords granted greater freedoms to their peasants in response. Grain prices had recovered by the outset of the sixteenth century, however, and landowners were keen to take back their fair share. They demanded tribute in kind rather than cash in order to sell it themselves, and restricted peasants' rights to the forests, grazing lands and hunting, all of which had hitherto secured the communal needs of the villages – the commons – in order to increase the yields of their lands.[65]

This renewed intervention into old rights and freedoms encountered fierce peasant resistance. These uprisings had flickered into life before, but grew in frequency towards the first quarter of the sixteenth century in south-west Germany, Austria and Switzerland, eventually igniting into the German Peasants' War.[66] Their self-dependent economic basis and awareness that they were defending previously recognized rights provided the peasantry with a high degree of mobilizing potential. Peasant protests found allies and developed links with urban class struggle and other forms of protest against the central state. Together with the growing strength of the Protestant Church, these movements posed a serious threat to the ruling order.

The peasant protests were squelched when the central state power – represented by the *Landesfürsten*, the local princes of the Holy Roman Empire – sided with the aristocratic ranks of landholders. The ensuing countermovement would cost 100,000 peasant lives between 1525 and 1526 alone. The Peasant Wars proved to be an opportunity for the rulers to push back militarily against the autonomy once granted to the nobility. While the rulers and the aristocrats reached a compromise, the peasants collapsed in defeat. A wide degree of regional variation existed between the burdens placed on the population by these new agricultural systems, but peasant households remained the basic unit of agricultural production in Central Europe across the board. Conflicts with landowners, protests and armed uprisings would continue to be the order of the day.

The characteristics of Western feudalism had deep roots among the German settlers of eastern Central Europe and the Magyars in Transylvania. These groups had been 'free' in that they were *immediately* subject to their ruler as opposed to facing *mediated* relations through aristocrats, and were thus relatively independent before 1500. The second Western element introduced by German and Magyar urban burghers was trade, exchanging Western European export goods for Eastern European raw materials. These two Western traits and their effects (independence and trade dependency) began to work against each other: as demand for eastern Central European exports rose, local nobility further tightened their grip on peasant producers. In many states, eastern colonization had established the German nobility as the supreme owner of most land. With the pressing demand for agrarian imports into Western Europe, eastern Central European nobles increasingly transformed their landed properties into estates producing for the export market. Formerly self-sufficient local producers were transformed from peasants into serfs. The oft-used term 'second serfdom' is misleading, however, as the kind of bondage seen in Western serfdom had been uncommon in eastern Central Europe with its looser, less coercive tributary relations.[67] Gradations can be observed with regard to the extent of forced labour, individual dependency and the peasantry's freedom to cultivate private land. Peasants were at least permitted to grow their own food in the rudimentary family economy existing alongside manorial estates. This also kept agricultural labour costs down, as the burden of sustenance was externalized onto the family household. Additionally, peasants continued to see themselves as such, although the work they performed on the estates often resembled agricultural wage labour in many ways. Resistance to bondage and taxation were manifest in efforts by dependent peasant populations to escape the yoke of serfdom by leaving to become free farmers or border guards (Cossacks) during Polish and Russian colonization of the steppe borderlands. This was a particularly tempting prospect for young men, as the Cossack camps erected after the Tatar Khanate's incorporation into the Tsardom of Russia (1550) were in effect largely warrior communities.[68] They formed the main line of defence against Crimean Tatar slave hunters and pressed forward with territorial expansion along the Volga and east to Siberia. In order to stop peasants from fleeing, the manorial landlords also built up a surveillance regime, giving work in this period a more coercive character.

Regional differentiation in agricultural economies was closely linked to developments in commerce. In Western Europe, commercialization of agriculture entailed commercial activities becoming separated from the family economy. English producers concentrated on wool, while in the Netherlands farmers specialized in the mass production of milk and vegetables, replacing the close entanglement of market and subsistence production. The urban populations working in the burgeoning commercial sector required foodstuff imports, mostly grain and livestock, to survive. This was also the case for mining regions, where demand for iron and precious metals drove the growth of a specialized mining profession without an agrarian subsistence base of its own.

Increasing demand for grain and livestock had a direct effect on the functioning of manorial farm economies in eastern Central Europe: the surplus gained from tributary payments and peasant labour rents could be increased by supplying foodstuffs to Western markets. Rising demand meant rising pressure on the peasantry. The nobility were not the only actors benefiting from this unequal division of labour, as Western European businesses profited from cheap supplies for their own families and those of their employees. This continental connection between functional areas marked by unequal labour relations as well as profits, first detailed for the Baltic region by Polish economic historians, also inspired Immanuel Wallerstein's world-system model.[69] Wallerstein views the West–East differential between North-Western and North-Eastern Europe as a fundamental pattern, which was also the basis of interactions between Western European industrial regions and their American colonies.[70]

Central and Eastern European goods generally arrived in Western

Europe unprocessed, reflecting unequal levels of participation in the expansion cycle of the sixteenth century. Commercial export specialization in urban crafts was rare for the East, and the local bourgeoisie were mainly active in trade. The high profit rates accrued from exporting raw materials kept impulses towards emancipation in the background among the agrarian nobility. In return for primary goods, high-quality processed goods were sent eastward from the West, mostly in the form of metalwares and textiles. Eastern Central European rulers often recruited craftsmen from Central and Western Europe to compensate for the lack of qualified professionals in their regions.

A semi-peripheral zone stretched between the Western and Central European cores and the eastern Central European periphery, i.e. from Saxony, Bohemia and the Austrian Alpine principalities across Habsburg Hungary to the northern Adriatic. Here, local commercial activity was largely geared towards regional markets, and often retained an agricultural component in the smaller towns. This region thus did not witness the North-Eastern European trend towards agricultural export specialization, but rather withdrew from interregional markets. Commercial and peasant goods were instead exchanged on local markets, and only particularly extraordinary goods left these regions through long-distance trade. This allowed for more mixed combinations of town and country, and agrarian and commercial, specialization to arise in Central Europe than in either the West or the East.

One such extraordinary product was woad, a plant used to make blue dye and the major source of the colour before indigo. This deep-blue dye can be understood as an intermediate product between agricultural raw material and semi-processed good, as turning it into coloured powder was a lengthy capital- and labour-intensive process. The German region of Thuringia became a major woad cultivator. Erfurt's woad merchants controlled the trade, and as land-cultivating citizens also enjoyed the right to brew and serve beer. The beer consumption of the city's copious drinkers allowed for the collection of urine, which was used in the fermentation process of drawing the blue pigment out of the woad. The next step was for woad wage labourers (*Waidknechte*, as they were known) to prepare the resulting mass of blue pigment into woad powder for transport.[71] Another area that produced woad, or *pastel* in French, was the region of Lauragais near Toulouse. This area provided Western woad merchants with their dyes.

Due to the diversity of livelihoods accessible to families, caring for the sick and disabled could be performed more easily in eastern Central Europe than in the West, where wage-dependent agricultural and commercial workers were more subject to fluctuations in demand and employment. There, public aid offered by the Poor Laws (England), parish-based poor relief (Netherlands) and poor houses (France) played a larger role. Domicile laws (*Heimatrecht*) in the Holy Roman Empire dating back to 1530 regulated institutional responsibility for poor relief, but mainly served the administrative accounting of a state's subjects. By assigning citizens to a community of domicile (*Heimatgemeinde*), they allowed for the deportation of those not entitled to social rights in their place of residence. This was mostly a concern for sixteenth-century towns, where large numbers of people resided outside their assigned district.[72]

Workers on manorial estates in eastern Central Europe had to do without public welfare of any kind. When their work was no longer needed on the manorial farm, family plots offered a form of social safety net. These were often overwhelmed, however, due to large families only having small plots with which to feed themselves.

A new form of enterprise and work organization also witnessed rapid growth at the end of the fifteenth century: mining. On one hand, mining supplied the necessary raw materials for the metalworking trades, while on the other providing the copper, gold and silver used to make the currency necessary as a means of circulation in the ongoing expansion of trade. The rise in demand was also related to state-building processes in the early modern period, as states increasingly needed money to finance administration, infrastructure and wars. The small groups of soldiers in service to the nobles were simply insufficient for early modern warfare, and paying mercenaries required cash. Mining sites were dictated by locations of ore deposits, but the division of labour in trade and transport continued to reflect the existing geography of inequality.

Early mining operations were based on older deposits, often densely packed into specific areas as ore yields were uncertain and transport was difficult. Even the smallest of deposits were exploited. The largest concentrations were located in the Alps and the Carpathians, while the most important Central European iron deposits were located around the Erzberg mines of Styria in Bohemian Saxony, and the Slovak Ore Mountains. The most important precious metal deposits were in Tyrol,

Styria and what is now central Slovakia. In addition to metals, salt mining played a central role.

Mining in Central Europe relied on a close symbiosis of feudal tenure, free enterprise and free wage labour. The *Landesfürsten*, who were royally entitled to mining rights (*Bergregal*), distributed mining concessions among nobles and wealthy merchants. Shareholders in early mining operations were known as *Gewerken* – vested with mining rights in the tradition of a fief, while also representing a mining-specific tradesman type. Vis-à-vis their workers, *Gewerken* were essentially the equivalent of landlords. Due to massive capital demand, local mining entrepreneurs quickly became dependent upon bankers from Upper Germany, particularly the Fugger family, who accrued enormous political influence by lending money to the German princes. Growing mining yields required high levels of workforce concentration, specialization and division of labour, all of which could not be achieved through peasants' side activities alone, as had previously been the norm. The town of Schwaz in Tyrol grew from two hundred to 15,000 inhabitants over the course of the fifteenth century due to silver mining, becoming the second-largest Austrian city after Vienna. Because its scattered miner settlements prevented the construction of a town wall, however, Schwaz did not enjoy town privileges until 1899.

An individual pit could require twenty-five to 250 workers, for whom the term *Knappen* gradually emerged. *Knappen* worked for hourly wages, or *Gedinge*, a typical form of piecework in mining. Miners could also be tenured workers who worked in the mines and paid tribute from the yields like peasant tenants, or self-employed small entrepreneurs (*Gewerke*). Working on the mountain was connected with long and difficult journeys. In summer, miners often lived in camps near the deposits. Women could also be found sorting and washing ore in the mines, either as day labourers themselves or as wives of bonded miners or self-employed *Gewerken* who helped their husbands, but were excluded from working as a *Knappe* or full member of the mining community, instead subject to patriarchal authority. Women workers who also worked outside the home were often unable to perform domestic work, at least periodically.[73]

Early capitalist mining was often integrated into a series of laws regulating ore extraction and processing, manufacturing of metal goods, food supply and trade routes. The Styrian Erzberg mine provides a good illustration of this system:[74] the mining areas were based on the locations of deposits, which could only be extracted with permission from the local sovereign. Land-rights policies were used to cultivate regions which promised high yields and exclude others. North and south of the Erzberg, extracted ore was separated from unwanted rock, processed and smelted in the two settlements of Hinternberg (known as Eisenerz today) and Vordernberg. These were connected to more distant, secondary processing regions, where the hammer mills and forges were operated by craftsmen organized in guilds. Provisioning networks were grouped around these iron-producing regions. Hardly any autonomous agriculture took place in the mountainous regions, nor in the areas where ore processing dominated. Even in the regions that specialized in metalwares, farming was secondary. The food supply for miners and craftsmen came from further adjoining regions with privileged outlets for agricultural products. This situation favoured market-driven production of food in peasant households far away from the mines, where it was carried out in connection with subsistence activities. In the mountainous regions where self-sufficiency was impossible, care for the sick, elderly and disabled was collectively addressed by the rudimentary forms of insurance, or *Bruderkassen*, developed by the *Knappen*.

Although the *Knappen* and their wives were placed in a form of servitude, this occupational group nevertheless anticipated industrial capitalist wage labour. This notion is also reflected in the organizational forms the miners developed to collectively provide for their colleagues, widows and orphans in case of need, and in the way they represented their interests against the *Gewerken* and political and ecclesiastical authorities. The parish church in Schwaz, Tyrol, provided the *Knappen* with their own nave. It was added on to the church, which had grown too small by 1500. These organizations, however, were dissolved after the miners fought alongside the peasants and urban bourgeoisie in the Peasants' War against the alliance between the nobility and mining enterprises.[75]

This small-scale division and purposing of land fit into the interregional division of labour. The towns to the north and south of the Erzberg – Leoben, Steyr and Waidhofen upon the Ybbs – became centres of local iron ore processing as well as points of contact for the distribution of cast iron and ironwares. Although the Erzberg and its iron-producing surroundings were an important centre of European mining, the region's position in the interregional division of labour was more intermediate.

High-quality finished products (knives, files, nails, scythes, and so on) were sent to Eastern and South-Eastern Europe; northern Italy, Upper Germany and the rest of North-Western Europe, however, required unprocessed raw iron and semi-finished goods to be finalized in Venice, Nuremberg or Antwerp.

Mining in Europe underwent a decline after 1550, due in part to competition from precious metals imported from overseas. Gold, silver and copper mining felt most of the impact, while the Erzberg and its surroundings remained a central mining region. The central Slovak mining region, which led the precious metals sector, would not survive overseas competition. As they were located in the area where the 'Ottoman Wars' were fought, early capitalist attempts there were ultimately extinguished by those wars.

Large-scale connections

Conquista and colonialization destroyed older ways of life for the indigenous people of the Americas. Contact with foreign diseases decimated their populations, followed by brutal assaults on the indigenous labour force, which further accelerated their decline. Populations were wiped out entirely on some islands and coastal areas, but not in the interior. In the Andean region, as well as the lands just beyond the coast, native agrarian societies were transformed in line with colonial needs.

European colonizers forced native communities to work and deliver agricultural goods for the colonial market. They also compelled the natives to use certain European imports in place of their own production. A basic form of colonial exploitation was the *encomienda* (from the Spanish verb for 'entrust'), which entitled owners to use the local labour force in exchange for certain protection and supply obligations. An *encomienda* could be inherited. King Charles V of Spain (and Holy Roman Emperor Charles I) banned the *encomienda* in order to prevent the development of feudal relations in 1542 with the so-called 'New Laws', stating that the *encomienda* system would no longer be hereditary. However, protests from colonists forced him to rescind his centralizing ambitions. Although the New Laws were only partially successful, they emancipated thousands of indigenous workers. The Spanish Crown also imposed taxation on indigenous populations. Thus, on top of tributary labour for the *conquistadors*, they were also obligated to pay tribute to the state. Massive fortunes could be accrued in colonial gold and silver mining as well as in the plantation economy, which had now become twin pillars of the colonial export economy.

Mining operations around mineral deposits in the Andean highlands and Mexico not only required a huge labour force, but also the necessary foodstuffs to feed it – this is how the Potosí mining range emerged as the nucleus of an interregional division of labour together with the colonial metropolis of Lima. By 1545, a far-reaching system of regions, workforces, foodstuffs and consumable items revolved around the largest silver mine in Latin America. The functional division of labour supported by mining is also known as the 'internal colonial market',[76] and included the farming communities providing the labour force. It also connected even further-off regions, which supplied foodstuffs, pack animals, luxury consumables (yerba, mate, wine, coca) and craft products to the mining region. Indigenous village communities, and the agricultural work performed by displaced native subjects on Spanish colonists' *haciendas*, constituted the basis of the mining industry.

Early on, some native entrepreneurs processed ore with traditional wind furnaces. However, silver mining soon became a capital- and technology-intensive business with the introduction of amalgamation, necessitating imports of mercury from Europe. Native populations were subsequently pushed into positions of dependency. Sending slaves into the mines, whether indigenous or African, proved neither effective nor tenable. Thus, to meet the increasing demand for labour, Potosí introduced the *mita* in 1573. This method for mobilizing the workforce required communities in the surrounding highland provinces to send one-seventh of their male population between the ages of fifteen and fifty to the silver mines every year. At the end of the year-long rotation, workers would return and be replaced with fresh men. On one hand, this ensured the availability of a replenished workforce. On the other, it compelled rural agriculture to send away part of its own workforce and do without its production, thus subordinating it to silver export production.[77] In the sixteenth century, over 16,000 *mitayos* were sent to Potosí annually. Natives could buy their way out of the *mita* by paying the mine operators. Overall, this meant a regular flow of labour and monetary tribute from the villages to the mines. In areas where there were no agricultural communities to draw from, or when qualified workers were needed, the mines hired wage labourers.

This explains why the colonial administration allowed indigenous village communities to retain their administrative structures. Wherever these structures tottered or collapsed due to the shock of colonialization, missionaries came in and regrouped the surviving indigenous inhabitants into new settlements, known as either *reducciones* or *congregationes*.[78] These settlements aimed to prepare them for producing foodstuffs to be sold for profit, or to work in the mines and *haciendas*.

On the Caribbean Islands, the first point of colonial contact, the native population was eradicated within a few decades. The islands initially served as a relay station for dealers, smugglers and colonizers before the sugar plantation became the dominant economic form in the seventeenth century.

Brazil was the first centre of the sugar cane economy.[79] Here, enslaving the native population proved insufficient to meet demand, and conditions were created for the machinery of the African slave trade to spring to life. The latest calculations estimate that 11 million people were trafficked to the Americas by the end of the nineteenth century, while another 2 million simply did not survive the journey.[80] Almost half of these slaves were put to work in Brazil. Procurement and transport of this workforce became its own business sector, where English merchants controlled the largest share.

Intensive mono-cultural export agriculture did not allow for the cultivation of food, nor the reproduction of the labour force. Therefore plantations have to be seen in connection with the great farms in the hinterlands, which produced the foodstuffs and livestock that sustained workers. This labour force was replenished by further slave transports from Africa.

In contrast to mining, which mobilized native village households to ensure its own reproduction and thereby subsidized the export of precious metals, plantations had no subsistence base to serve the same purpose. Ways of life, languages, rituals and memories from the African region of origin accompanied slaves along their forced emigration and were necessary souvenirs that allowed them to endure the tribulations and humiliations of forced labour.

Development of the Latin American provinces into outlets for colonial settlers, export markets, and suppliers of gold, silver, sugar and cotton extended the territorial base of the European economy. Further processing was concentrated in the industrial regions of the Netherlands and England, while even the precious metals ended up with the North-Western European creditors and investors due to the high levels of debt and the underdeveloped commercial sector on the Iberian peninsula. Gold and silver were available for trade with Asia; Portuguese, English and Dutch traders bridged the Spanish colonial economy and Asian industrial production. The South American precious metals put European long-distance traders and merchant companies into a position to acquire coveted spices and prestigious goods from Asia for European consumers, as well as provide them to other regions of the world.

Transatlantic expansion helped to shift the existing cores of the European economy, once dominated by the network of Upper German and northern Italian towns, westward: Seville and Lisbon became points of departure for overseas trade; Antwerp replaced Bruges as the hub between the Mediterranean, Atlantic, North Sea and Baltic trade.[81] This development pushed aside the Habsburgs' erstwhile financial backers, Upper German bankers and merchants such as the Fuggers and Welsers who were also active as mining financiers in the Alpine and Carpathian regions.[82] Other than regions affected by the Habsburg–Ottoman front (like Slovakia), however, this in no way entailed decline for the Central European regions. Rather, it set in motion a process of regionalization that strengthened local and regional integration vis-à-vis interregional developments, in contrast to Northern Europe, where the Polish and German Baltic feudal estates benefited from growing sales opportunities for agriculture and maritime goods to Western Europe. Here, magnates resorted to a cheap labour force by transforming their tributary peasants into serfs.[83]

The unfree and coerced labour of the North-Eastern European manorial economy has on many occasions been compared to slave labour on the South American and Caribbean plantations. Indeed, parallels can be observed in relation to the use of forced labour in the production of cash crops, processed in the Western European industrial cores or used to supply local workers with low-cost food. We also find parallels, however, between *encomienda*, *mita* and the market-oriented coerced labour of the manorial economy: in both arrangements, indigenous workforces were put to work without completely destroying their subsistence base. Instead, these became an additional source of supply for the workers mobilized to work in the mines and *haciendas* and in the manorial surplus economy.

The historical cross-section for 1500 focused primarily on physical

space and labour relations incorporated into the systemic intercon-
nectedness of the 'European world-system'. The regional and unequal
functional division of labour between the individual world regions is
seen as both characteristic of and the necessary precondition for 'capitalism'. This entails an understanding of capitalism that is not bound to
one region but to the entire systemic context. If we date the beginning
of 'historical capitalism'[84] to its incipient penetration into America and
North-Western Europe around 1500, then the sixteenth century can be
seen as 'early capitalism'. This world-systemic definition stands in opposition to a concept of 'early capitalism' that merely situates its emergence in
the wage labour of mining companies and commercial export, which in
turn is seen as a predecessor of wage labour's later generalization, as considered typical of labour relations under 'capitalism'. Nevertheless, there
is no reason not to see the miners forced to work under the *mita* system
in Potosí as a manifestation of early capitalism, any less than the Tyrolian
or Slovak miner *Knappen*.

Russia is not dealt with in this cross-section due to the view of major
world-systems scholars that it was excluded from the interregional division of labour at the time. Hans-Heinrich Nolte, however, views Russia as
semi-peripheral to the European world-system, due to its close religious
and political ties.[85]

In many cases, European behaviour in such 'external arenas' of the
world-system is nevertheless reminiscent of the attitudes of colonial
superiority and prevalence of coercion, clearly exemplified in the colonies in the Americas. The Portuguese regime of the *estado da India* in
Goa is likely to have followed South American–type colonial models.
The Portuguese colonial regime replaced the balanced relationship that
had typically been maintained with such external arenas with one-sided
activities that only benefited the colonial European power.[86]

1700

Characteristics

The expansive global economic dynamic characterizing the 'long' sixteenth century had reached its limits by the mid-seventeenth century.
Population growth, economic growth and overall demand began to
decline, and with them prices and profits. In Europe, the crisis is often

associated with the Thirty Years War, which had particularly disastrous effects on Central Europe. Globally speaking, however, we find no evidence for an overall negative or backwards developmental trend. Important parameters of development remained in effect: the division of labour between North-Western and North-Eastern Europe continued to provide inexpensive grain from the manorial economy. Dutch agriculture benefited from a cheap seasonal workforce, the northern German *Hollandgänger* who brought home their additional income to supplement their peasant existence. In the Americas, precious metals and agricultural products were supplied for export to Western Europe by native unfree labourers forced to work under the *mita* colonial contract with the Spanish rulers, and black plantation slaves. Following the War of the Spanish Succession which reflected ongoing rivalries between Britain and France, the United Kingdom secured a monopoly over the transatlantic slave trade, the so-called *Asiento* (1713). The slave trade would reach its peak under the British in the eighteenth century; about half of the ten to twelve million slaves who survived the journey are estimated to have been brought over from Africa in the 1700s. The North American colonies were also based on slave labour, most notably the tobacco plantations of Virginia. Central European traders who themselves had little to do with the slave trade nonetheless profited from colonial slavery through the means of exchange.

Until 1700, Spaniards and Portuguese had constituted the largest settler group in Latin America, with over a million people. The initially low number of British immigrants, however, now rose in the American colonies, to 800,000 between 1700 and 1800 alone.[87] In addition to religious refugees who founded agricultural settlements, other immigrant groups mainly comprised the impoverished, criminal and social fringes, employed as contract workers on colonial farms as servants and maids. This contract work is known as indentured servitude. As the name suggests, indentured servitude meant that contracts could not be terminated at will, nor was their choice to work free. This was an elaborate system, often based on expulsions and deportations. Workers could not change their place of employment or quit during the indentured period, usually between five and ten years. The first black settlers in North America were originally indentured servants as well, until slavery was legally institutionalized and their aspirations for eventual freedom extinguished. Sugar cane and cotton were the two main cash crops. Cotton spurred the growth of the European textile industry. The New England colonies extended the transatlantic trade network, receiving English finished products in exchange for fish and timber, which they in turn traded for Caribbean sugar and molasses.

The availability of cotton changed the Western European textile industry.[88] Cotton overtook the other raw materials of Central Europe as well, particularly in conjunction with flax (fustian). This cotton, however, came from Syria and Egypt, the spoils of victory enjoyed by the Habsburgs after defeating the Ottomans.[89] Rising pressure on prices and profits, stemming from stagnant or declining population growth across various regions, allowed new forms of enterprise to emerge and with them new organizational forms. A key difference was that these companies viewed the old guild rules as obstacles to growth. Local rulers did their part by offering exemptions (privileges) to businesses in certain sectors, freeing them from guild regulations. In return, they expected growing production to bring higher tax revenues into state coffers. The new entrepreneurs, above all in textile manufacturing but also in metal processing, moved their operations into rural areas beyond the reach of the guilds which dominated the cities. The result was the emergence of a competitor to craft production: the so-called manufactory and 'putting-out system'.[90] While central manufactories achieved productivity gains through economies of scale and internal divisions of labour, putting out allowed labour-intensive processing to be relocated into workers' homes, thereby saving wage, social and setup costs. Manufactory and putting-out production usually emerged in close connection: until now, concentrating commercial production around one site had been difficult due to the lack of adequate workforces at any one location. Centralized manufacturing was thus limited to management, labour preparation, finishing and distribution, while the most labour-intensive steps were given to workers to perform within their own household. Accordingly, the decentralized form of work found in the putting-out system is also called home industry or cottage industry. The transition to a growth-oriented mode of production therefore occurred less as a result of centralization as such, than through the combination of centralized logistics at the manufactory headquarters and decentralized cottage industry. This shift also changed the geographical landscape of commercial production: while urban craft production remained in the hands of the guilds, manufacturers availed themselves of the workers available in rural commercial regions.

The geography of export trade changed with the introduction of new products as well: English weavers, for example, were able to corner the Flemish and Dutch markets with their lightweight and more comfortable 'new draperies'.[91] Cotton and cotton-blended fabrics began to surpass pure wool and linen fabrics. As cotton had to be imported, proximity to ports and interregional transport routes was a crucial factor in the development of cotton-processing centres.

None of the movement occurring in European manufacturing and putting out in the textile sector managed to unseat the primacy of Asian producers, however. In 1700, Chinese silk, fine Indian muslins and painted and printed calico, as well as Persian and Ottoman carpets, were the undisputed market leaders in textiles. Asian export production operated similarly to the European putting-out system, structured around centralized workshops and households which were coordinated by wholesalers and their middlemen. While production remained an Asian affair, distribution was handled by European merchants over existing Indian Ocean trade routes. Thus, like the production sector, European trade companies enjoyed state guarantees and privileges with monopoly rights and military protection for their ships. Over the course of the seventeenth century, several European trading companies were established to conduct trade with Asia: the British East India Company in 1600 and the United East India Company founded by the Dutch in 1601. These two were joined in 1664 by the French Compagnie des Indes orientales. Their initial customer base remained limited to wealthy elites, but gradually an ever-growing audience enjoyed access to the coveted goods. Trade was by no means limited to imports for internal markets, but was also a means to re-export articles to various export markets. The Indian subcontinent enjoyed relative trade freedom in this process, while export to and from China remained under strict state regulation. While cotton processing was done in peasant households supplying the internal market, porcelain, wallpaper and silk industries were highly export-oriented. Triangular Atlantic trade also provided outlets for Asian textiles, which could be exchanged for slaves in Africa, plantation products and precious metals in Latin America and the Caribbean, or for cod and whale in North America. The price of a slave was set either in gold or in cotton fabric. A strong male slave in the eighteenth century, for example, was valued at three thousand grams of gold or a *pièce d'Inde* (ten to fifteen yards of cotton fabric).[92]

Merchant capital's economic predominance began to wane by 1700. The consolidation of modern European states, which relied on growing tax revenues to build administration, infrastructure and armies, occurred under the aegis of mercantilism. Policies sought to keep gold and precious metals in the country and strengthen domestic production and exports, thereby achieving a positive trade balance and high corporate profits as the primary basis for taxation. England (united with Scotland since 1707) and France deployed successful mercantilist strategies promoting and protecting domestic producers and markets, and thereby gaining the upper hand over the Netherlands. The cores of the European world economy shifted from Amsterdam – in competition with Paris – to London. The gateway to the global economy where Asian and Atlantic trade converged was Liverpool, rivalled by Nantes.

According to Immanuel Wallerstein, the 'European world-system' in 1700 now consisted of the North-Western European cores, the Central European semi-periphery, and the periphery in eastern Central Europe and the Americas. The incorporation of South and South East Asia, the Ottoman and Persian Empires and Russia would only come to be in the second half of the eighteenth century, with China and Africa following later in the nineteenth century.[93] Critics object that the incorporation of these regions into the global unequal division of labour had already begun by 1700.

Russia's victory over Sweden in the Battle of Poltava (1709) allowed the Russian Empire to expand across the Baltic coast. The Russian capital was moved from Moscow to the new city of Saint Petersburg, modelled after the grandeur of Amsterdam. Western Europe became the developmental role model for Peter the Great and subsequent Russian rulers, treated as a standard against which to measure their own progress.[94] Mining and industry underwent a comprehensive modernization, albeit only around Moscow, Saint Petersburg and the Urals. In cultural terms, Russia had long felt connected to the system of Christianity – a connection long hindered by the split between the Latin Catholic and Byzantine Orthodox Churches (the Schism of 1054), by two hundred years of Mongol occupation, and by Russia's exclusion from the great European alliances. In order to win Russian support for the Holy Alliance's advance against the Ottoman Empire following their defeat in the Battle of Vienna (1683), Russia was integrated – albeit with reservations – into the circle of European powers in 1685.[95] This can be interpreted as political incorporation.

The concerted push against the Ottoman Empire culminated in the Habsburg conquest of northern Serbia and Belgrade along with Lesser Wallachia in 1718. A trade agreement following the Treaty of Passarowitz/Požarevac established the foundation for intensification of trade and exchange, which had largely ceased during the Ottoman Wars. In earlier times, Ottoman exports had consisted of high-quality, luxury commercial products. Now, the tide had turned: the Sublime Porte's military weakness was reflected in terms of trade, as exports shifted to raw materials and semi-finished goods, relegating the empire to a peripheral role in the global economy.[96]

The year 1700 also marks a turning point for the Indian subcontinent. In 1701, England closed its domestic market to imports of printed cotton fabrics. Around the same time, France (1696) and Spain (1717) – states with highly developed textile industries – imposed similar cotton import bans.[97] The English prohibition concerned only the internal market; re-export of calico, or *indiennes* – a primary East India Company export – was excluded. English, French, Dutch and Catalan entrepreneurs had only just begun to produce cotton prints, and enforced protectionist measures in line with the emerging mercantilist spirit to protect their products against (vastly superior) Indian competitors in their respective states. This can be seen as the beginning of the end of Indian superiority as the global leader in the textile market. The ban initially only targeted the last step in the processing chain, textile printing, which was particularly sensitive to consumer wants and fluctuations in demand. At the time, Europe was incapable of producing the plain cotton fabrics needed for this step in the required amount or quality, and thus remained unaffected by the ban and continued to source its cotton from South Asia. Demand from European printers led to an export boom in Bengal, where plain weavers were concentrated. Gujarat and the Coromandel Coast, by contrast, specialized in calicos and subsequently lost their European export markets. The Indian cotton industry thus remained a global player throughout the eighteenth century. The substitution of calico imports with European production, however, resulted in regional shifts, as well as specialization in the market niches increasingly in demand among European buyers.

Local conditions and labour relations

The various activities of the household-based economy in its peasant village and urban craft forms have already been described in the section on 1250. The newly emerging centralized sites of production, or manufactories, differed from peasant and craft commercial production in that work was performed at a workplace outside the home. Workers no longer received successive training in the various steps of production, mastering one task after another until they had learned the entire production process. Instead, they were employed in companies that divided the production process into individual steps – specific, repetitive processes that required little or no training. In *The Wealth of Nations*, Adam Smith gives a detailed description of the eighteen steps needed to produce a nail in a southern British nail factory, highlighting the productivity-enhancing effects of the division of labour and specialization.[98] The encyclopedias of the time devoted a great deal of space to illustrations of each work step along with necessary machines and equipment, thereby influencing subsequent ideas of manufacturing production. In artisanal craft production, such unqualified activities removed from the context of the overall work process were only the norm among unskilled labourers, rather than apprentices, journeymen or masters.

Production sites that gathered production processes (now disassembled into individual steps) in one central location were commonly called manufactories, or factories (French *fabrique*, German *Fabrik*, from the French *fabriquer*, 'to make'). One particular manufactured good was, as we have seen, fabric, which received this title in the 1750s. The term 'factory' reflected the other side of production, namely the centralizing office coordinating the various work processes, and stemmed from the Latin *factorum* – an 'office for agents' ('*factors*' – doers, makers). Following the introduction of external energy sources, line shafts and, especially, combustion-powered machinery around the end of the eighteenth century, the term 'factory' was restricted to these newer operations, whereas it had once been used interchangeably alongside 'manufactory'. Water-powered machinery had sometimes been used for certain tasks, but was not necessarily a unique feature of manufacturing; mills and sawworks also featured the use of such machines, as did various artisanal craft operations.

Until now, separation of work from the household context had largely been limited to the mining sector, where the distance between mine locations and households was a simple fact of life. Building sites, courtly workshops and merchant shipping also required work performed outside the household. Centralized manufactories, however, brought forth a particular kind of workforce whose tasks were removed from knowledge of the production process and whose workplace had been separated from their place of living and reproduction. Manufactories were not bound to any minimum size, and were often founded by individual nobles, industrial producers, merchants or even shareholder consortiums. Because the level of financing involved usually exceeded the resources of individual founders, banks, guarantors and lenders were also involved in their establishment.

In practice, this new phenomenon was extremely rare. Centralization of the labour force in one place was usually only found in state-run workhouses, where economic considerations existed alongside social discipline and the use of asylum inmates and prisoners as workers. Manufactories also operated in the luxury goods markets, such as porcelain, tapestries, silk, leather, mirrors, clocks, wallpaper or weapons. These acted as model mercantilist companies, like the royal tapestry maker Manufacture nationale des Gobelins in Paris, founded in 1607 as a private company; another was the Königlich-Polnische und Kurfürstlich-Sächsische Porzellan-Manufaktur in Meissen. Outside major cities, mobilizing large groups of workers into one place was simply not possible. Major mass production of goods for interregional markets occurred less in manufactories themselves, instead operating largely through the decentralized form of the putting-out system. The principal employers here were mostly merchants who owned no production facilities of their own. Sometimes, production was coordinated by a central manufactory.

The political and social power of the craft trades and the guilds in European cities made hiring workers outside guild control rather difficult. To get around this, some manufacturers relocated or 'put out' commercial production to the rural areas. Thus the putting-out system was a decentralized form of manufacturing: individual work processes (spinning, spooling, weaving, knitting and making bobbin lace for textiles; filing, drawing, hammering for metalwares) were performed in peasant farms and small rural households that worked independently and were paid for piecework, hourly wages or a combination of the two. On one hand, these household contractors functioned as outsourced company departments.

On the other, putting-out work was only one of several activities they pursued, which fit into rhythms of daily or seasonal work and the familial division of labour. Yet the very separation of labour processes, reflected in allocating specific tasks to specific households, was turned on its head in the putting-out system, as the work process became integrated into the undivided and indeed indivisible workload of the family household and was thus given a new contextual framework within people's lives. The organizational aims of the division of labour, namely time savings and standardization through monitoring, repetition and factors of scale, could not come to fruition in the putting-out system. This was offset by other benefits: workers provided their own workspaces, and usually their own tools as well. Their agricultural activity usually kept them supplied with food, allowing them to accept lower wages. As all types of work were incorporated into the household unit, reconstructing precise household proportions of subsistence work and putting-out work is quite impossible. The employer profited from the fact that true costs could only partially be accounted for. In other words, the putting-out contractors profited not simply from the added value of commercial employment and subcontracted labour, but also from the transfer value from unpaid subsistence work provided by rural households. This extra value flowed into commercial goods production within the putting-out system. Fundamentally, workers in the putting-out system stabilized their households with peasant market production. Should rural households manage to sell agricultural products on the market, they gained another income stream that strengthened their position vis-à-vis the putting-out agent.[99] Similar conditions applied for domestic family economies in Asian commercial regions.[100]

The households of rural commercial producers are the most illuminating examples of the interplay of forces in the household family economy context,[101] exhibiting a special flexibility for adapting traditional roles and distributions of labour when it became necessary due to changing demands for specific operations or skills.[102] The putting-out work provided in peasant households only constituted a fraction of total working time. Dexterous fingers were the greatest occupational capital of spinner and weaver households, whose main source of income was putting-out work. Socialization ensured that women and girls were the most skilled in this area, and thus performed most of the paid work. Men were responsible for the agricultural side of subsistence. They also earned extra income with migratory work or looked over the household when the women were occupied by commercial activities – this included traditional women's work like preparing food, taking care of children or raising chickens.

Manufacturers contracted the whole household represented by the head of the house, the *Hausvater* ('house father'). To illustrate this arrangement, it helps to look at a contract for spinning work from the Linzer Wollzeugfabrik, founded in 1672, which contracted spinning and weaving labour in Upper Austria and the north-western Waldviertel region, as well as southern Bohemia. The written contracts obliged putting-out partners to dedicate all of their available time to working for the company, in order to prevent other manufacturers from poaching these families' labour:

> A contractual agreement has been established between the k. k. Linzer Wollenzeugfabrik and the subsequent spinner people and their domestic servants, according to which the k. k. Fabrik undertakes to provide enough wool to the spinners and their house servants under voluntary conditions for the usual spinner wage for 8 years, in order to contribute steadily to the earnings of the household … For which in return the Spinner as House Father along with all of his house servants are bound … to dedicate all of the time remaining after their household and field work and flax spinning to the spinning of wool for the k. k. Fabrik.[103]

This contract illustrates the various pillars of a peasant household in a rural textile-producing region: the household and all its members were active both in farming and in the household economy and flax spinning, while no distinction was made between activities for their own production and those for market. The contract is only concerned with the time they have left over, which is to be used to spin wool for the manufacturer in return for payment. This wage constitutes income supplementing agricultural market production; in cases of simple subsistence farming, the wage would represent the household's main income. This period lacked a professional ethos ranking individual areas of activity above others or valuing certain areas more than others. The household was a living and working collective distributing all needed work as well as earnings and income in terms of one indivisible collective income.

Manufactory and putting out peaked between 1650 and 1800, exhibiting a distinct geography in which sources of raw materials (metals, wool, flax, silk), markets (large towns, capitals, export trade routes), and finally regional employment conditions each mattered immensely. Peasants in agriculturally favourable regions were less willing to take on putting-out work than those in less favourable areas. Particularly noteworthy putting-out regions for textile production in Central Europe were eastern Switzerland, Vorarlberg and southern Germany, Upper and Lower Austria, northern Bohemia and northern Moravia, and the Moravian–Silesian–Polish and the Czech–Saxon border regions, as well as Rhineland and Westphalia.[104] It nevertheless ceased to be the predominant form of enterprise at the end of the eighteenth century, as putting out was replaced in Western and Central Europe by the centralization and mechanization of cotton spinning. For the next thirty to fifty years, putting out focused on weaving, which lagged behind spinning in terms of its degree of mechanization. When weaving and textile printing became mechanized and centralized in factories around 1840, putting out – now called 'homework' – shifted to cover periods of demand, custom orders and manufacturing niches which proved difficult or impossible to mechanize.

The demand from manufactories and putting-out entrepreneurs reorganized the way rural households managed their livelihood, and encouraged the establishment of new rural lower-class households known, according to region, as *Häusler, Keuschler, Chalupner, Käthner*, and so on, corresponding to the English 'cottager'. Each term stems from a kind of small house or hut – the *Haus* in the German *Häusler* is evident. A *chalupa*, for instance, was a kind of west Slavic hut. These names addressed the fact that while they may have owned houses, these families had little or no land to live off. They thus represent a type of rural sub-peasantry that arose through the demand for putting-out labour and was encouraged by population and marriage laws, allowing former servants and non-possessing family members to own houses and start families of their own. Given the exploding demand for labour, lower peasant households turned textile production into their primary livelihood. This new composition of work types did nothing, however, to change the undivided nature of family income and the incorporation of all areas of work activity into one household.

Interregional connections

The households of rural commercial producers in Central Europe were incorporated into the interregional network of the putting-out system. In contrast to the trade connections based on the urban guild's control over the production process, production itself was now organized as an interregional combination of different locations. Both organizational forms coexisted over a long transitional period, in constant competition for raw materials, markets and workers. With guilds and magistrates on one side and non-guild industrialists on the other, the eighteenth century was a period of intensive government lobbying to shape legal and institutional frameworks in the interests of each side.[105] In the Austrian lands, local commercial activity under guild control, known as *Polizeygewerbe*, was legally distinguished from export, *Kommerzialgewerbe*, in 1754. Guild craftsmen nonetheless functioned as suppliers for the putting-out system as well.

Some of these commodity chains were very locally oriented and concentrated on one seigneurial estate, as was the case in the Bohemian lands.[106] Oftentimes, small-scale putting-out systems linked up to commodity chains which reached much further, across regional and state borders. In the strict sense, such a commodity chain encompassed all processing steps from raw materials to the finished product. When raw-material extraction and distribution are included into this process, the radius of such chains expands enormously, particularly when raw materials must be imported from distant lands. The European transition from linen and wool to cotton was necessarily linked to this geographical expansion.

St Gallen, Switzerland, provides a telling example of a commodity chain transitioning from local to transregional control. Until 1650, the urban crafts controlled the entire process of urban textile production from raw-material preparation to the finished product.[107] In order to circumvent the requirements of the guilds and the city's own municipal finishing workshops, merchant capital entered into the production process in the second half of the seventeenth century. This was associated with the shift to rural sites as individual work steps were subcontracted out. The expansion of production went hand in hand with the transition to cheap mass-produced goods – linen yarn was increasingly blended with and eventually replaced by cotton. Eastern Swiss households largely focused on in-house weaving, although the tedious preparatory work was often passed on to subcontractors. Several refining businesses arose as well, such as bleaching, dyeing and printing. These manufactories were centrally organized and employed dependent wage labourers. Poorly paid spinning work was sent further off to more agricultural regions, weaving Toggenburg, Thurgau, Allgäu and Swabia, as well as Vorarlberg, into the eastern Swiss putting-out system. Local villagers constituted the labour force necessary to fulfil orders for spun yarn, while peasant households also delivered flax, grain, livestock and milk products to the urban textile producers. The unequal value creation along the textile commodity chain, characterized by higher wages at its core and lower wages on the periphery, also spilled over into specialization of agricultural work. Here, the division of labour found in peasant households provided cheap means of sustenance to the rural workforce, in turn adding greater value to the upper end of the textile chain.

As linen yarn grew scarce at the end of the seventeenth century due to the overall expansion of production, the supply chain was expanded north-east to Silesia; this link would later fray with the proliferation of cotton in the eighteenth century. Eastern Swiss textile makers received their cotton supply from long-established Swiss merchants with access to French and Spanish overseas markets via Lyon and Marseille. European woad, hitherto the primary source of blue dye, suddenly found itself competing with overseas indigo imports during this period.

In the Austrian and Bohemian lands, the urban linen export trade in the fifteenth and sixteenth centuries was no match for Zurich and St Gallen's immense reach. Exports travelled via Krems-Stein, Linz, Reichenberg/Liberec, Chemnitz and Augsburg. The diminished importance of the Upper German cities resulted in the regionalization of the aforementioned supply regions. This mass production of textiles in the Austrian countryside was conducted by companies granted privileges by the *Landesfürsten*, allowing them to circumvent guild regulations. In their initial phase, they were given monopoly rights over processing sheep's wool (Linzer Wollzeugfabrik, founded in 1672) as well as cotton (Schwechater Baumwollmanufaktur, founded in 1724). Schwechat, an estate owned directly by the Austrian *Landesfürst*, proved to be the ideal location on Vienna's outskirts to avoid the influence of the capital city's guilds. While Swiss merchant capital assumed the role of coordinating the commodity chain without owning production facilities, Austrian textile putting out emanated from the manufactories headquartered in Linz and Schwechat, where management, purchasing, raw-material processing, work distribution, refining and sales were located.[108]

Spinning, spooling and weaving work was distributed over several hundred kilometres among peasant households, all controlled from the manufacturing centres in Schwechat and Linz. A rise in labour demand in the eighteenth century triggered conflicts between the now numerous manufacturing companies, in turn leading to several population-growth-oriented reforms such as state support for new families, which then facilitated a rise in the number of small peasant and cottager households, whose main occupation became spinning and weaving. A geographical distinction between spinner and weaver districts did not exist. 'Factors' were mercantile agents who made contact with the putting-out workers. They recruited households and supplied them with raw materials, inspected finished products for quality, and brought these back to the manufactory headquarters where trained craft specialists such as dyers and printers made the final touches together with their assistants. Guild weavers who employed apprentices and journeymen competed with the manufactories for spinners in particular. Spinning yarn was among the most labour-intensive activities: it took eight to twelve workers on the spinning wheels just to supply one weaver. When we consider that spinning was rarely a person's primary livelihood, the explosive demand for workforces that accompanied any expansion of production becomes easier to imagine.

Large-scale connections

The Central European region was involved in large-scale textile trade in many ways. Asian goods were held in high esteem – some were introduced into the market directly, others arrived as English re-exports. Since the beginning of the eighteenth century, however, the most prevalent textile products were domestic, depending on raw materials (cotton, silk and dyes) on the one hand, and market outlets on the other. While Central European participation in textile markets was limited to buying and selling through overseas trade, the British, Dutch and French East India Companies went a step further: these began to employ their own textile putting-out systems in South and South East Asia, over which they maintained direct control.

Depending on the textile region (interregional connections being our interest), cotton was sourced from various corners of the globe. In Switzerland and northern Germany, markets were supplied with American cotton. Ottoman wool and cotton supplied the Austrian and Bohemian textile industry. The end of the seventeenth century saw the establishment of the first smaller manufactories, owned by aristocrats and municipal workhouses. The 1719 trade agreement with the Ottoman Empire marked the rise of large-scale manufactories and putting out, causing textile putting out to expand into more and more households until the introduction of mechanical spinning around 1800. By 1750, the Linz and the Schwechater manufactories each employed between 30,000 and 60,000 spinners and weavers. At the height of putting out around 1790, over 180,000 people were registered as waged industrial workers in Lower Austria alone, mostly as spinners. Due to the density of textile production, every third person in the Mühlviertel and Waldviertel textile regions participated.[109]

The beginnings of Austrian manufacturing and putting out were closely associated with the Imperial Privileged Oriental Company, founded immediately after the peace and trade treaty was signed with the Ottoman Empire (1719). Although its shareholders consisted of noble landowners and merchants, it can be understood as a governmental institution promoting both manufacturing and export. The company was not only awarded the rights to trade with the Ottoman Empire, but would go on to found companies in various strategic sectors.[110] Along with ship, rope, sail and copperware production, this mandate also extended to large-scale textile production. The Oriental Company acquired the already established Linzer Wollzeugmanufaktur and was given permission to establish the Schwechater Baumwollmanufaktur, which was continued as an independent enterprise after 1731 following the state-sponsored company's bankruptcy. Responsibility for securing raw material supplies and the processing industries, restructuring the commercial landscape according to mass production, and sales were united at the beginning of the putting-out system and placed under state control.

The Habsburg Army was responsible for driving the Ottoman Empire out of the Balkans. In contrast to the invasions of indigenous societies, this was a dispute between major imperial powers. The Sublime Porte had been militarily superior to the Christian powers until the end of the sixteenth century – accordingly, the empire dictated conditions of trade, and political alliances allowed for reductions in customs duties for some European states. As that page of history began to turn around the outset of the eighteenth century, the commodity structure of trade also underwent major changes.[111] Ottoman exports consisted increasingly of raw and semi-finished goods, while the Europeans began to export finished products. Political sovereignty prevented the transformation of the Ottoman Empire into a colony in the wake of this commodity structure deterioration; however, Austrian merchants did their part in bringing about the empire's peripheralization.

Not so for the case of Austrian expansion into East Asian markets. With territorial gains from the formerly Spanish Netherlands, the other Austrian imperial trade operation – the Privileged East Indian Company (based in the Belgian town of Ostend) – launched Austria into the East Indies trade in 1722. This endeavour was short-lived, however, as the British, Dutch and French managed to squeeze them out by 1731.[112] Giving up East Asian trade was the bargaining chip played to guarantee European recognition of Maria Theresia's succession to the Habsburg throne, a clear priority for Austria's rulers. Subsequently, interested parties from the Habsburg Monarchy depended on the British, the Dutch, the French or the Ottomans as intermediaries for South and East Asian goods. The Austrian government, as well as the merchants who used Austrian ships for East Asian trade, sought to bypass this suspension by handing over the vessels to another maritime power: the Free and Hanseatic City of Hamburg. Hamburg had sought to develop independent colonial trade since 1720, and hoped to achieve this goal as the successor of the Austrian East Indian Company. This move was blocked by the British and Danish, however. Prussia soon intervened, flying its flag in protection of an Austrian ship at the port of Hamburg in September 1731.[113] Ultimately, the Habsburgs shifted their shipping and maritime ambitions (following a brief pause to build a navy to protect merchant shipping in Naples) to Trieste.

Central Europe simply could not build a company large enough to compete with the grand Western European East India companies. Central and Eastern European merchants were nonetheless very involved in transatlantic trade with the Spanish colonies, in which networks of trade outposts and envoys along the Mediterranean and European Atlantic coasts played a significant role. These all converged in Cádiz, replacing Seville as the privileged Spanish seaport in 1717.[114] Commercial relations between Central European regions and the Asian and Atlantic worlds were limited to trade; Central European merchants did not outsource or subcontract in these regions, and thus did not intervene in the local conditions of production.

A closer look at the British East India Company's approach on the Indian subcontinent reveals a very different pattern.[115] The first hundred years after its founding in 1600 exhibit balanced relations between the mutual interests of Indian producers, landowners and merchants on the one side, and company shareholders (who enjoyed strong protection under the English Crown) on the other. Indian spices and commercial goods were purchased without recourse to coercion, overreaching or even company interventions into local processes. By establishing global distribution through re-export, British traders spread Indian products throughout the globe. Indian textile production, for example, was able to realize huge increases in output through the *dadni* system, a local institution which resembled the putting-out system and made it possible to meet growing international demand.[116] Merchants simply distributed incoming orders through middlemen to village weaver households, who either wove as their main source of income or conducted other activities alongside. *Dadni* denotes the monetary and material advances given to weavers. Spinning was either performed directly within the weaver's household or outsourced even further. Applying the decorative patterns, which often entailed a combination of dyeing and painting, was the most complicated step in the work process and required a great deal of knowledge, experience and skill. European buyers gained access to Indian producers by adopting the *dadni* system. Their primary concern was keeping up with growing demand, which meant finding new suppliers or convincing current suppliers to dedicate more time to textile labour. Merchants also faced the fact that British customers had their own ideas about the oriental patterns and fabrics they so desired, but conveying these to the Indian designers and printers was not always easy.[117] At first, the Europeans asked middlemen to deal with increases in demand and pass on the design patterns that customers wanted. As pressures rose, the Europeans were increasingly forced to act as contractors, transforming a trade relationship into a putting-out operation in which they saw themselves as organizers of local commodity chains for which they controlled the market through sales. This forced them to specify quantities, schedules and design templates, and to monitor quality. They granted credit to households that could not afford the initial investment, or offered advances in the form of yarn and then forced the household into supply contracts. To repay the loans, household members had to perform more textile labour at the expense of household work, and thus fell into growing dependency on British merchants, not infrequently leaving the household in the debt bondage of the so-called 'thread and money' system.[118] This process constituted the gradual conversion of a balanced relationship into a one-sided relationship of dependence.

Wallerstein situates India's transition from an external arena to a periphery of the 'European world-system' in 1765 with the British East India Company's assumption of administrative functions on the subcontinent.[119] This occurred in the wake of the British victory over the Nawab of Bengal in the Battle of Plassey (1757); the Mughal Empire bestowed upon the East India Company the *Diwani* – administrative and tax jurisdiction over the province. British governors introduced a new tax system in Bengal which allowed them to influence the production of desired export goods. This also made it possible for the British to force the local population to pay for British rule, mediated by the East India Company.[120]

The process of incorporation, however, had begun much earlier. It could be observed in the East India Company's creeping establishment of a global putting-out system since 1700, which slowly subordinated the autonomy of local producers to British demands. There are blatant parallels with today's commodity chains, in which 'global buyers' face off against local producers. The shift is also reflected in the simultaneous ban on imports of high-quality Indian calico to Europe to the benefit of domestic European entrepreneurs, who substituted Indian prints by establishing their own workshops, while Indian producers were forced into less lucrative sectors of semi-finished goods. Now they suddenly found themselves supplying the plain raw fabrics for European printers to finish. The regions specializing in calico printing suffered while other weavers of plain fabrics boomed, but this too brought forth a one-sided mono-structure. Although Indian textile imports were completely excluded from the domestic British market as the British cotton industry further expanded from fabric printing to mechanized spinning and weaving at the end of the eighteenth century, the subordination of Indian producers to British interests had begun one hundred years earlier.[121]

1800

Characteristics

The Industrial Revolution, i.e. the replacement of craftsmanship with machines and the centralization of commercial production in factories which took place in the British cotton industry between 1780 and 1800, is often regarded as characteristic of the transition to capitalism. This, however, seems too narrow a definition in light of the unequal transnational division of labour favouring capital accumulation in the cores of the European world-system since 1500. One might also ask whether signs of the transition from subsistence-oriented to capitalist – that is, profit- and growth-oriented modes of production – could have appeared outside the context of European accumulation, such as in the Chinese silk industry, considered the nucleus of Chinese capitalism.[122] In eighteenth-century China, large-scale manufactory and putting-out systems in the cities of Jiangsu and Zhejiang provinces expanded to include industrial households, specialist workshops and free labour markets. In Suzhou, specialists organized into their own guilds stood on various bridges throughout the city, which served as day-labourer markets. Here, they gathered to compete for contracts. A government document from the time describes the market:

> The inhabitants of the eastern section of the prefectural city (Soochow) are all textile workers … Each weaver has a special skill, and each has a regular employer, who pays him a daily wage. Should anything happen (to the regular weaver) the employer will get a worker who is without regular employment to take his place; this is known as 'calling a substitute'. The weavers without regular employers go to the city's bridges each day at dawn to await the calls. Satin weavers stand on Flower Bridge, damask weavers on Kuang-hua Temple Bridge, and spinners who make silk yarn at Lin-shi Ward. They gather by the score and by the hundred, scanning around expectantly with outstretched necks, resembling groups of famine refugees. They will stay until after the breakfast hour.[123]

That said, these considerations do not diminish the dramatic break represented by mechanization and centralization of industrial production in the factories in any way.

These developments dislodged the most striking characteristic of the pre-industrial economy: the incorporation of production within the family economy of the household. The rise of centralized energy supplies moved work – and the workers – into the factory halls. Work remaining to be done in the households underwent an ideological reinterpretation: now it was considered reproduction, women's work and motherly obliga- tion, relegated to the private realm. Beginning around 1800, this transition initially remained confined to a small group of industrial workers in the cotton mills, the leading sector of industrial transformation. At first, the group remained a tiny minority even in Great Britain, where the trend began. The European continent would have to wait until 1820 for the factory system to really establish a foothold and begin drawing in other industries and wider layers of the working class. In many Central European regions, in the whole of Eastern Europe and in the rest of the non-European world, factories were simply not built. Commercial pro- duction remained connected to rural market economies and subsistence farming. The Industrial Revolution and the new understanding of work it entailed nevertheless reverberated far beyond the borders of Western Europe. Putting-out and family economies came under immense pres- sure to abandon their various sources of income in favour of specializing in supplying raw materials to large-scale industry.

By introducing factory production into the leading sector of the Indus- trial Revolution, the cotton industry, the United Kingdom managed to achieve a position which would pave the way for its global economic hegemony in the nineteenth century. Napoleon's defeat had left its largest European challenger, France, standing in the shadow of British domi- nance, expressed not only in the empire's territorial consolidation but also in its control over the global economy's means of communication: finance, transport and information transmission.

Against the backdrop of later developments, it may seem rather sur- prising that England failed to dominate iron production in 1780 (40,000 tons per year). In fact, Russia was the true iron champion in this depart- ment (140,000 tons). How was this possible? In 1735, Abraham Darby discovered how to smelt pig iron in coke ovens, and indeed, English black coal and iron supplies would later ensure that England became the leading country in heavy industry. But the devil is in the details, so to speak, as pig iron could only be purified and refined in direct contact with charcoal until the discovery of the puddling process (1784). Because England had no more forests to speak of, British ironworks were forced to rely on iron from Russia and Sweden, where wood for charcoal burning was abundant. Russia used this export opportunity to expand its mining and iron operations in the Ural mountains with expert help from the Germans and the Dutch. Success depended on the web of state funding, Russian entrepreneurs, Western smelters and peasants who worked in the mines as serfs.[124] As soon as the technological gap closed, the flow of pig iron imports was eliminated. Within a short time, production reversed: by producing 173,000 more metric tons, England was ahead of Russia (165,000) by 1800. To be on the safe side, Great Britain implemented steep iron tariffs in 1803, and fifty years later its iron output was twenty times greater than Russia's. As in the substitution of calico imports from India, this was a gradual process in which imports of semi-finished goods were favoured until domestic production had come into its own. Customs protections then came into play, as competitors were pushed out from export markets (sometimes militarily) in order to secure them for domestic producers. By 1840, iron production had supplanted the cotton industry as the leading sector of industrial progress.

The declarations of independence signed by former Spanish colonies in Latin America (except Cuba) at the beginning of the nineteenth century aligned with British interests, granting them access to raw materials and colonial export markets independently of Spain's attempted monopolies.

Back to the year 1800: commercial textile exports around the world were suddenly flooded with cheaper English factory goods, driving governments in Western and Central Europe to enact prohibitions and customs barriers against English goods. At the same time, they sought to promote factory growth through a combination of imitation and innovation. The continental blockade imposed by Napoleon, temporarily slowing down English competition, fostered Central European catch-up efforts in industrialization in various spheres. Mechanization accentuated the technological gap between Eastern Europe and the non-European regions, which were considered backward due to the absence of mechanical production.

The displacement of Asian industrial products from European import and re-export markets had greatly reduced textile putting-out and artisanry in the Asian export regions, but full-scale deindustrialization was still not the case in South and West Asia by 1800. Rather than in export, artisanal and household commercial production found a market inside the country, although products were often considered inferior to

European imports. It is notable that Asian producers made no move to mechanize production along English lines, but instead held on to crafts- manship. Weavers and putting-out workers, however, increasingly relied on European machine-spun yarn imports over hand spinning.[125] This testifies to local producers' wide-ranging flexibility in adapting work processes and flows to changes in the general conditions, integrating the mechanical European cotton mill into a commodity chain con- trolled by regional putting-out entrepreneurs and weavers. They reacted to the Industrial Revolution in the cotton industry, therefore, without decoupling industrial production from the household economy (as was otherwise typical for the factory system). They relied on small workshops instead of mechanization and factory centralization. The drastic collapse of India's textile exports after 1800, on the other hand, shows that only a small part of the former productive capacity could be retained, and would continue to decline. The loss of income associated with the dis- placement of the world market nurtured Indian producers' willingness to become contract workers (coolies) on overseas colonial plantations.[126]

The European factory industry's hunger for raw materials and food- stuffs pointed to the new strategic role that non-(factory)industrialized regions would now play. Whether as formal colony, independent state or inner periphery, these regions were incorporated into the large-scale division of labour as agricultural suppliers. Plantation production in the Caribbean, the southern United States and Brazil not only expanded but also underwent major intensification, as work became increasingly subject to the requirements of the industrial system. The term 'second slavery' has been used to emphasize this intensification and the aggra- vated work regimes that went along with it.[127] Integration now extended to regions – whether small state or great empire – which had hitherto maintained independent economies and trade structures. While British interests had been represented by the East India Company (EIC) in earlier times, British rule gradually expanded across the Indian subcon- tinent until formal colonization (1858). Rather than commercial goods, the EIC now exported cotton, indigo and opium to China, which in turn satisfied the demand for tea in England, driven forward by the industrial way of life.[128] In China, demand for Indian raw cotton was strong due to the region's high population growth. According to the traditions of rural agricultural society, processing was done during the winter months. The eighteenth century saw more and more families turn to spinning and weaving as their main source of income, without market production enhancement towards technical innovation or mechanization.[129] China's foreign trade monopoly set narrow limits on its incorporation into the world economy. This barrier was only lifted by the Opium Wars, which ignited in 1842. If we compare the Chinese share of gross world product to that of India, which saw a decrease from 24.4 to 16 per cent between 1700 and 1820, we see that China's share rose from 22.3 to 32.9 per cent in the same time frame.[130] Moreover, the European textile industry preferred long-fibre American or Egyptian cotton to India's short-fibre cotton, as it was easier to process with machines. American cotton also owed its advances to the young country's deeply racist attitudes, which allowed for the indigenous people to be pushed ever deeper into the continent's seemingly inexhaustible interior on the one hand, and recourse to a workforce of uprooted black plantation slaves on the other – with relatively little resistance from either group.[131] Ambitious state promotion of industry began in Egypt under Governor Muhammed Ali, who sought his country's independence from Ottoman rule through the establishment of a domestic textile industry modelled on Britain's success. Forced peasant labour to supply raw cotton was part of this programme. Ali's military defeat (the Oriental Crisis of 1840) at the hands of the Ottoman Army with British, French and Austrian support spelled the end of his industrial catch-up attempt, and Egyptian cotton was re-channelled into raw-material export.

Africa did its part to sustain British industrial society by supplying palm oil and peanuts, which were grown on large plantations operating under conditions resembling slavery. Suddenly, the British grew reluctant to lose this valuable resource – African workers – to the American slave plantations,[132] and thus enacted the 1807 ban on the slave trade in accordance with the demands of the bourgeois abolitionist movement. Formal abolition of slavery in the British colonies would have to wait until 1833. The slaves of French colonies in the Caribbean had already taken the French Revolution at its word and ended slavery there in 1794. What caught them off guard was the normalization of French power that occurred under Napoleon, which reversed the situation in 1802. Only Sainte Domingue (present-day Haiti) declared itself independent and thus escaped the restoration of slavery.[133] While slavery was officially abolished at the Congress of Vienna in 1815, 3.3 million slaves were still sold to the Americas in the nineteenth century nonetheless. Slavery held out in the French colonies until 1848 and in the southern United States until 1863, in Spanish colonies until 1880 and in Brazil until 1888.[134] The American Civil War and subsequent abolition of slavery put the raw-cotton supply in danger. Frantic efforts began to spread cotton plantations around the southern hemisphere. Brazil, Egypt, India and Africa were pushed ever further into monocultural agriculture, and more farmers became suppliers of cash crops.[135]

Parallel to the abolition of slavery arose a pushback against the state's power over Western and Central European peasants. The privileges of feudal fiefdom that restricted subjects' freedom of movement were now a hindrance to state authorities and the companies that relied on labour mobility – the same reason Western European subjugation had begun transforming into land tenancy, agricultural wage labour and the migration of rural peasants into the industrial factories from the fifteenth century onwards. This emancipation stopped, however, before it reached the indigenous inhabitants of the colonies. In Central Europe, the seigneurial system reliant on rents from independent peasant subjects continued, while the export-oriented manorial system of Eastern Europe led to a delayed enforcement of serfdom and mobility restrictions.[136] Russia only began to subjugate its serfs in the seventeenth century, making it the law of the land in 1723 – a mark of Peter the Great's modernization efforts.[137]

The French Revolution's version of peasant liberation was also short-lived, but managed, through Napoleon's advances, to inspire developments in the occupied territories of Europe. In the states of the Holy Roman Empire, the strengthening of peasant rights vis-à-vis seigneurial lords went hand in hand with modern state building in the second half of the eighteenth century – driven forward by the ruling authorities to allow direct state access to the peasantry, rather than mediated access through the landlords. For peasant subjects, this meant, on the one hand, emancipation from the noble landowner, permitting them to marry as they pleased (i.e. without the landlord's consent), own property, work for wages and enjoy freedom of movement. On the other hand, however, all areas of peasant life increasingly came under state supervision. Emancipation of the peasantry was carried out in several steps: first, the institution of serfdom was abolished, feudal work services and levies were limited, and subjects' civil rights were extended, while hereditary servitude and tributary obligations remained in effect.[138] Major regional differences can be observed in terms of when exactly changes began, how the particulars played out, and how the process concluded – even within Central Europe. Factors shaping this process included the existing agrarian system, the speed of state reform, estate owners' resistance, and finally a given region's location and position in the face of Napoleon's advance. Two pioneers of peasant emancipation under French influence were the Rhenish Confederation and Prussia, which abolished hereditary servitude in the Stein–Hardenberg Reforms after their defeat by Napoleon in 1807. Other German states would only take this step much later, until finally personal freedom was established as a civil right throughout the German states and the Habsburg Monarchy in the wake of the 1848 revolution. Serfdom in Russia ended in 1861. A decisive factor in this late abolition was not least the contribution made by forced labour to maintaining low agricultural prices, as cheap grain exports were necessary to fund nineteenth-century state investment in the subsidized metal and arms industries.[139]

On the whole, the abolition of servitude led peasants into new forms of dependency. Emancipation meant that peasants holding feudal tenure became legal owners, but were still obliged to compensate the seigneurial owner. This contributed to peasant indebtedness and wide-scale pauperization, and thus, finally, to a concentration of ownership in the hands of big landowners who were able to modernize their estates with the help of reparations payments. Moreover, abolishing the overlapping ownership of supreme property (nobles) and usage rights (peasants) robbed peasants and the rural poor of access to the commons, and thus forced them into agricultural labour. Rather than peasants working the land, they were now merely an agrarian labour force for even larger estates. On top of that, they were also freed up to enter the non-agrarian labour market. Former slaves in the United States were also confronted with the prospect of freedom gained in abolition without a parcel of land to call their own: they were limited to plantation wage labour, sharecropping and the rural exodus that drew black workers to the industrialized North.

Local conditions and labour relations

The first mechanical cotton mills of continental Europe were founded around 1800. From an architectural point of view, these were completely new production facilities: multistorey buildings with machines driven by waterwheels and central transmission systems. These required rivers and streams with strong currents, canals, dams and water regulation systems. Rural areas were thus predestined to become factory sites. These massive buildings with their towering chimneys were often called the 'cathedrals' of the new epoch.

For the workers inside, however, these structures could better be described as a prison. Local populations were too small to provide the necessary workforce, prompting the importation of workers from the surrounding areas and even further. Poor families, orphanages, parish priests and even seigneurial lords were pressured to send the children and youth under their authority to work in the factories. Most of the factory workers were young, single and inexperienced; dormitories were built in which men, women and children were separately housed. Initially, no regulations were in place concerning the length of the working day, and sixteen-hour shifts were common. Within a few years, workers' bodies would be exhausted from the long working days, pressure of the machines, the din, the dust, the monotony, and the employers' surveillance regime which followed them into their dormitories. They were quickly replaced.

Cotton yarn was the motor of the Industrial Revolution. By 1830, thirty mechanical cotton mills and ten printing factories had emerged south of Vienna in what has since become known as the Lower Austrian industrial district, which altogether employed 10,000 women, men and children. At this early stage only professionals, technicians and administrative staff could entertain the prospect of starting a family, while unskilled workers could only marry after leaving the factory floor. This changed in the 1850s, when housing estates began to be built for working-class families. Whole families could now live together near the factory, ensuring replenishment of the workforce through on-site reproduction. The rise of steam power finally allowed factories to be built away from rivers and other sources of water power.

Factory work in Central Europe was limited to certain regions and thus affected only a small segment of the working class. The majority of people continued to live and work in agriculture, crafts and the putting-out system, and thus retained their familial work and life economies.

Mechanization put an abrupt end to supplementary income through hand spinning. Early industrial statistics show an expansion of 'industrial labour' in Lower Austria from 19,733 workers in 1762 to 182,473 by 1790.[140] The increase was primarily due to spinner work, as eight to twelve workers were needed to supply one hand weaver. The number of spinners rose from 14,560 in 1762 to 119,906 by 1790, the majority of whom were women and girls. While the number of men counted in the statistics rose between 1790 and 1811 (from 35,825 to 43,054), the number of female spinners sank from 119,906 to 14,693. Spinning machines had definitively replaced spinners. As the machines were introduced into the mechanized spinning factories of southern Lower Austria, thousands of women and girls involved in the putting-out system lost their opportunity to earn extra income.

Depending upon the importance of spinning in a given household, various strategies were marshalled in response. When markets were close by, peasant households increased agricultural production, whether subsistence farming or to produce more for the growing urban markets. They specialized in agricultural production, and many gave up other commercial pursuits – a transformation called agriculturalization. Peasants intensified winemaking in the wine districts of north-eastern Lower Austria, while elsewhere grain production or dairies proliferated. Those who could not count on inheriting the family farm left for the growing cities and industrial areas to try their luck. This changed both their work and their lifestyle: farmers became workers with no way of securing their own sustenance and were drawn to paid factory work. Whether or not they started a family no longer mattered in terms of foodstuff production, as time and space for such activities were limited by the long working hours and cramped living conditions. Nor can we forget that women spent long hours shopping, cooking, cleaning and caring for children in these small working-class households – often in addition to wage labour.

Other migrant workers in the nineteenth century found jobs as commercial assistants, in construction, or in specialized agricultural regions. These positions were often temporary and workers frequently had to find new jobs, making founding a stable household largely impossible. Another option was for workers to become servants in a bourgeois or noble household, a growing sector in the era of industrialization and urbanization. In a way, servants were considered part of the 'family'. This could entail some integration at the lower rungs of the social hierarchy, in that the 'master's' family became a surrogate family to the servant – or it could mean a marginalized, oppressed existence at the edges of the aristocratic or bourgeois household. The bourgeois ideology surrounding the family envisioned women as wives and mothers, counterparts to the male heads of the family, and usually rested on the shoulders of the servants who carried out the difficult domestic labour. Petty bourgeois households, on the other hand, relied on wives alone, although they usually did not participate in wage labour. Proletarian households also oriented themselves towards the ideal that paid work and family were separate worlds, in turn placing enormous burdens on wage-labouring wives.

In the first half of the nineteenth century, home weaving offered an alternative path. Weaving lagged behind spinning in the mechanization of production, and weaving orders were still largely passed onto home weavers by putting-out agents on behalf of merchant capitalists. These textile entrepreneurs did not own their own factories, but instead bought yarn from the spinning mills and put weaving out to rural households, where weavers then enlisted their whole families in the work. The Waldviertel textile region in north-western Lower Austria serves as a perfect example: once a putting-out region for spinning and weaving for the manufactories, it would develop into the main stronghold of home weaving over the first half of the nineteenth century.[141] Comparable home weaving regions were found in the Swabian Jura.[142] While peasant families increasingly turned to agriculture and textile production for their own use, the landless lower social strata clung to home weaving. After the decline of the putting-out manufactories, these weavers looked towards Vienna to take on contract work, or worked independently for textile entrepreneurs. Their yarn was spun by machine in the industrial districts of Lower Austria. Family members supported the weavers in textile production, either with preparatory work or as hands-on assistants, or worked their small subsistence farms.

The humble potato would assume a central role in both the organization of work and workers' diets, rising in popularity as the favourite food of small-scale weaver families. Previously, the tuber had been viewed with disdain by the peasant population. Although potato cultivation is quite labour-intensive, its yields are also high, making it excellently suited to the small parcels of land farmed by homeworkers who could not charge their employers for the hours spent growing it for sustenance. This independent food supply enabled them to live on very low wages – a circumstance which helped them to continue on into the second half of the nineteenth century as supplemental labour, as weaving became mechanized but factories still failed to keep up with fluctuations in demand. A similar development occurred in lace production, becoming an important source of income for households in Vorarlberg in eastern Switzerland and Vogtland in southern Saxony. All members of a given family participated in the spirit of supplementing each other's efforts, but this extra familial help was no longer reflected in commercial statistics as it had been with spinners in the putting-out system. They became invisible appendages of their gainfully employed family members, whose contribution to the product, household income and regional output figures went unaccounted for.

With growing commodification and downward wage pressures caused by factory prices, localized income pooling by rural households soon grew insufficient to provide enough money to live on. Some family members had to leave or were sent away to work outside the home; for many, the lack of suitable employment in their home region meant migration. Family members were chosen for migration based on their age, marital status, how useful they were within the family economy, and the demands of external labour markets. Most labour migration was temporary, based on income supplementation and a later return to the family household.[143] The reaction to the break-up of local supply circuits in the rural regions of Central Europe bore many similarities to that in Asian putting-out regions. If they failed to fulfil a new function within the interregional commodity chain in order to survive, migration was inevitable.

Interregional connections

The geography of intra-European migration in the early modern period exhibits three types of space: first, urban centres, or mining or agricultural export regions, which required mostly seasonal or temporary workers; second, regions unsuitable for agrarian production, whose inhabitants could not supply themselves with enough to eat and were thus mobilized as migrant labour into the core regions. The third type was the largest in terms of surface area, where artisans, temporary workers and servants migrated between clusters of clients, but where the 'push of duty and the pull of desire' proved less influential than interregional seasonal migration.[144]

Several migration systems stand out among the regional networks, exhibiting particularly high workforce movement around 1800.[145] Cities were not the only places in need of migrant labour, as the agricultural regions that supplied the cities with foodstuffs also relied on these movements. In the Paris basin, for instance, some 60,000 workers participated in the annual grain harvest. Madrid and the plateaux of Castile attracted at least 30,000 migrant workers from the mountainous north, Galicia and the Basque country. Similarly, 100,000 seasonal labourers came year after year to central Italy for the wheat harvest. Eastern England and London attracted workers as well, particularly from Ireland. Other urban zones, each requiring over 30,000 seasonal workers annually, included the Po valley and the Dutch–German North Sea region – dense urban landscapes surrounded by agricultural market production. Seasonal workers came down from the Alps and the Apennine mountains into the Po valley to harvest rice for export. Livestock, dairy and horticulture were the primary importers of migrant labour along the North Sea coast. Dikes and drainage systems had to be built and maintained in order to grow any sort of foodstuffs in this region, requiring even more workers from the German hinterlands.

Alongside these larger movements were migration cycles with only small groups of participants. In mountainous regions, seasonal migration was simply part of the annual work cycle: a number of household members accompanied their cattle up to the Alpine pastures and produced dairy products there. An alternative to stationary Alpine farming was transhumance, the practice of moving sheep or goats to graze on various pastures, which primarily served wool and meat production. Those living in regions unfavourable to agricultural production often sent their workforce to nearby valleys with higher yields, where they would work as servants for several years, or as day labourers during seasonal peaks. Southern Germany, for example, attracted migrant workers from the southern Alpine regions (Tyrol, Vorarlberg). The legendary Swabian children, who regularly came to help southern German farmer households in the summer months, were one such group.

Wage and price gaps were the prerequisite for the emergence of migration between regions in need of work and regions with surplus populations to send off to work. The opportunity to work in a distant region depended heavily on existing relations of servitude, and largely excluded serfs and other indentured workers; sometimes, transfers of serfs were organized between manorial estates in place of free migration. The nobility's supreme property rights continued to apply throughout the Holy Roman Empire and the states formed after its dissolution in 1806, for which the peasantry had to pay feudal rent or duties. However, the abolition of bondage and freedom of movement in the eighteenth century would push noble disposition over their subjects back far enough to enable labour migration in Central Europe. Relations between work in the family household and supplemental income from migratory work was contingent not only upon the different agrarian systems – the size of a given estate and local inheritance customs were also determining factors. Regions with small farms where partible inheritance was common played a larger role in supplemental income migration than those with closed inheritance systems.

Industrialization and urbanization shook up established migration systems between economic cores and surrounding areas, which were generally of a smaller scale. On the one hand, demand rose in some central areas, thus mobilizing immigration from further afar than was previously the case. On the other, new relations of competition in industry, the service sector and agriculture affected hitherto independent households, which now required additional income to survive. The new type of rural household that resulted was forced to incorporate emigration or supplemental migration by certain family members into their survival strategies.

This was particularly true for the small peasants and cottagers discussed in the last chapter, whose existence had been secured through eighteenth-century putting-out work. It also affected small rural economies which could no longer compete with regions practising intensive agrarian strategies.

The liberalization of family and household formation associated with the putting-out system had increased the number of rural lower classes, which relied primarily on non-agricultural livelihoods. If one's putting-out work disappeared, one had to follow income to other regions in need of industrial labour, seasonal agricultural labour, transport and construction workers, or household servants. Women day labourers and servants could also turn to prostitution as a means of extra income. Love for sale was rarely a woman's main source of income, however, but rather a form of (more or less voluntary) side-employment,[146] potentially unknown to the other members of the household.

Owning a house, even if small with little farmland, constituted a good reason to make it the basis for familial mobility and indeed the focal point of one's life. The household functioned not only as a supply node, but also as a place of identification that gave meaning to the long stays in foreign lands and provided migrant family members with a point of orientation. Such a household was imbued with interregional significance, combining family members who stayed in the home and other migrating workers who took up and passed on the baton at different points in their life cycles. While one member sent back remittances, others provided a reproductive safety net that prepared some family members for work abroad while offering others care in case of illness or job loss. The reciprocal relations of the extended household often survived well into the nineteenth century, as subsistence migration transformed into permanent emigration.[147]

Those without houses or who felt unwelcome in their household often found it easier to leave – and leave they did, with greater expectations, as long-term emigrants. These migrants were not in search of supplemental income but escaping households with simply too many mouths to feed, and were thus literally forced into emigration. Ties to households of origin frayed significantly.

It is difficult to reconstruct who exactly had the greatest decision-making power among family and village communities regarding who was to emigrate, or how much pressure, coercion, fear, volition or enthusiasm to escape one's domestic confines played a role. These emigrants joined the growing populations of urban centres at the end of the eighteenth century, a trend which continues to this day. We should not forget that for every worker who managed to become a permanent city dweller, a much greater number of migrants only remained temporarily, moved on voluntarily or were deported or threatened with deportation due to the old residency laws.[148]

Those who could neither find work nor return home joined the jobless and sustenanceless, whose ranks exploded due to early nineteenth-century armed conflict, and whose only way to get by consisted of odd jobs, street performances or begging. Regardless of their reasons for emigration, every person under the Habsburg Monarchy who moved from one administrative district to another or abroad required a passport. For most states, passport obligations for internal movement were only lifted over the course of the nineteenth century. The state authorities issuing (or refusing) passports often faced a difficult decision: although they had to ensure personal mobility in the context of labour demand, this hindered their ability to restrict the movements of people who could become dependent on public relief. Not obtaining a passport, however, was no reason not to try one's luck elsewhere. As authorities lacked the means to enforce travel and residency laws, huge numbers of people migrated 'illegally'. History has only recorded those arrested and sent back to their communities of origin as 'beggars', 'vagabonds' or 'passport-, destination- or subsistenceless'. Women were often deported for 'prostitution', 'fornication' and 'licentiousness'.[149]

A study of interregional connections in terms of the movements of commodities and people must necessarily take transport into account. By 1800, Great Britain boasted a close-knit network of canals for moving goods. Efforts to integrate the European continent through canal systems, however, were often left unfinished. In 1797, a canal was to be built between Vienna and the port city of Trieste, one of the main transport routes in the Habsburg Monarchy, but would ultimately only extend sixty kilometres south from the capital to the nearby coal mines around Wiener Neustadt. Similarly, the proposed Ludwig–Donau–Main Canal, or the Ludwig Canal, was abandoned after only about sixty kilometres in 1846. This left the continent's great rivers – the Rhine, Main, Danube, Elbe and Oder – as the most effective axes for long-distance traffic, flanked by a network of roads and trails for carriages and pedestrians. The railway era would only arrive in 1830 with the connection between Liverpool and Manchester. The first steam railway in the German states chugged to life in 1834 from Nuremberg to Fürth, followed in 1838 by the track from Vienna to Lundenburg/Břeclav. Transportation thus remained confined to a pre-industrial pace. The exchange of rural servants limited itself to a range of fifty kilometres, distances easily traversed on foot. Agricultural wage labourers or construction workers travelling to the growing cities similarly limited themselves to manageable distances. Travelling artisans in special trades with access to strong interregional professional networks were one of few groups who regularly travelled further, along with soldiers, both active and demobilized, and deserters.

Nevertheless, the extent of specialization and division of labour between regions continued with industrialization and the growth of the cities, particularly after the Napoleonic Wars, which had posed major obstacles to the continental system of international exchange. This also led to growth in the overall volume of interregional commodity exchange – in small-scale town–country exchange between agrarian regions, industrial regions and urban consumer cores, as well as on a larger scale between areas of raw-material procurement, processing regions and export markets. These developments were facilitated by the abolition of internal tariffs and the establishment of import and export duties at state borders. Protectionist tariffs and absolute trade bans on certain goods were implemented throughout Europe in the eighteenth century. As a whole, these constituted a major part of state efforts aimed at economic integration, and led to the compression of the flow of goods within state borders. Developments in the Western European maritime powers, whose merchants and ships were active in overseas trading and possessed colonial bases and territories, differed from those in the Central European states where overseas trade relations were quite weak (with the exceptions of Hamburg, Bremen and Trieste). Poland had disappeared from the map as an independent state, divided among Prussia, Russia and Habsburg Austria (1772–95). Russia now encompassed the Baltic coast and Finland, and fought the Ottoman Empire in numerous wars over access to the Black Sea coast. The German states generally oriented towards Russia in their foreign relations, while the Habsburg Monarchy looked towards the south-eastern Danube and Black Sea regions. Trieste and Venice provided the Habsburgs access to the sea, although intercontinental trade over the Mediterranean was a very weak substitute for the Atlantic indeed.

The moves towards integration being taken in the German Confederation, which succeeded the Holy Roman Empire after 1815, came into conflict with Habsburg ambitions towards territorial integration of the countries decreed part of the Austro-Hungarian Empire in 1804, which included Hungary, Galicia, Lombardy, Venetia and Dalmatia and thus extended beyond the German Confederation. Again, we find a regionalization of trade and migration networks, following the lines of the Confederation's and the Empire's respective integration projects, although these areas overlapped to some extent until the Battle of Königgrätz/Hradec Kralove, where Prussian forces defeated the Habsburgs (1866). As a consequence, commodity and migration flows were channelled within the political boundaries of both entities.

The Archduchy of Upper and Lower Austria, with Vienna as its imperial capital and resident city, exerted a strong pull on both temporary and permanent migrants. These came mostly from the Austrian Alpine and Bohemian lands following the establishment of the empire, whereas migration from southern German regions subsequently dwindled.[150] Alpine and Bohemian migration into the German states declined in return, with the exception of the border regions. This reorientation of migration routes and networks also altered the character of migration. Traditional artisan migration – generally structured around training, communication and knowledge transfer for particular occupational groups – continued in the first half of the nineteenth century, but became less significant than the subsistence migration practised by the impoverished underclass driven by job loss and the reduced competitiveness of regional products. The mechanization of spinning drove them from the rural putting-out regions of Bohemia and Austria, where they had lost their main or extra sources of income, or they came from Alpine regions unable to sustain so many inhabitants. These migrations centred around migrant workers seeking supplemental income to secure the family household, as well as their own return journey.

Small-scale supplemental migration failed to play a comparable role in Hungary and Galicia around 1800. The manorial system stayed intact much longer there, and proved simply incompatible with the small-scale migration systems of Western and Central Europe. Subjects were bound to the soil as serfs. Some migrated nonetheless by escaping to neighbouring regions in the east or as an organized transfer to another estate, but this also severed the connection between the old and the new home. Unconnected to the serfs, the settlement system developed in Transylvania and the Banat since the victories against the Ottomans (1699) had spread to Galicia and Bukovina by the end of the eighteenth century. It brought with it rural settlers to whom land was made available, as well as craftsmen from German, Austrian and Bohemian lands to colonize the expansion areas. Between 13,000 and 18,000 colonists settled in the first years after these areas were absorbed by the Habsburg Empire in Galicia and Bukovina alone (1772–75). Similar to the escaped serfs, however, connections to the settlers' old homes were largely broken in the process. Legal settlement incentives were created for Jews in Bukovina, setting in motion a wave of emigration out of the Habsburg Monarchy and Russia.[151] Supplementing one's income with subsistence migration arose in Hungary and Galicia only after the abolition of bondage in 1848. The freedom to choose one's place of residency was enshrined in the 1867 constitution, enabling the mobilization of huge numbers of family members unable to make a living in the household alone. Small-scale migration systems formed in Hungary, particularly within the lands belonging to the Hungarian Crown. Migrants from Galicia mostly worked as seasonal labourers on farms east of the Elbe river from the 1880s on. Polish workers from eastern German regions, rather, went to work in the industrial areas of the Ruhr and the Rhine.[152]

Large-scale connections

The form of global economic integration emerging around 1800 increasingly ordered regions which had hitherto operated rather independently into a macro-systemic context shaped by trade, migration and commodity chains. In turn, the spectrum of labour relations affected and connected by these transactions grew enormously. The introduction of free wage labour in factories pressured guild and craft producers to adapt. The goods of the United Kingdom's highly developed factory system, the first of its kind, put pressure on other export regions to imitate the islanders' methods. This led to industrialization along the lines of the English factory industry in Western and Central Europe, while Asian commercial cores continued to reject factory mechanization and centralization. The Asian cores instead maintained the manufactory and putting-out system for domestic markets, integrating European factory-spun yarn as a semi-finished import. However, they lost their erstwhile position as top producers for the global market to the Europeans.[153] Direct colonial rule was not always necessary to eliminate Asian commercial competition and transform Asian regions into suppliers and markets for Western exports, as the same goal could sometimes be achieved under conditions of formal independence. It was only in the second half of the eighteenth century that growing competition between the European industrial nations triggered the shift from informal to formal colonial rule.

Asian and African exports now largely comprised agricultural products and raw materials sent to Western and Central European industry for processing. Low-paid farm work became more and more important on the cash-crop plantations, but getting erstwhile peasants to make the transition from primarily subsistence economies with livelihoods of the kinds typical of such systems to a wage labour system for agricultural mass production was no easy task. Additional leverage was often necessary, an essential tool of which was tax jurisdiction, which allowed the East India Company, for instance, to tax crops in Bengal, thereby influencing planting and the ways that Indian subjects went about their work.[154] The Permanent Settlement Act of 1793 established these new tax rates in Bengal, but also prompted numerous uprisings.[155] In Africa, the population was also coerced into selling their labour to plantations through poll taxes and other similar means.

The German states and the Habsburg Monarchy were not involved in the peripheralization of the South Asian kingdoms, as no significant exchange existed between them and the little trade that did occur was conducted through intermediary merchants. Exchange with the Ottoman Empire, however, had become a mainstay of Austrian merchants by the eighteenth century. Their demand for raw materials exerted a decisive influence on economic structures, price pressures and the modes of production in agricultural export. The existing prebendary economy, in which the nobility lived off tax farming and influenced rural economic life only minimally, now went through a process of commercialization as production began to orient towards global markets. Foreign trade remained in the hands of non-Muslim minorities (Greeks, Armenians, Jews) as a result of the *millet* system, but the delicate ethno-religious balance it struck was gradually undermined as Christian merchants increasingly placed themselves under the protection of European states.[156]

The Habsburgs' efforts to catch up to Great Britain in terms of modernization were not only based on an advantageous position in foreign trade, but also involved the empire's emergence as a colonizing power vis-à-vis neighbouring territories in Eastern and South-Eastern Europe: carving Bukovina out of western Moldavia in 1775, an Ottoman province at the time, and dividing Poland with the Habsburgs, the Russian Empire and the Prussian Kingdom between 1775 and 1795. This expansion not only secured the three continental superpowers' spheres of influence in strategic terms, but also turned these territories into internal peripheries to compensate for a lack of external colonies and presence on the global market. Annexation thus introduced the agricultural export economy based on the prebendary economy (Bukovina) and serfdom (Galicia) into the Habsburg Monarchy as a variation of already existing systems of bondage. Although the core regions of the empire all abolished bondage in the 1780s, new forms of servitude and forced market-oriented labour arose in the zones of colonial expansion. Forced labour was simultaneously suppressed and expanded by the same state structure, ensuring unequal exchange between the industrial production of the western and the agricultural production of the eastern Crown lands.

A similar interaction between elements of abolition and the bolstering of forced labour can be observed in plantation slavery. Slavery would only emerge on African plantations after Great Britain banned the slave trade (1807) and slave labour (1833), while trade with the United States continued to boom despite the ban.[157] The US produced the cash crops necessary to both fuel Western European industry and feed its workers: sugar, coffee, cocoa, cotton and tobacco. Growing demand for cotton meant growing demand for territory, and the American slavery system expanded westward, displacing the indigenous populations in its path. As supplies of new slaves from Africa were no longer readily available, slave labourers were encouraged to start families and permitted private gardens, in this way securing local reproduction of the slave labour force.[158] Removing the seeds from the cotton plant was a tiresome and time-consuming job, soon revolutionized by the invention of the cotton gin (1793), which also enabled producers to use the short-fibre variety of cotton grown in the interior. The cotton gin brought rationalization to the plantation, but excluded the introduction of free wage labour that accompanied such developments in other regions. Unfree labourers made redundant by the cotton gin were simply put to work in the new cotton fields that rapidly expanded to the west in the first half of the nineteenth century.

The rapid upswing of the cotton textile industry in Britain, France and Catalonia, as well as in the northern New England states, would have been impossible without cotton from Brazil, the Caribbean and the southern US. Forced labour on the plantations and free wage labour in the factories functioned in vital symbiosis to drive the rise of the industrial system in the nineteenth century. Central European textile factories met their cotton needs with imports mainly from the Ottoman Empire, and were involved in overseas colonies and trade to a much lesser degree. In terms of the nineteenth-century transatlantic slave trade which continued despite the ban, Central European merchants were not involved at all. However, this did not prevent colonial goods based on slave labour from playing a role in the workshops and domestic consumption of Central Europe. As a cog in the grand industrial machine, they also drew from these commodities, with or without their own territories, transport routes or methods of procurement. They could thus be described as part of the semi-periphery, which still participated in the global economy, albeit in the shadow – and waterways – of the Western colonial industrial powers. With regard to their territorial gains from eastern and south-eastern expansion and the decimated Ottoman Empire, Central Europe was made up of imperial core regions that created their own peripheries in order to develop peripheral procurement and export markets for industrialization in the core.

For workers looking towards long-distance migration, Central Europe offered two options: settlement of the Danube and Black Sea region, which most migrants chose, or emigration abroad, particularly to the United States.

As with short-distance migration, emigration was mostly under-taken by small-scale farmers and lower sub-peasant classes, who largely enjoyed freedom of movement – by no means a given at the time, when the rural population was still bound by strict servitude and emigration was never really an option. Therefore the south-western German regions (Rhineland, Pfalz, Swabia, Baden, Württemberg) emerged as areas from which people were sent off to find their fortune in Central Europe. This was due to the regions' inheritance laws and customs, as discussed above. The northern German regions sent workers to Holland for supplemental income, and were thus less affected by emigration.

As many of those willing to emigrate lacked the financial means to do so, they often resorted to agents who advanced them the money needed for their journey.[159] A contract would be signed in return for credit to be worked off within a specified amount of time. These contract workers, called indentured servants, would mostly go off to work on farmlands in the United States. American commerce and industry adopted indenture contracts defining terms of work between master and apprentice in place of the old guild ways, which offered apprentices the prospect of starting their own farming or commercial operation later on. European systems of servitude were thus transplanted into the New World, ironically affecting groups who had enjoyed the greatest freedom of movement in the Old World. Now most of these immigrants became the semi-free servants of agricultural entrepreneurs, bound by contract to their job. To finance German immigrants' voyages, indentured servitude was replaced in the eighteenth century by the 'redemptioner' system, which offered a degree more freedom in their choice of work. Many dreamed of working themselves up to self-employment, but realizing this dream often meant participating in the westward expansion, which drove indigenous populations even further from their land. Another prospect for servants and maids, as well as children from peasant families, was to take up wage labour in the textile factories of New England, which had sprouted in the early nineteenth century backed by massive state aid.

Compared to the colonization of Eastern and South-Eastern Europe, eighteenth-century German emigration remained relatively mild. About 130,000 people, or one-sixth of all emigrants, landed in North America (compared with 350,000 in Hungary, 300,000 in Prussia, 50,000 in the Polish areas),[160] two-thirds of whom arrived via Philadelphia, Pennsylvania. German-speaking emigrants also left for the southern Russian territories along the Dniester and Don rivers.

The term 'indentured labour' was used exclusively for white European contract workers. Workers contracted from India, China, South East Asia and Oceania after the British slavery ban were called 'coolies'. Coolies constituted the replacement workforces on plantations in American and other colonies where the labour force could no longer be replenished from Africa. Around 30 million people from India and five to six million from other Asian areas came to the West as coolies between 1830 and 1930. The word's origin, however, is unclear: it could come from the Chinese word for 'bitter labour', the Urdu word for 'slave', Tamil for 'rent', or the name of an Indian tribe whose members are considered thieves, robbers and looters.[161]

The differing designations for the same labour relations, strictly speaking, reflect the racist lens through which 'white', 'yellow' and 'brown' workforces were viewed. While Asian migrants were seen as forced labourers, most clung to the illusion that European migrants, by contrast, were free. In fact, coercion was the defining feature of both groups' departure for the New Worlds of the Caribbean, Oceania, the Pacific and the Indian Ocean, brought on by economic hardship, the cost of financing the voyage, job placement and contract-bound labour relations. Nonetheless, unlike for slaves, forced deportation did not play a role in the lives of indentured servants and coolies. They entered into these contracts of their own volition, even if the labour relations they faced in light of their decision would turn out to resemble slavery.

1900

Characteristics

By 1900, the incorporation of external arenas into the capitalist world-system was complete: a worldwide network of capital, commodity and communication flows had emerged under British hegemony, constituting something like a first high point of globalization. The fact that everything was connected to everything else (in more or less direct ways) had implications for labour relations, as well. The notion that relations began to converge across world regions (as some historians claim) is not true – it is true, however, that events in one location had consequences for and connections to the rest of the world-system. As time went on, Britain's leading role in the global economy faced new challengers, as Germany and the United States took the lead in key sectors and production processes, namely the chemical, electrical and machine industries. Although the great powers of Europe shared a common interest in maintaining the imperial – or rather imperialist – order of the day, this joint cause was undermined by their ongoing competition for market share in a world economy increasingly dominated by monopolies. Informal domination of the global market may have been more elegant and less of a burden on state coffers, but the fight for market share soon set in motion the race to establish colonies in far-flung regions nonetheless, which were then turned into sales, procurement and investment markets for the colonizers. Thus came about the carving up of Africa between the European colonial powers, shortly after India was named a Crown Colony in 1857. In the case of the old Asian empires, the great powers pursued a different strategy: they assisted local Ottoman and Persian forces whenever enemies attacked in order to prevent imperial competitors from making territorial gains, but used this position to obtain huge swathes of territory in the form of protectorates and exercise strategic influence over aided countries' economy and infrastructure. A joint European effort forced China to accept Western influence over the country's export sector in 1900.

The only non-European state to successfully manage catch-up industrialization as occurred in Central Europe and the United States was Japan. This was due to the government's industrial policies established in the eighteenth century and the first half of nineteenth, which could no longer be reversed after the United States forced Japan by gunboat diplomacy to open their markets and sign the Japan–US Treaty of Peace and Amity in 1854. Military defeat led to regime change – the Meiji Restoration – ushering in a phase of industrialization along Western lines. Japan has belonged to the circle of industrial countries ever since.

The global South functioned as a supplier of raw materials in this international division of labour. Plantation slavery was replaced by free and semi-free labour. Workers either were driven into wage labour by the silent compulsion of economic relations or, when there was no necessity to hire out their labour such as in colonial Africa, were forced into wage labour through all kind of dubious means, like conscription or poll taxes known as hut taxes. Moreover, classical forms of slavery and slavery-like conditions continue to exist.[162]

Former industrial–commercial cores in Asia's commercial regions were forced to sacrifice their export industries and thereby relegated to producing primary commodities. India's and China's share of global industrial production showed them to be the world leaders in 1750 with 32.8 and 24.5 per cent respectively, but had fallen to 6.2 and 1.7 per cent around 1900.[163] In the colonies as well as the states that managed to stay politically independent, however, there existed modern enclaves employing wage labourers in the mines, on the burgeoning oilfields, in the factories and above all in the transport and port facilities necessary for shipping the products extracted from the countries' interiors to the harbour cities, and from there to the industrial countries.

The insignificance of domestic industrial manufacturing was due to the fact that colonial administrators and the indigenous upper classes who copied the colonial lifestyle mostly consumed imported goods. Locals, however, consumed locally and supplied themselves through subsistence production. Households satisfied their monetary needs by supplying labour for the export-oriented, mining, plantation, agricultural, industrial and infrastructural sectors. This labour force was composed of migrant labourers who moved between ancestral settlements, reduced to a supportive role for the poles of growth and zones now specialized for export production. The severe working conditions they encountered here often exhausted workers within several years, prompting them to return to their places of origin in the hinterlands when distances and transport conditions allowed. If return was not possible, they could always join the informal workforce, a belt of reserve labour surrounding the poles of growth. The pattern of circular labour rotation between poles of growth, informal sectors and hinterlands was something that repeated itself locally, at mid-range and at more remote locations. Steamships had made transcontinental migration so much faster by 1900 that family reunification, return and renewed labour migration were now possible in this context as well.

Exchange between industrial and developing countries mirrored the core–periphery relations characteristic of classical imperialism between 1870 and 1930: capital flowed from north to south as investments in the extractive sectors and infrastructure, accompanied by technical know-how, experts, administrators and Western imaginaries of work and labour, consumption and a comfortable life. In exchange, primary commodities flowed northward to be processed in the industries of the North. Market power and low wage costs meant that every transaction represented a value transfer based on unequal terms of trade and unpaid work hidden in every product. On top of that were the profits transferred by investment capital, interest flowing to the banks, and the patents that went to the research and development departments of companies based in the industrial countries.

As soon as industrial factory production became the standard for productivity and paid employment the standard for work, a conception of development emerged which depicted the industrial countries as the naturally 'developed countries', distinguished by the rise of heavy industry and service sectors, the industrialization of agriculture, and the generalization of paid extra-domestic employment as the basis for survival. Regions that could not compete due to the liberalization of their internal markets and international free trade underwent peripheralization. Small-scale agriculture and business were now subject to interregional competition, which often led to greater polarization between areas of emigration and areas of agglomeration. While migration had initially been a way for people to supplement their household income, it now became a growing and irreversible flow into Europe's industrial areas and cities. By the turn of the century, a fast-growing segment of the European population began migrating across the ocean. This can be attributed, on the one hand, to the fact that European migration networks were already firmly established and hard to access for newcomers from other regions. It also stemmed, however, from growing pressure to emigrate from peripheral rural regions due to the rationalization of agriculture. At the same time, demand was rising in the United States for European workforces to man the emerging industries and populate newly conquered western territories with loyal settlers.

The number of European overseas migrants between 1830 and 1930 is estimated at 60 million, only one-fourth of whom ever returned.[164] Several waves can be distinguished: European overseas migration in the first decade of the nineteenth century reached, on average, about 50,000 people per year. The following waves were 1846–50 (250,000 per year), 1871–5 (370,000 per year), 1880–90 (780,000 per year) and 1906–15 (1.4 million per year). Migrants' origins shifted over time, from the Western and Northern European regions which dominated until the 1880s to the South, South-Eastern, eastern Central and Eastern European regions later on.

With the consolidation of gainful employment as a separate sphere outside the domestic context, social relations required a degree of reordering. The pre-industrial security, sustenance and control mechanisms provided by households, village communities and the feudal system faced growing pressure from the industrial mode of production and liberal economic legislation.

By the middle of the century, the literal physical exhaustion of young people in the darkness of the mines and factories was gradually mitigated through forms of worker mutual aid along the lines of the mutual insurance associations (*Bruderkassen*) set up by journeymen, and paternalistic social activities initiated by the entrepreneurs themselves. The last quarter of the nineteenth century in all industrialized countries was characterized by hectic moves to bandage the wounds of social relations, rubbed raw by unhindered exploitation of the labour force, by creating legal and institutional frameworks to regulate and protect employment. Ideas of how viable social consensus for life in industrial society ought to look were diametrically opposed, and as ill-conceived as they were radical. Elite snobbery and die-hard fiscal frugality faced off against social redistribution policies, revolutionary ideas of common ownership and visions of a utopian society free of domination and exploitation. The urgency of the problems at hand, the ongoing conceptual clashes, and the opposing interests of workers and entrepreneurs as expressed in rallies, strikes, lock-outs, police operations and arrests called for a political response. A plethora of government regulations pertaining to wages, work rules and health and safety soon followed, limiting capital's total hold over the workforce and allowing it to withstand the demands of industrial labour for longer periods of time. Although certain companies and sectors bitterly opposed protective measures for their workers, these measures actually served capital's interests, as it sought qualified workers whose wages would also allow them to become consumers. Under this new framework, working hours were shortened, child labour was banned, women's work was restricted and protective measures and periods of rest were codified in employment regulations. Workers were granted the freedoms of assembly and association and permitted to organize trade unions.

A particularly noteworthy social-policy milestone was the statutory health and accident insurance introduced for industrial workers in Germany, Austria and Hungary in the 1880s (German Reich 1884–5, Austria 1888–9, Hungary 1891–1907). These reforms created the first social safety net independent of family and poor relief, based on a legal entitlement stemming from the labour contract. The system was financed through employee and employer contributions as well as state subsidies. In cases of illness or accident, employees now continued to receive payment. The insured also received access to drugs and medical care, along with their families. Part of the security and care once provided by the family household was thus transferred to professional public institutions. The costs for reproducing this good – the labour force – increased. Other European industrial countries and the US, however, decided not to base their welfare policy on a compulsory insurance system, opting for a combination of private and governmental assistance and voluntary insurance instead. Even the social insurance systems widely introduced during the New Deal or in Great Britain and France after the Second World War failed to measure up to the level of services and security offered by the social-democratic and Christian-social models of Scandinavian countries, Germany and Austria.

Despite regional differences between welfare regimes, work was reconstituted as a new social relation through regulations that came about at the end of the nineteenth century. Some authors interpret this as the 'invention of work'.[165] Others see this change as the 'production of work'[166] or 'career'.[167] This new understanding of work was anchored through legal definitions, defining the basis of labour legislation and negotiations between government agencies, companies and trade unions. An abundance of institutions and commissions appeared to deal with the definition of work and the establishment, implementation and review of standards, policies and labour laws. Statistics contributed to the formation and cementing of categories, as censuses and company counts beginning in the second half of the nineteenth century were thought to offer a systematic overview of the population. The classification of companies according to individual economic areas, sectors, classes and company size took on a central role, as did assigning people to professions, careers and positions in the workplace. Industrial associations conducted their own surveys. Official agencies and scientific communities subjected the data to detailed analyses, which were subsequently published in academic journals. The publications of the German Verein für Socialpolitik and the Austrian monthly *Österreichische Statistische Monatsschrift* exhibited a high level of expertise. Individual branches of industry were measured in large-scale surveys based on visits to companies and conversations with owners as well as employees. Journalistic reports of a socially critical nature written for the workers' papers rounded out public insights into the industrial world of work.

It was also around this time that economics would emerge as an academic discipline,[168] supported by industrial initiatives and associations which financed both practical and theoretical research. While (neoclassical) business economics focused on individual companies and declared the state a troublemaker in the free reign of market forces, (classical) political economics included companies, the state, labour relations and sociopolitical aspects in its analysis of political economy. Despite their extremely different regulatory concepts, both neoclassical and classical economics shared a common view of work – namely that work was only relevant in terms of business or the economy when carried out as paid labour. Only as such would it fit into national accounts and thus create added value, and only as such could it carry a price (expressed in wages). Whether labour's value depends upon supply and demand as neoclassical theory claimed, or on the amount of working time materialized in labour as Marxist theory postulates, remains an open point of contention. What both liberal and socialist positions had in common, on the other hand, was their shared rejection of non-work, which excluded not only those unable to work, but everyone who worked without pay: housewives, subsistence farmers, non-paid helpers and informal workers of all kinds. Moreover, it also meant all workers without access to the latest technology whose productivity thus failed to keep up with the average rate of profit: artisans, craftsmen, small farmers, day labourers, homeworkers, and so on.

The income they received from their (employed or independent) work was often far lower than that of workers in modern industry, and their labour expenditure – or at least any portion of it that failed to compete with the level of productivity – was thus 'worthless'. This contribution was conceived neither as value creation nor as exploitation (surplus going to the entrepreneur or contractor), but was rather seen as a relic from an outdated mode of production in which commodified and reciprocal activities had not yet been differentiated from one another. Consequently, these workers were paid less than what their labour was worth, that is to say, they were underpaid. In contrast to the proletarianized strata, these work characters could be seen as semi-proletarianized. The organized labour movements, representing 'real proletarians', treated day labourers and homeworkers with disdain, as their class position could not be clearly ascertained and they were often deemed the 'lumpen proletariat': class-unconscious outcasts.

The categorization of work was pursued differently in the field of scientific management. Motion, time and load studies like those of Frederick W. Taylor (1856–1915) and others in the US steel industry became the basis for dividing work processes into small steps among differing groups with specific responsibilities, thereby increasing the efficiency of work processes overall. Work in these studies was first and foremost defined according to the body of the individual in order to maximize said body's performance. In later years, it was extended to psychology and occupational hygiene. State institutions welcomed and promoted labour studies to lift burdens and verify standards and laws. Industry and state institutions shared an interest in boosting economic productivity. Trade unions opposed the workplace pressures that came with this segmentation and streamlining, but often agreed to participate in return for efficiency bonuses. Taylorism only came to full fruition with the rise of the assembly line, which saw widespread use in Europe after the First World War.

The process occurring here can be understood as an instrumentalization of work in the interests of capital valorization. The popular understanding of work was divorced from its earlier meanings and various religious guises as a blessing or a curse, as shame or honour, and instead reduced to a cost factor. From the perspective of unfolding and differentiating Western industrial societies, this was expressed in the triumph of paid, legally regulated and socially secured work. Wages, working conditions and social services for a segment of the working class (the regularly employed) were expanded to include education and the protection, preservation or restoration of one's ability to work, as well as purchasing power befitting their status. Still open to negotiation were how much employers were expected to provide and accept, where the state should take on responsibility, when and how much wage labourers were expected to contribute, and, finally, what could be left to the family.

This corresponds to the notion of an inevitable, quasi-automatic connection between proletarianization and social protection through commodified social security financed by the state or insurance contributions. Upon closer inspection, however, it becomes quite clear that regulation and increasing social security coverage only applied to a portion of the labour force. The codification of work as employment was a major factor in imposing a completely new conception of work based on inclusion and exclusion in equal degrees. This shift was also reflected in language, which from then on made much clearer distinctions between commodified, gainful work and other activities. This new categorical definition of work made it possible to distinguish various classes of workers according to the extent to which they fulfilled the ideal of productive, commercially and economically meaningful work. It also enabled a clear distinction between work and non-work, thereby providing an answer to questions of poverty and social responsibility.

By no means were all workers entitled to health and accident insurance. Except for state employees, pension insurance in most industrialized countries was only introduced after the First World War, while compensation for unemployment remained out of reach. Depending on the degree of industrialization, economic structure and level of technical development, some segments of the workforce were included in insurance schemes, while others were excluded. No country in 1900 included servants and farm labourers in obligatory insurance schemes. In Austria, workers in small businesses as well as homeworkers were excluded from accident insurance. In Hungary, such insurance was only introduced in 1907, while the health insurance system established in 1891 excluded day labourers. Thousands of lawsuits were carried out to determine which working conditions and labour relations should include commodified social security and which ones should leave reproduction to the family or poverty relief.[169]

Belonging completely or even partially to the sphere of non-work also meant exclusion from social insurance, making family members without regular employment who lived and performed unpaid work in the household dependent on the insured breadwinner. In cases where no connection to an insured wage labourer existed, poor relief was often the only option. Demographic developments in the cities at the end of the nineteenth century had resulted in a great number of people in need of temporary or permanent social support in their new places of residence. These people were regarded as lacking means of subsistence, and vagrancy laws were enacted to distinguish between those willing to work and those who were not, i.e. those who ought to be imprisoned rather than granted poor relief. The notion of re-education through work was brought to bear in the reformatories, jails and work camps of this period, which ascribed to hard work a certain pedagogical quality. In wider society, the view that unemployment could be overcome through job placement and employment policies became increasingly popular. Those who were employed but failed to live up to price-determining productivity levels were considered to be working at less than their full value. These small-scale commodity producers, traders and day labourers had one foot in the commodified sphere and the other in the reciprocal sphere, and were classified as individuals whose sustenance ought to be fulfilled by the reciprocal sphere. Social responsibility fell on the household's ability to provide sustenance.

To what extent a given society's working population was engaged in regulated and secured wage labour depended on each country's level of development, socio-economic potential and the specific combination of social interests at play. Paid employment as free wage labour was by no means the most common labour relation around 1900 – outside areas of major industrial concentration, that is. The majority still lived in the countryside and in small towns, eking out a makeshift existence with a mixture of independent and dependent, formal and informal, paid and unpaid activity in agriculture, commerce and the service sector – essentially defying any concrete categorization. They provided sustenance to a wide circle of family, household members and the village poor (if they were able to) with various forms of assistance. In the larger cities, there were more small craftsmen and merchants, day labourers and people whose only means were irregular work than people with fixed, socially insured contracts.

Regulation and social insurance encompassed a greater portion of the working population in the German Reich, where heavy industry was most developed, than in the Austro-Hungarian territories where small businesses and cottage industries remained widespread. The 1891 Gesetz betreffend der Invaliditäts- und Altersversicherung, or Act Relating to Invalidity and Old-Age Insurance, played a major role here. In 1900, 18.3 per cent of the German population had health insurance, 33.9 per cent had accident insurance, and 23.8 per cent had invalidity and old-age insurance. In the Austrian half of the Habsburg Monarchy, by contrast, only 9.6 per cent of the population had health insurance; in the Hungarian half of the empire, where precarious day labour remained common in both industry and agriculture, the figure only reached 3.6 per cent.[170] With this came the fact that services were poor and, in practice, hardly functioned. Outside Europe, institutional social insurance played no role whatsoever. Social security was either provided by familial, neighbourly or paternalistic structures, or workers provided their own security by saving money.

Although the reduction of work to gainful employment failed to correspond to the realities of most people, they were nevertheless forced to grapple with the legal definitions and social constructs of work in opposition to non-work, as social identities and social demands could henceforth only find articulation in the codified categories of work. As soon as legal standards were set for what kinds of work would receive what wage, what sorts of protection were entailed or which insurance benefits included, individuals had an ideal type against which to measure their own situation: did their social reality correspond to the standards set for their category of work? To what were they still entitled? Who else were they expected to provide for? From the perspective of non-employed family members, the question was rather to whom must one attach oneself for security and sustenance, both now and in the future?

This proletarian conception of work restricted to gainful employment was then applied to other regions of the world where work was not understood in terms of industrialization and commodification, at least outside small enclaves. Here, most of the population lived and worked within a domestic family context which produced, beyond self-sufficiency, for the market to a greater or lesser degree, or in which individual family members worked in the export-oriented extractive economy. These individuals were paid, but no legal obligations existed for anyone – state, company or worker – to finance social services of any kind. Rather, these wage labourers were forced to rely on their families for support in illness and old age. To the extent that families were overwhelmed by these care obligations, misery and hunger grew among households and villages. Although these populations were incorporated into the world economy as cheap labour, consumption remained the domain of those who benefited from their low-cost labour inputs, namely the entrepreneurs of the industrializing states which processed the incoming raw materials, as well as the proletarians who earned family wages and enjoyed access to commodified social services.

One characteristic of Western hegemony (which, through imperialism, acquired decisive influence throughout the world) was the codification and formalization of work as socially secured gainful employment. Even if this categorization only applied to a minority within Europe itself, it became the standard for progress and model of development par excellence. Colonial administrations adopted their home countries' definition of work, but encountered significant obstacles when applying it to the entirely different labour relations found among their colonial subjects. Peripheral states which retained political independence discussed notions of backwardness and modernization targets in terms set by the alleged Western pioneers.

Work as paid and legally regulated, socially secured gainful employment was a phenomenon of industrializing countries, but established a model that would go on to occupy popular concepts of development and progress more broadly. This process did not occur independently of the global context, however. The Other, often depicted with recourse to colonial analogies, reached into the heart of Europe itself: by projecting the perceived gap between East and West onto the agrarian Eastern European regions, Eastern Europe was often equated with South America, India or Asia, as was also reflected in relations between the urban, industrial cores and the agrarian periphery. The industrial conception of work facilitated the construction of a belief in Western superiority, which legitimized the industrial societies' interventions into the affairs of 'primitive cultures'. These were classified as 'primitive peoples' in need of civilizing, and what they created was not regarded as a product of work or labour, but as a part of nature to be expropriated – a raw material, the processing of which could only be carried out in factory industry. This construct obscured the exploitation and expropriation inherent to colonial rule. Indeed, it is telling that the German word for processing,

Verarbeitung, consists of the nominal form for work, *Arbeit*, with a prefix meaning 'to give form'. Edward Said described the discursive processes of othering that cemented the notion of Western superiority as 'Orientalism', highlighting how the Other is created not only by colonialism but also by denying them their own cultural achievements. The Other is constructed by deficits, by the absence and the lack of what makes the West succeed. In practice, orientalization and peripheralization formed an inseparable unit.

Local conditions and labour relations

According to the bourgeois family ideology of separate domestic and gainful spheres, no 'work' was to be performed within the family. This necessitated a distinction between family and non-family members of the household, the latter having a place in the house but not in the family itself. For them, working was not a flaw but a duty. Breastfeeding, changing nappies, cooking, serving food, hosting, cleaning, walking, playing, teaching – all of these activities were considered 'work', as long as they were performed by servants. When wives or daughters participated, they did so out of love. The ideal-typical bourgeois family consisted of several generations who often lived scattered over several residences. Male members provided the income, while female members directed the servants, maintained family and social contacts, engaged in charitable work, and practised handicraft and fine arts.

The world of work could be found in the company, the branch office, the public institution and the lawyer's or doctor's practice, where different social conventions and hierarchies applied. The self-employed lived their working lives in the context of their professional organizations and interest groups. While workers could only attend club activities and participate in union or political work in their free time, maintaining networks, carrying out political interventions and lobbying belonged to the entrepreneur's occupational profile. Professional employees often found themselves caught between both worlds. The working life of the bourgeois professions also extended into political, social and cultural spheres, where public office, philanthropy, support for the arts and attending social functions were facts of life for a successful businessman, official, scientist or politician. Here, wives, daughters and sons were permitted and indeed expected to appear at his side. Volunteer and charitable activities were thus largely integrated into working life. To the extent that such activities entered the premises of one's own house, the world of work enveloped this sphere as well, serving as a stage upon which the age-old household unit could be re-enacted for a short time.

Limiting housewives to the role of a non-working, obedient being self-lessly devoted to her husband, who in turn enjoyed the social advancement and professional success tied to gainful employment, led to growing tensions between the sexes. One wing of the bourgeois feminist movement, generally labelled conservative, sought social recognition for women's work in the family and in public life, essentially demanding the elevation of their activities to the level of work. The other, so-called radical wing opposed women's exclusion from education, academia and professional life. By the turn of the twentieth century, both the European and the American women's movements had succeeded in opening up numerous schools, fields of study and professional careers previously reserved for unmarried women to both sexes. Employment and professional careers, however, would remain the exception for bourgeois women.

Working-class women often had no other choice than to work, obligated as they were to earn money. Because women in the workforce were now viewed as a temporary means of extra income (a product of bourgeois family ideology), women's wages regardless of occupation were always lower than those of their male counterparts. Justifications for paying women less were not limited to lower qualifications, but also pertained to the way in which women's work was perceived in society, downgrading every kind of employment accessible to women on the pay scale. Many women found jobs in nursing and care professions due to the increase in public and private care facilities in the new health care and welfare apparatus. A familial aura coalesced around these professions, which commodification and professionalization failed to extinguish. This work was said to be done out of love in working life as well, and thus did not require the same level of financial compensation. Socialist and bourgeois liberal women had already begun fighting for equal pay for equal work in the nineteenth century. For many proletarian women forced to combine work and family life, as well as domestic service workers deprived of such family life, a housewife's existence could seem like an attractive alternative to their double burden, and many working-class families adopted the bourgeois ideal. Even in cases where a worker or low-level professional's wage (now measured in terms of a 'family wage') sufficed to allow his wife to stay home, she was by no means free from work. Not only that, she enjoyed neither the amenities of a bourgeois apartment nor servants to assist her. Beyond not pursuing an occupation, some worker's wives also imitated their bourgeois peers by connecting their own prosperity with the social advancement of their husbands. These women not only provided their husbands' meals and made their beds, but also urged them to be diligent, obedient and compliant at the workplace.

The labour relations surveys conducted in the various branches and sectors of the economy around this time provide us with a clear picture of the work and daily life of these workers. In Austria alone, the Labour Statistics Office of the Department of Commerce carried out surveys between 1896 and 1906 among Viennese wage labourers (1896), on labour relations in the clothing and linen industry (1899, 1906), in the Austro-Hungarian Navy (1900), in the Trieste Lloyd Arsenal (1902) and in the shoemaking industry (1904, 1906). The office also investigated the findings of employment agencies (1903–5), hires and lockouts (1899, 1906) and factory working hours (1907). Special surveys were devoted to women's work (1896), child labour (1908) and cottage industry (1900–1, 1904).

What stands out here is that the most extensive studies were dedicated not to heavy industry, but to branches and sectors in which industrialization and mechanization were not or only partially implemented. The high proportion of small businesses and home and cottage industries reflects the specificities of the Austrian industrial structure, where large firms were the exception, not the rule. The reports reveal a wide variety of company forms and worker types as well as labour relations in which the 'normal' labour relation with obligatory social insurance (as understood in economics, statistics and scientific management) only applied to a small proportion of workers. The following passage, taken from a report by the Habsburg industrial inspectors into the cottage industry in Austria, describes an exemplary cottage industry family:

> The family has five members. The husband and the sixteen-year-old daughter work at home, each at a loom. The wife helps them if the business of housekeeping and supervision of their two small children allows. As the survey official entered the room inhabited by this family, only the girl was working her loom; upon being asked, the wife reported that the husband was recovering from a severe, protracted illness, but was still unable to

work, and that despite the weekly earnings of her daughter, they would be unable to afford the cost of living without her husband's illness benefits.[171]

By contrast, if we look at reports from the chambers of commerce and industry, the yearbooks of large companies and world fairs, or the ceremonial publications commemorating the fiftieth and sixtieth anniversaries of Kaiser Franz Joseph's coronation, *Die österreichische Großindustrie* (1898–1908), we see evidence of Austria's industrial modernity. The reader finds panels and photos of impressive factory facilities, smoke billowing from their chimneys, sparkling halls, rows of neatly arranged machines, powerful line shafts, happy men and women workers looking up to their supervisors in awe. Group photos of the workforce show concentric rings of workers, arranged respectfully around their owners or managers. The configuration reflects their positions in the company, as well as their age and sex. How workers dealt with their work and daily life is not revealed.

The sectoral studies conducted on behalf of the authorities and labour inspection agencies were not written as celebratory texts, but rather sought to identify where problems existed and what action was needed in both technical and social policy areas. When reading these, it becomes clear that the analytical distinction between employment and family reproduction was simply not viable in practice. Family and household did not allow themselves to be pushed entirely into the private realm. Therefore it makes sense to unpack local conditions, here with reference to the German and Habsburg Austrian examples, in terms of what they meant for the household.

To begin with, the ideal of the bourgeois family with its clear separation between the gainful economic and private spheres simply did not hold for men and women without families. Even smaller bourgeois families unable to afford servants due to the breadwinner's low wages failed to live up to the ideal. Housewives lived in the isolation of their houses or small apartments, often overwhelmed by their household duties and the internalized expectation to live up to a standard befitting their status. Forms of neighbourly or familial assistance offered a way out.

Proletarian households whose members pursued regulated wage labour were also overburdened. By the turn of the century, eleven-hour days were finally enforced across most industries; remaining free time and work-free Sundays were now for shopping, housekeeping and maintenance of housing and clothing. Laundry, a particularly large burden on women and girls, marked a difference between city and small-town or rural living conditions. Life in metropolitan apartments was tight due to the small size of rooms and kitchens. Most floors only had one water tap located in the hallway which allowed residents to take care of the bare necessities. Working women's household duties thus required strict management of time and finances. Numerous homemaker's guides advised homemakers to maintain a household budget to prevent spending from outpacing income. Rooms or beds were often rented out to lodgers to relieve the pressure. In the case of lost wages or other unforeseeable circumstances, it was not uncommon for people to fall into debt, mortgage their belongings or lose their apartment entirely. Homelessness was not uncommon. Socially critical journalism from the time offers insight into subproletarian Vienna or Berlin, where people lived in shelters, ate at soup kitchens and slept under bridges or in drainage canals.

This kind of agglomeration of proletarian misery was unknown in rural factory settlements, as housing was generally provided by employers and the pace of life remained more or less manageable. These residential apartment complexes were located in close proximity to the factories and, depending on the size of the company and number of employees, often featured in-house canteens, pubs and grocery stores. In villages where one or several companies dominated, the industrialist often sponsored schools, churches and recreation or social facilities. Classic attributes of workers' settlements in rural areas included small garden plots, communal laundry rooms and tool sheds. These facilitated working-class families' sustenance and made them less susceptible to wage fluctuations and losses. The courtyards and garden plots expanded workers' radius of activity, and served as spaces for gathering and socializing, particularly in the summer months. Supervision of children was also greatly simplified by these communal spaces. The tight-knit nature of communal life in the workers' settlements helped to socialize the household and break up the confines of nuclear-family isolation. This was the precondition for working-class women who were not employed themselves to participate more easily in political action and trade union campaigning on behalf of their husbands. Of course, rent contracts were only valid as long as the employment relationship remained in effect.

While work in heavy industry was limited to a minority of workers, the norm for large swathes of Central Europe continued to be the extended households that company owners sought to compensate for with kitchen gardens. This was true for farmers whose market production and wage labour were embedded in a broad range of self-sustaining household types, as well as for small commercial producers and cottage industry operators whose gainful activities took place in the household. Depending on the extent of one's access to land and means of self-sustenance, subsistence work took up more or less of the workday. Should combined income and subsistence basis prove insufficient, then labour migration and income supplementation came into play. Although many people from rural areas had already moved to the cities permanently by 1900, migratory income supplementation continued. Ties between migrant workers and their families at home remained strong on both sides. They replenished the urban workforce, but also increased the absorptive capacity of rural and urban households for the elderly, sick and unemployed. This meant that the extended household also offered the prospect of integration for those with no family, those who did not start their own or had somehow lost it. In rural areas of the Habsburg Monarchy where no social institutions existed, officials placed strangers in families' homes as charity cases in accordance with prevailing residency laws.

The extended household's capacity for social absorption, its limits and its durability can be accounted for through the combination of incomes, subsistence farming, interregional expansion through labour migration and access to public support in the form of social and poverty policies. The parameters of income combination, subsistence, social transfer and translocality tell us more about what life was like for a worker in Europe around 1900 than the conception of work as a secured occupation limited to gainful employment could. They allow us to view regulated and secured wage labour in industrial society as a regional and temporary variety of work, advancing within a much broader context.

Interregional small- and large-scale connections

Due to the shrinking of the world that resulted from transport's increasing acceleration, density and frequency, the interregional connections originating from Central Europe will not be classified according to distance and range. Rather, emphasis will be placed on the effects of travel and migration on labour relations.

When discussing changes in labour migration from rural regions into urban spaces in the nineteenth century, what mostly comes to the fore is the transition from temporary and circular migration to permanent emigration and settlement in the destination region. The stabilization of immigration into the emerging European metropolises is often cited as proof for this claim. Often obscured, however, is that migration-based population growth stems from the surplus of those who remain over those who leave after a time. The growth of these big cities is the result of constant coming and going. In the case of Vienna, four out of five newcomers left the city within one year between 1880 and 1910.[172]

European overseas emigration, a mass phenomenon by the 1870s, represented an irreversible decision in its early years given the high costs and difficulties entailed. However, as overseas travel grew faster and more affordable, even this form of migration became a circular means of income supplementation. Countries of destination often modified entry and residency requirements in times of economic crisis. The 1908 economic slump in the United States, for example, caused many migrants to lose their jobs and return home. In the 1880s, racially motivated halts on immigration were imposed on Chinese and Japanese workers, driving many of them to settle in South American countries and improving prospects for Eastern European immigrants in North America. In the Habsburg Monarchy, emigration restrictions were lifted by the 1867 December Constitution.

Economic interest was the primary reason for emigration and the motivation behind one's choice of destination. Nevertheless, this interest was not limited to migrants' quest for earnings or even demand for migrant labour. Recruitment and transport became big business, with growing numbers of employees. Emigration, consulting and translation agencies, ocean liners and travel outfitters all offered their services to potential emigrants, each promoting their own routes and destinations. These were complemented by the public authorities, job placement offices and emigration associations, which occupied an immense amount of resources in the state and private service sectors, as well as the voluntary sector.

Requirements for migrant workers around 1900 differed significantly from pre-industrialization migration systems.[173] Centres of mining and heavy-industry processing along the Rhine, Ruhr, Saar and Mosel rivers required a constant flow of permanent workers. Agricultural workers from east of the Elbe river, largely ethnic Poles, established themselves as an important recruitment pool. As agriculture mechanized, the constant need for workers there dwindled to seasonal peaks during harvests. Farms were now manned by cheap seasonal workers. Now that the local labour force had moved west to become miners and industrial workers, new workers were brought in from the Austrian and Russian partitions of Poland, the largely Russian-controlled Kingdom of Poland, and Galicia. German demand, however, came into direct conflict with the landowners back in migrants' homelands, as Russian colonization in Central Asia and Siberia also needed more workers. Furthermore, other Western European states fuelled competition for Eastern European industrial and agricultural workers.

The seasonal model was dominant in industrialized agriculture east of the Elbe. Small farmers and peasants with smallholdings were recruited to do the threshing or work the sugar beet harvest and other peak phases in intensive agriculture. One politically influential organization responsible for this was the Zentralstelle zur Beschaffung deutscher Ansiedler und Feldarbeiter, the Central Authority for Procurement of German Settlers and Field Labourers. This was a subgroup within the German Eastern Marches Society (founded in 1884), an extreme nationalist group dedicated to the promotion of German over Polish culture in the areas of eastern expansion.[174] Workers were only permitted to stay for a maximum of eight to ten months to ensure their return; family migration, permanent residency or marrying into a family were all forbidden. Due to fears within nationalist circles that eastern Germany would undergo 'Polonization', Germans often exhibited a preference for Ruthenian workers from Eastern Galicia. The Ukrainian-speaking Ruthenians who worked on Polish estates took advantage of seasonal work in Germany, migrating in droves. When over 100,000 of them held a strike against the Polish estate owners in Galicia in 1902, the German Eastern Marches Society stirred up anti-Polish sentiment to attract the striking Ruthenians to German estates.[175] The Ruthenian Greek Catholic clergy, a leading force in the Ukrainian nationalist movement, took part in organizing labour migration to Germany by declaring working the Polish soil rather than travelling back and forth to work in German fields one of the 'seven sins'.

Roughly 100,000 Ruthenians went to work seasonally in the expansive German agricultural region east of the Elbe each year around 1900. Another 200,000 to 250,000 Poles came from Galicia and 380,00 to 400,000 from the Russian partition, despite the rather cold reception given to them by German nationalists.[176] Hungarian Germans, Slovaks and Austrian Italians also worked in Germany. Russian and Austrian authorities made several attempts to curtail migration and prevent labour drain, but were hindered by political interventions and concessions – Germany even offered to reduce import duties on Russian wheat, while Austria–Hungary was offered German support in their plans to annex Bosnia–Herzegovina. The Galician government also became involved in recruitment, with its labour authority in Lwów/Lviv/Lemberg. Consulates and associations were opened in Germany's seasonal labour regions to offer protection to Austrian migrant labourers. In France, 40,000 seasonal workers travelled from Galicia in 1910; another 80,000 went to the Netherlands and Scandinavia. Seasonal labour forces were a commodity in high demand, and proved a major source of contention between the countries of origin and destination. This generally had little impact on the working conditions of seasonal workers, however, who returned home with their savings.

The poles of attraction in Habsburg interior migration patterns were the Lower and Upper Austrian and Styrian cities and industrial zones, which were in turn plugged into the network of immigrants from the rural Bohemian and Alpine regions. Meanwhile, overseas migration offered an alternative to landless peasants from the Carpathian mountains in the north-east, and the Dinaric Alps in the monarchy's south-east. The states under the Hungarian Crown comprised their own internal migration areas, with the agglomeration in and around Budapest serving as the main pole of attraction. Overseas migration was more important in Hungary than in the Austrian half of the empire. From 1870 to 1910, around 3.5 million people emigrated overseas from Austria–Hungary, 3 million of which went to the US. Of the 2 million who made the journey between 1900 and 1910, 18.6 per cent were Poles, 16.1 per cent were South Slavs, 15.4 per cent were Slovaks, and 14.7 per cent were Magyars. The share of emigrants among the respective national groups was greatest among the Poles (9.3 per cent), followed by the South Slavs (6.8 per cent) and Jews (6.8 per cent).[177]

Recruitment was done by the same means. Who took what offer depended largely on the efforts of local recruiters and migration agencies, but also on the impressions garnered from migrants who had already made the journey. Chance, of course, also played a role. Thus migration concentrated in spatial terms along the transport routes leading to emigration ports, where medical care, lodging, provisions and travel equipment took on significance in the service sector.[178] The highest value creation was netted by the shipping companies, which not only supplied overseas transit but also organized transport to the harbours and carried out immigration controls on behalf of the American authorities. The Hamburg America Line, or Hamburg-Amerikanische Paketfahrt-Actien-Gesellschaft (HAPAG for short), built huge barracks into a veritable town: Ballin-Stadt, named for the passenger line's director, Alfred Ballin. Fierce competition among the ocean liner companies fostered processes of concentration, price fixing and monopolization. Most emigrants from the German Reich, the Habsburg Monarchy and Russia left the Old World via the German North Sea harbours of Hamburg and Bremen, but also via Holland, Belgium and England. The German and Dutch companies banded together in 1892 to form the Nord-Atlantischer Dampfer-Linien-Verband (North Atlantic Steamer Line Association). Fiume/Rijeka had been built up by the British-American Cunard Steamship Company to offer Hungarian emigrants an alternative since the turn of the century, but neither Rijeka nor Trieste could rival Hamburg or Bremen as the monarchy's main ports of emigration.

Along with migration within Europe or off to American shores, a third destination was possible: the colonial settlements being established by the migrant's home countries. This type of migration was most strongly tied to states' political interests, and exhibited stark variations between the German Reich and the Habsburg Monarchy. While Germany took part in the colonial partitioning of Africa, acquiring German South West Africa (1884) and German East Africa (1885), Austria–Hungary held no overseas territories. Both states, however, had internal peripheries tied to core areas through relations of dependency: inhabitants from peripheral regions who migrated to the cores were citizens and therefore seen as civic equals; conversely, many state officials, investors and scientists in the provinces were recruited from the imperial cores, representing the interest of central government in the periphery.

In order to demonstrate its colonial presence in Africa, Germany was obliged to dispatch at least some colonial settlers. The duties of settlers in German colonies were very different from those of the workers and settlers who went to America. For one thing, women were indispensable. These settlers were sent to appropriate lands over the long term, to run plantations and man the colonial administration, while the indigenous populations were displaced and sent to reservations. In 1904, German colonial troops would become infamous for their repression of the Herero uprising in German South West Africa (present-day Namibia). Anti-colonial resistance fighters who fled to the British colonies around the Cape or Portuguese Angola were subsequently liquidated by German troops, in cooperation with the other colonial powers.[179] Attitudes towards the black workforce were of a drastically different calibre than in Eastern Europe. This mass murder was to serve as an example that any further anti-colonial resistance would be suppressed, and it was only through these means that the indigenous peoples finally permitted themselves to be pushed onto reservations, becoming migrant labour for colonial agriculture.

When comparing conquest and colonization in Eastern Europe on the one hand and colonialism on the other, we would be well advised to keep this distinction in mind. However, let it be said that the occupation of Bosnia–Herzegovina by Austria–Hungary closely resembled the scramble for Africa. Six years before the Berlin Conference (1884), which later regulated colonial borders in Africa, the 1878 Congress of Berlin institutionalized Austro-Hungarian rule of Bosnia–Herzegovina, technically under Ottoman jurisdiction until formal annexation in 1908. In contrast to other Habsburg conquests, Bosnia–Herzegovina was not integrated into the state as a province but rather governed as a protectorate. Only after armed resistance was put down here as well did the native peoples accept their lot. Bosnia provided its Austro-Hungarian occupiers with a large-scale colonization project, preventing the loss of settlers overseas and replacing the need for colonies elsewhere. Peasants willing to migrate to these new farmlands numbered 10,000, while others worked in forestry, mining or infrastructural development. Bosnia was home to huge forests and large mineral deposits. The elimination of Ottoman legal traditions permitted the expropriation of land from native peasants (*kmetr*) who lacked proper documents to verify their usage rights; they were driven from the land and their plots given to settler families, mainly Croats, Poles and Ruthenians.[180]

Further fields of action tying Central Europe to other world regions through work were trade, transport, investment and military intervention, which secured raw materials, procurement and sales markets, as well as transport routes. The German Reich, Austria–Hungary, Switzerland, Italy and the Scandinavian countries were all underrepresented in terms of capital exports, trade volumes and colonial territories compared to the Western European maritime powers, making it all the more important for their governments and industrial companies to secure global interests even without recourse to direct colonization. One possibility was to take part in the colonial scramble, as Germany and Italy did in Africa, or through economic engagement in the colonial powers' wake and through accords with them. This allowed semi-peripheral states to take part in the uneven international division of labour as industrial countries without their own sizable colonial conquests.

Hamburg, Bremen and Trieste were not only ports of emigration, but also ports of call for the merchant fleet engaged in the unequal trade of Central European manufacturing exports for commodity imports from overseas. Austrian maritime transport was carried out by Austrian Lloyd, the Austrian equivalent to HAPAG, by the North German Lloyd in Hamburg, or by the Holland America Line (HAL) in Rotterdam. Located in Trieste, the shipping company boasted over seventy steamships in 1870 and serviced the Mediterranean, the Atlantic and, after completion of the Suez Canal, the Indian Ocean. It was among the largest companies in the Mediterranean, while Austria–Hungary was the Ottoman Empire's most important trading partner. Around this time, a delicate dispute with Great Britain emerged over whether Austria–Hungary had permitted or perhaps even favoured the transport of African slaves on Lloyd vessels from Alexandria to Istanbul, violating the ban on the slave trade. The British ambassador in Smyrna had raised the accusation.[181] Inspection of one Lloyd steamer by a British patrol boat prompted further suspicion, although no proof that the passengers were to become house slaves at their destination was found. The Mediterranean had become an important slave trafficking area following the nineteenth-century reduction in the transatlantic slave trade. In the first third of the century, 16,000 to 18,000 slaves are estimated to have been brought to the Ottoman Empire annually, amounting to 1.3 million in the years of intensive trade between 1850 and 1870. In fact, the Mediterranean Sea was not even mentioned in Great Britain's 1807 ban, which only specified the Atlantic. From the Ottoman perspective, the ban was not considered binding until the British occupation of Egypt forced the Sultan to accept the ban for the Mediterranean as well in the 1880s.

In light of this, the response of the ship's captain, as well as that of the Austrian authorities confronted with the case, is illustrative. They evaded accusations of supporting slavery, first, by arguing formally that the possession of and trade in slaves were explicitly forbidden by both the Austrian criminal code and various international Acts from the Congress of Vienna to the Quadripartite Treaty of 1841; thus no person aboard a ship flying the Austrian flag could be viewed as a slave. Second, they claimed, the authorities had no right to intervene in a private company's conditions of carriage. Although the complaint came to nothing, there was no escaping the relations of dependency between colonial areas and industrial countries for transport businesses and trade. Austria–Hungary had claimed the role of a great industrial power, and Lloyd committed itself to carrying out the unequal exchange despite being itself dependent upon the goodwill of Great Britain, the global organizing and regulating force of the day.

Another example of this riding in the greater colonial powers' wake to secure global interests can be seen in the participation of German and Austro-Hungarian warships in the defeat of the Boxer Rebellion in China (1900–1), as part of a military alliance between Europe and the United States. The uprising itself was directed against the selling out of China in the wake of its military defeat in the Opium Wars, manifested in 'unequal treaties' as well as in the extraterritorial economic zones granted to Western powers. This Chinese rebellion targeted symbols of the West: embassies, missionaries and Chinese Christians. Sending off the troops of the German Expedition Corps, Kaiser Wilhelm II held his infamous 'Hun Speech', filled with a mix of racist hubris and orders to brutally anni-hilate the enemy.[182] After defeating the rebels, the allied forces engaged in a spectacle of punitive looting and plundering. As compensation for their contribution to the dominance of the Western powers and Russia, Germany and Austria–Hungary were guaranteed territorial spheres of influence of their own. For the Habsburg Monarchy, the newly acquired quasi-colonial enclave of Tianjin, a port city, was its only such over-seas territory.[183] Even today, the Austrian Military Museum in Vienna proudly displays the spoils of that plunder: weapons, clothes and even severed braids of hair, bearing shameless witness to the humiliation of the Chinese.

Last but not least, the ambivalent connection between Central Euro-pean regions and the hierarchies of global inequality can be seen in the emigrants who came from poverty-stricken conditions in Germany or Switzerland, yet went to Great Britain or the US and managed to become mining tycoons.[184] The poster child for such success stories was the Guggenheim family. Once a family of Swiss peddler merchants, their ancestor Meyer Guggenheim emigrated to the US in 1847 to lay the foundations of an international mining empire which would soon account for 80 per cent of global copper, silver and lead extraction, complemented by wide-ranging land grabs, militarized labour regimes and a brutal physical workload. Once comfortably atop the zenith of high finance and big business, the bosses' connection to their countries of origin was usually severed. They acted above all in the interests of profit. When they did choose to align themselves politically with states, it was with the leading industrial and colonial powers which ensured the global capitalist order. Rarely did they utilize their business success to benefit their home nation. In the case of the English pastor Rhodes, family matters were somewhat different. His sons had acquired one of the first South African cotton plantations before joining De Beers in the diamond business. Cecil Rhodes (1853–1902) in particular, who studied law in London, rose to be a diamond king whose business was always closely linked with that of the British Crown. In a symbiotic relationship, state and capital accelerated land grabs and acted against rival colonial powers as if against economic competitors. The diamond boom was followed in the 1880s by gold mining. Rhodes became prime minister of the Cape Colony in 1890, and still graces the company's garden in Cape Town today in the form of a towering statue. The monument bears the inscription 'Your hinterland is here'. He brought the independent kingdoms of northern South Africa under the control of his Consolidated Diamond Mines, which soon achieved a monopoly over diamond production in southern Africa. The company pioneered infrastructural development and acted as a colonial administration until the areas of northern and southern Rhodesia were officially incorporated into the British Empire as colonies (until the independence of Zambia in 1964 and Zimbabwe in 1980).

TODAY

Characteristics

Allow us to recapitulate – briefly – the twentieth century from today's perspective. The escalation of imperialist rivalry culminating in the First World War was followed by the disintegration of the German, Habsburg,

Russian and Ottoman Empires. The confrontation to determine who would succeed the British as the hegemonic world power intensified during the Second World War, ending with the occupation and division of Germany. Japan, which had pursued conquests in East Asia similar to those of Nazi Germany in Europe, also suffered defeat. Both states were folded into the post-war order under American hegemony. Its range was limited, however, by the Soviet Bloc and the People's Republic of China, which remained allies until 1960.

Both world wars contributed significantly to the consolidation of industrial management, the rationalization (as well as destruction) of human life, and the future of warfare itself. The factory system began its global advance after the First World War, boosted by Henry Ford's scientific management practices in the United States. The Soviet Union also adopted productivity intensification through division of labour in its pursuit of catch-up industrialization, subordinating human hands to the pace of the conveyor belt in the process. The lack of capital, technology, know-how and mass purchasing power among the traditionally non-industrial states impeded the formation of viable industrial structures and domestic markets in the interwar period. Many of these states remained agrarian in character or were only able to catch up industrially in select sectors, remaining dependent on foreign capital, loans, imports and technology transfer. Nevertheless, the vision of economic development via the factory system had been nearly universally adopted in political discourse, so that when the global economic crisis of the 1930s weakened established industrial states, an opening emerged for certain newly industrialized countries (NICs) – such as Brazil, Mexico, Turkey, South Africa, India and Romania – to engage in import substitution industrialization.

Post–Second World War reconstruction bolstered desires to build a modern, coherent industrial society practically everywhere, including in the newly independent states of the periphery. Traditional economies, self-sufficiency and familial security systems were regarded as residual, to be replaced as quickly as possible with regular gainful employment and social services for the broadest majority of the population.

This vision would become a reality in the industrialized capitalist states of the West after the Second World War. Riding the wave of the reconstruction boom, industrial bases and service sectors were spread and diversified, complemented by the expansion of gainful employment as well as social security, welfare, education and mass purchasing power. Ever greater numbers of women joined the workforce, while activities around childcare and care for the elderly were 'outsourced' to so-called professional institutions financed by public coffers or social insurance institutions. Social insurance or public social services such as assisted living for seniors spread to new sectors in Western European welfare states, and successively extended to new social groups like farmers and the self-employed. In the US, on the other hand, private insurance and private pensions became the norm. The household transformed into a retreat into the private sphere, a space requiring ever less physically strenuous domestic work due to the rise of technical appliances. Domestic activity in the now-predominant nuclear family shifted to the arena of family reproduction, child-rearing and leisure time. The fact that supporting the social mobility of husbands and children fell to working housewives and mothers as a new, additional burden was largely ignored.

Growth was driven by the ongoing commodification of an ever-increasing number of social needs; this new world of commodities was perceived as an increase in prosperity, and set the standard for groups not yet able to participate.

The state socialist countries of the Soviet Bloc (with the exception of the East German and Czech industrial regions) began the post–Second World War period as agrarian states; the destruction of the war placed them in a difficult starting position. Socialist industrialization policies pursued under the political primacy of communist parties, however, were able to mobilize these states' limited resources through a mixture of political enthusiasm and coercion. The state socialist ideal deviated from the Western model: every man and woman was to be integrated as wage labourers into gainful activities organized within the planned economy, entitling them to the social funds made available to the whole society. Forms of social insurance which distinguished between entitled and non-entitled individuals were, in this context, simply unnecessary. Work-centred socialist society treated the worker as the social ideal, and thus also provided social services in the form of company facilities such as free factory kitchens, kindergartens, clubs and (modest) vacation resorts. Child-rearing, sustenance and nursing activities were outsourced to public institutions to a much greater extent than in the West. Wherever this arrangement actually managed to function, household and domestic work diminished in importance. To overcome the supply shortages characteristic of planned economies, however, household provisioning and personal networks played a central role in accessing essential goods. In this regard, and similar to the West, conditions varied greatly between rural and urban zones.

The hopes of post-colonial states staking their claim to catch-up development after the Second World War as non-aligned, developing or 'Third World' countries were massively disappointed. Their role as suppliers of raw materials in the international division of labour continued largely unabated, while industrial development was limited to restricted enclaves. Access to social security through gainful employment was reserved for civil servants and small circles of fully proletarianized workers. The bulk of the population remained dependent in terms of income, as well as social sustenance, on traditional sectors characterized by subsistence and informality, which had now been relegated to the social fringes. Society was characterized by social division and polarization.

The global economic crisis of the 1970s triggered by the end of the reconstruction cycle marked a major turning point, intensifying economic competition worldwide. The lack of innovation and dynamism in the state socialist countries led many to import Western technologies, which, however, brought about enormous debt levels rather than the desired economic upgrades, due to the borrowing necessary to acquire such technology in the first place. Additionally, the East also began to function as an extended workbench for Western corporations, eroding political primacy in economic management and eventually triggering a process of system transformation. Consequently, Eastern Europe fell back to the peripheral status it had held before its socialist transformation.[185]

In the capitalist West, the profit squeeze initiated a renewed push towards cost-cutting and rationalization. New digital technologies and the outsourcing of fully established industrial mass production to low-wage locations across the global South precipitated a collapse of the Fordist industrial world, as well as the social securities and mass purchasing power associated with it. The industrial age had been characterized by stable employment relations and the strong bargaining power of unions and labour parties. This arrangement had seemed to be a permanent fixture of social life for decades, but was now suddenly being replaced by new divisions of labour and a new flexibility in labour relations. The abandonment of social partnership consensus and the introduction of policies with negative impacts on the working classes who had only recently become middle classes met with strong resistance and could only be implemented in gradual steps.

A new constellation favourable to capitalist interests arose with the collapse of state socialism after 1989. The political turn accompanying the fall of the Iron Curtain unlocked new labour, procurement and sales markets for Western capital seeking valorization through privatization and the collapse of social structures, soon ushering in a new economic upswing. Furthermore, the discrediting of social issues and workers' rights in the wake of state socialism's collapse had knock-on effects for Western work and conflict culture, not least due to migrants' willingness to accept lower wages and less job security.

Another instrument of bringing national achievements into disrepute and discrediting them as distortions of competition was to shift economic and social regulatory competencies over to inter-, trans- and supranational organizations like the World Bank, the International Monetary Fund and the World Trade Organization. The liberalization of trade, services and investment protections pushed through by major global players in regional economic blocs and countless bilateral agreements between individual states was intended to prevent any future political limitations or barriers to capital valorization. However, the global financial crisis of excessive accumulation beginning in 2007–8, the cost of which was again shouldered by the world's poor and peripheral regions, has caused many to doubt neo-liberalism's 'There Is No Alternative' mantra.

The relocation of labour-intensive basic and consumer goods industries to the 'Third World' allowed these countries to overcome their total economic orientation towards raw materials. In practice, this meant that a number of NICs became home to huge factory complexes, often located in special economic zones producing basic materials and consumer goods for export. By shouldering the burden of development costs and enacting capital-friendly labour, environmental and tax laws, governments sought to attract foreign direct investment into their countries, expecting job creation, technology transfer and modernization of their economic structures in return. Hard and precarious working conditions, low wages, extreme exploitation and bans on trade union activity were accepted as the price of entry into modern industrial society. Most hopes of rising from the low end of the global commodity chain to a position with advanced technology and intensive value creation with higher skill requirements and a diversified industrial landscape were disappointed.

Corporate headquarters, logistics and research and development remained in the old industrial countries, allowing them to complete the transition to post-industrial, knowledge-based sectors – the new measure of global economic development. Back in the NICs, when component production suddenly leaves one site for another with more favourable conditions, destruction is left in its wake.

Several 'Third World' countries, however, strengthened their position as emerging economies through the globalization of industrial production. These include larger and wealthier NICs with access to raw materials, qualified workers and a developed industrial base, such as Brazil, India, China and South Africa. Boosted by rising global demand for industrial capacity since the 1980s, these countries abandoned their internal market-oriented import substitution strategies of catch-up development and instead assumed the role of suppliers in the new international division of labour. Supply was not limited to industrial components, but in fact encompassed all sorts of services and development jobs, such as call centres and universities in India. Following system change and the disintegration of the Soviet Union, Russia can also be included in this group of emerging countries, which coordinate their international presence since 2009 as the BRIC countries, amended to BRICS (Brazil, Russia, India, China, South Africa) with South Africa's admission in 2010.[186] Despite their differences, the BRICS and several other emerging countries, known as NEXT-11 (Egypt, Bangladesh, Indonesia, Iran, Mexico, Nigeria, Pakistan, the Philippines, South Korea, Turkey, Vietnam) or the 'global swing states', are characterized by high growth rates, industrial expansion and growing industrial employment, strong commodification and a rising middle class, accompanied by deep social and regional divisions within society. The economic weight of the new industrial countries in relation to their older industrial counterparts has risen. These countries have in turn strengthened their own position at the expense of smaller, more disadvantaged developing countries by siphoning off their orders or forcing them into a position of dependency as suppliers of raw material, sales markets or extended workbenches. This has resulted in new rivalries and conflicts with the old colonial powers, which had hitherto largely monopolized relations with their former colonies, and with the US, whose core position as the global hegemon is being challenged – not only by regional blocs like the European Union, but also by the emerging countries themselves. China's position vis-à-vis the United States, for example, is both that of a financial backer, as it holds most of its export surplus in US treasury bonds, and that of an economic competitor and ultimately threat.

Local conditions and labour relations

Allow us to return to the post-industrial world of Central and Western European states, where mass production of consumer goods and basic industries have largely disappeared from the scene and high-quality, intelligent products like the German, Swiss and Italian machinery industries have prevailed. There are thus still factories and qualified industrial workers, as well as qualified work in the service sector. Job security and secured social rights for the core layers of the working class, however, are increasingly a thing of the past. These have been eroded by flexibilization and the use of subcontractors, temporary workers and freelancers on the one hand, and by partial or total outsourcing of production to locations that appear more willing to fulfil companies' demands on the other. As most major corporations are embedded in complex structures of ownership across multiple locations, it has become a widespread business practice to play industrializing host countries against one another in terms of optimizing conditions for capital valorization. The task of politicians has shifted from regulating labour relations and working conditions to a form of regional marketing operation, seeking to draw the largest investments possible to their respective countries.[187]

Working conditions and employment biographies are now highly fragmentary. Essentially, five work characters can be identified: the remaining classical workers and office employees; the post-industrial upwardly mobile; stagnating precarious pieceworkers or temporary workers; foreign migrant workers; and, lastly, those dependent upon charity or unemployment and social assistance.

The working class and the employed middle class socialized under conditions of social partnership continue to occupy key positions in industry, as well as the health care, transport and communication sectors, which were once typically state-owned but have now mostly been privatized or placed under private management. Civil servants, teaching and educational staff find themselves in a similar position, belonging to segments of the non-self-employed workforce who were able to retain the labour and social rights gained during their countries' welfare state phase.

When unions and other organizations representing their interests attempt to mitigate the loss of existing social rights, they are often demonized in the media as trying to take advantage of privileges or waging class warfare. Air traffic controllers, train conductors, teachers, and so on – these groups ought to accept collapsing wages and job security along with the rest of society, rather than seek to extend this security to other parts of the working population. It is often the case, in fact, that a sense of solidarity with the precariat is rather weak and diffuse, while elitism and arrogance towards society's lower rungs are firmly anchored in the minds of civil servants and the proletarian avant-garde. The ongoing process of rationalization via digital technologies and changes in employment contracts seem to be sending this kind of worker into extinction, which in turn would eliminate the social base upon which trade unions build their negotiating power – both for these and other groups of workers.

Organized labour's position has gradually been replaced by the emerging upwardly mobile groups. These new social climbers are helping to create a new kind of middle class whose members are well educated, master digital working processes and communication, internalize new career demands and show no interest in union organization. They demonstrate high levels of loyalty, flexibility and strong commitment, and for that they are well paid – compensation for the lack of social security due to short-term contracts and frequent changes of employer. With this compensation, they are expected to make private provisions for hard times, relying on their own savings rather than unemployment assistance or buying into private pension schemes. Their company position obliges them to enforce cost, time and adaptation pressures among their subordinates, and consumer codes and recreational facilities are decisive social incentives for them. However, they are kept on their toes by the drive towards constant self-promotion and availability via their smartphones, turning their mobility into a physical and psychological burden. Freedom of location and collaborative work through the use of information technologies open up global career paths, but also expose them to competition through offshoring and outsourcing to their highly qualified colleagues in the global South. Standardization and modularization of working tasks entail a new form of Taylorism from which not even the new knowledge workers are immune.

The most prevalent work characters in the new post-industrial and post-Fordist world of work belong to the precarious, flexibilized workforce.

These consist of local residents and so-called 'persons with migrant backgrounds' who have permanently settled in their destination country. Even for a small business operation, constant adaptation to fluctuating order levels, cost structures and relations of competition in production make flexibility more important than long-term experience and worker loyalty in the eyes of bosses and company shareholders. Older, long-term employees are replaced by younger short-term and part-time employees, and fixed employment contracts by freelancer contracts. Financial and social security are thrust upon the (often only nominally) self-employed worker. Employing temporary labour brings differing classes of workers together to perform the same tasks: temporary workers are often classified into another profile, subject to different payment agreements, and are usually the first to go – hoping that their employment agency will be able to place them elsewhere, as reinforcement workers with low levels of job retention. Part-time and marginal employment offer additional ways to reduce wage costs and other expenses. These elements of flexibilization all required certain forms of labour deregulation which, depending on the specific labour relations of the state concerned, have granted companies a great deal of room to design employment contracts to their liking. In recent years, an observable tendency has emerged to award work orders online through so-called 'crowd-working' platforms, where payment, labour exchange and workplace are completely and utterly decoupled. Here, the employment contract disappears into an uncontrolled grey zone outside state regulation or legal certainty.

As long as the old labour laws remain in force for at least the remaining segment of permanent employees, this degradation of labour rights can be viewed as informalization. The moment regulatory cutback is enshrined in a new law, however, whatever already existed informally becomes the new standard form of work. In some cases, flexibilization and informalization suit those who prefer to determine their own work schedules, such as by combining gainful work with child-rearing, care of the elderly or volunteering. From the employer's perspective, the right to interrupt a work process or part-time work are social standards which prevent the flexible use of labour, and are thus generally opposed. Insecure part-time contracts and marginal employment for low pay result in growing numbers of workers who cannot survive on the income of a single job, and take on several at once to compensate for the individual shortcomings and uncertainties of each. Not all jobs are subject to social insurance contributions and not every employer registers these jobs with social insurance institutions in the first place, further excluding these workers from secure relations of employment. A real danger exists for the working poor to fall into poverty traps.

A specific case of flexibilization and informalization is represented by workforces whose family network is centred in countries where lower wages and a lack of jobs constitute good reasons for migrating to better-paying countries to supplement one's income.[188] The wages in their country of destination are attractive, while the lack of social services, particularly for irregular migrant workers, is compensated by workforce rotation in the context of the transnational household. In the Western European core, European freedom-of-movement regulations allow workers from low-wage EU countries to compete with migrants from outside the EU. These workers are available for all the jobs that even the local precariat refuse to take, but place additional wage pressures on these workers through their willingness to do so. It is thus not surprising that fears of wage dumping by importing foreign workers is greatest among the socially disenfranchised and downwardly mobile. In many cases, the children of the first generation of migrant workers are unable to break out of the lowest labour market segments. This competition leads to a downward spiral, which could only be solved by legal regulations to harmonize working conditions. This, in turn, automatically raises the question of selection criteria for admission to the national labour market.

Seasonal-worker regulations modelled on the imperial-era German Farm Workers Agency (Feldarbeiterzentrale) of the 1900s, which repeal residency rules for short-term workers, undermine such harmonization and instead of codify difference. This is true of the Austrian Home Care Act (Hausbetreuungsgesetz, 2007) as well as the Healthcare and Nursing Act (Gesundheits- und Krankenpflegegesetz, 2008), which hastily constituted irregularly employed domestic nurses as freelance entrepreneurs in order to legalize the services they had hitherto provided as undocumented wage labourers.[189]

These regulatory changes push a segment of the workforce out of the labour market for various periods of time. Nurses who paid into social insurance while employed receive unemployment benefits and can participate in retraining and further qualification programmes. After a certain – increasingly short – period, benefits payments are conditioned upon recipients' assets and those of their close family or household, and only those who can prove a lack of assets and income are entitled to continue receiving state support. Recipients of unemployment benefits are obliged to participate in job placement through the employment agencies and prove their willingness to work by attending regular meetings and submitting job applications.

State provisions for those who have not paid into social insurance consist of a different social safety net not financed by social insurance contributions, namely public social assistance. This represents a modern form of poor relief, which depends greatly on the economic strength and political composition of a given state. Benefits can be issued in the form of money, vouchers or assistance in kind, and recipients are subjected to very strict evaluations.

In 2002, Germany's Social Democratic–Green coalition, led by Chancellor Gerhard Schröder, launched a groundbreaking initiative to transform the country's 'long-term unemployment' and social assistance programmes into a second labour market, bundled into a series of legislative packages known as 'Agenda 2010'. These reforms effectively destroyed the labour and social rights won by the old working class.[190] The new programme's architect was Peter Hartz, personnel director at the Volkswagen corporation in Wolfsburg, where the federal state of Lower Saxony holds a legally enshrined blocking minority share in the company. Initiated by the Hartz Commission and continued by Angela Merkel's subsequent governments, this move caused wages to collapse between 1990 and 1998 in a country once considered a role model in terms of social policy; ongoing wage stagnation has been the rule ever since.[191] As wages sank, the profit share of the national product rose.

The long-term unemployed and recipients of social assistance were grouped together under the official category of 'Unemployment Benefits II' (Arbeitslosengeld II, or ALG II), popularly referred to as 'Hartz IV' after its namesake. This recategorization reduced recipients of unemployment benefits to the level of 'welfare cases'. Living off benefits was from then on known as *hartzen*, a new German verb. *Hartzen* has two implications: first, one's income and that of one's immediate family (their household) is strictly evaluated and monitored, while the level of their assets has an impact on their benefits – one's house, jewellery or even financial savings are up for liquidation. Second, in order to foster their reintegration into the labour market, recipients of ALG II can be assigned what is officially termed 'additional working opportunities with extra remuneration', notoriously known as 'one-euro jobs' for their hourly wage of €1.00 to €2.50. This is by no means a 'normal' employment relation. Through administrative act, the employment agency can assign benefits recipients to elderly care and nursing jobs, cleaning, or municipal maintenance work (such as street cleaning) for non-profit service providers. Because recipients are threatened with losing their benefits should they refuse an 'additional working opportunity', we can speak of coercive labour relations. In the year of its introduction, 2005, 604,000 Germans found themselves in one-euro jobs. One-euro jobbers are not counted in official unemployment statistics,[192] and thus find themselves on a secondary labour market managed by the employment agencies, the primary function of which is to put pressure on regular employees and job seekers to sell their labour for less. The effort has been a success in Germany, where wages have been in sharp decline for several years. German exports rose just as sharply, with both their southern and new eastern EU neighbours purchasing a great deal thanks to EU internal-market liberalization.

Despite its comparable starting position, Austria has not (yet) gone down such an aggressive path in pressuring its recipients of unemployment and social assistance to become complicit in wage dumping. Although Austria has ratcheted up the pressure by softening provisions on reasonable entitlement to unemployment insurance, it has not been able to level this with 'emergency assistance' (as long-term unemployment benefits are known in Austria) and social assistance, due to resistance from state governments and municipalities. Benefiting from emergency assistance and basic social assistance is not tied to performing compulsory non-profit labour. Moreover, the level of monthly basic assistance – €838.00 for single adults (2016) – is significantly higher than the ordinary rate of Germany's Hartz IV law, €404.00. This demonstrates that a range of variations are possible within national labour market and social policies. The increase in social welfare claims from asylum seekers and refugees, however, has placed additional pressures on the system's financial viability since 2015.

What effects do status in professional life and the character of social insurance and public social services have for work performed in the context of the household and family? How much volunteering is compatible with employment? The extended household with domestic subsistence production and family incomes has virtually disappeared. Agricultural specialization has meant that even rural family businesses no longer produce all of the food they consume, but rather shop at the supermarket like urban families. Women's employment, longer education and training periods, and multiple jobs leave no time for gardening, provisioning, foodstuff conservation, nursing and child-rearing.

The meaning of the traditional nuclear family has greatly decreased in western Central Europe: in 2012, the average number of children per woman was 1.38 in Germany and 1.44 in Austria. The number of childless couples, temporary relationships and singles continues to rise, in turn causing the total number of households to skyrocket. As the individual household's capacity to supply its members declines, today's households instead represent a growing demand factor. Location and partner changes as well as double housekeeping for couples living apart often force people to buy new furniture and household items multiple times throughout their lives. Mobility and flexibility are connected to work, and the household has shifted its social meaning to new areas. Rather than subsistence, households concentrate more and more on monetary income, upon which they depend to participate in new areas of activity. In this sense, modern households can be seen as agents of commodification. Depending upon a household's purchasing power and consumption type, demand concentrates more heavily in classic consumer and educational goods (among the old working class and long-term employed), chic extravagancies, sometimes linked to tokenistic environmental awareness and events (among the upwardly mobile), and games and cheap junk from the factories of the world market (the precariat, the unemployed and social- assistance dependents). The lifestyles and consumption patterns of these fragmented workforces are as far apart from one another as their places of residence. Foreign migrant workers remain the only group able to maintain family subsistence in the context of transnational households, helping them to compensate for their low wages, fluctuating employment and lack of access to social services. This is, of course, further limited to those families who have a rural subsistence basis within travelling distance of their workplace; in the case of Central European workers, these would be workers from East and South-Eastern Europe and Turkey. In these circles, provisioning, foodstuff conservation and personal involvement in family celebrations and community events are commonplace, sometimes involving even the second and third generation. Independent migrant retailers and shop owners are also open to people from outside their ethnic community. Their trades, street markets and grocery stores provide services which would have long disappeared from the market if not for the migrant-family business model.

Partial subsistence activities of non-foreign resident populations are largely limited to knitting, tending herb gardens, making jam, house construction and car repair. The unemployed, insofar as they are not writing job applications, involved in various training programmes or forced to perform non-profit labour, could potentially have time for such self-sustaining activities. But do they have the knowledge and resources to do so? Not much ought to be expected here, given that social welfare authorities require one to abandon the pursuit of means of subsistence beyond the bare minimum. Experimentation with alternative ways of living thus remains restricted to well-off unconventional thinkers who can afford working without pay for a time – unless, that is, some sort of movement arises which, in the face of hardship, social spending cuts and the pressure to perform coerced labour, favours land occupations, community gardening and barter systems over the bureaucratic administration of social transfers. These subsistence, community and commons activists are pioneers in developing new forms of social reciprocity.

At the same time, we see an explosion of shadow work associated with online shopping, online banking and online administration and agencies. Even in cases where physical locations (stores, banks, offices) continue to exist, clients and customers increasingly replace personnel. Calling information hotlines has become an automated gauntlet of artificial voices. In the spirit of Ivan Illich's description of 'unpaid drudgery in industrial society/unpaid contribution to the managed economy',[193] unpaid shadow activities are quickly adapting to the digital transformation. With the general availability of smartphones and wireless Internet, personal consumption and financial management now extend octopus-like into every aspect of life, leaving absolutely no time for work-free free time. Its tentacles wrap around one's wage-earning activities and working times as well, but neither use value nor exchange value are created; conversely, participating in social life in the Internet age is increasingly impossible without this do-it-yourself shadow work. For online store owners, banks and authorities, shadow work performed by clients and consumers represents a substantial boon replacing the need for more civil servants, bank employees, representatives, consultants and salespeople. Massive economic advantages are gained through cost savings on personnel, branch offices and franchise networks as value transfer is sapped from the non-valued work of the customer. Along the way, the ambitious networkers offer a stream of constant data for targeted advertising as well as mass surveillance. In German, this process is often described as a transformation into *gläserne Menschen*, 'glass people' transparently carrying on our shadow work.

Interregional connections

Developments in Western and Central Europe occur against the backdrop of rising global challenges from the newly industrializing countries and competitive regional bloc formation in North America and the European Union. Competition for global leadership is heating up due to the current global economic crisis, accentuated by the polarization between cores and peripheries within the European Union. Germany, the driving force and flagship for concentration and expansion of the union, pursues a mixed strategy in order to preserve its competitiveness as a producer of high-value capital goods. Through internationalization of production sites by means of outsourcing, mergers and foreign direct investment, German companies exploit global wage differentials to reduce costs, while driving down unit costs through flexibilization and deregulation at the same time. This has made German exports highly competitive once again. Meanwhile, real wages in the southern and eastern member states have risen, but strong disparities in wages and taxes ensure that relocation and outsourcing remain lucrative options,[194] and that migrant workers continue to be drawn from the periphery to the core.

In Eastern Europe, this peripheralizing effect can be traced back to EU accession. The fully integrated factory combines erected under state socialism were subsequently shuttered or privatized and retooled to take up a position at the lower end of the commodity chain as component supply production sites.[195] Meanwhile, the flood of Western European export goods into Eastern markets dislodged a wide swathe of the labour force. Labour legislation followed the World Bank's recommendations in its 1995 annual report, which claimed that restriction of labour mobility was a crucial obstacle to transformation:

> Inflexible wages could undermine the restructuring of employment ... A lot is changing here but even in a liberalized environment there are often limitations to wage flexibility that could seriously slow the restructuring of employment ... Minimum wages that are too high prevent downward wage distribution and restrict new wage formation at a market-clearing price.[196]

Societies hitherto based on the notion of work for all thus subordinated themselves to the demands of capital accumulation.

The public social systems established under state socialism were abolished and replaced with social insurance schemes, albeit only to a very fragmentary degree. State health care and nursing facilities are generally in deplorable condition due to state spending cuts associated with joining the EU. Most suffer from a lack of infrastructure, personnel and operational necessities – from drugs to bed sheets, to canteen plates and the meals meant to be served on them – which are only provided for additional payment, or if the family decides to provide them. For those who can afford it, it is often best to avoid the public health system altogether.

These and other factors have fostered a widespread willingness to migrate to work in higher-paid countries. Substantial demand in Central and Western Europe exists within the health care and nursing sector (alongside gastronomy and construction), siphoning off qualified workers from Eastern European countries. At this point, even health care and nursing facilities offering regular contracts can no longer afford to dispense with Eastern European doctors, nurses and orderlies. This dynamic also extends into the informal sector in the form of private, home-based care. Nannies, housekeepers and cleaners replace employed mothers in the household. With twenty-four-hour nursing for seniors, a model for the transnational household has arisen in which nurses divide their lives between working for clients in Austria and Germany on the one hand, and caring for their families back home on the other. Depending on the distance travelled, two nurses will 'tag-team' for fourteen-day, monthly or multi-month stints in either location. In any case, the country of origin loses a person desperately needed in their home country as a paid worker in the state health care system where brain drain is sending away trained personnel, not to mention the impact felt by their families who must do without the care of their mothers and daughters.[197]

In Greece, Spain and Portugal, which all joined the European Community between 1981 and 1986, domestic agriculture, small businesses and the meagrely developed industry of these countries have failed to compete with import pressures from the Northern European industrial nations, a consequence of liberalization through the single market. Although tourism constituted an economic counterweight, it was concentrated on the coasts and islands, while the inland areas were left to haemorrhage. As long as imports could be financed on credit, internal migrants displaced from industry and agriculture found work in tourism and public service, and alternately, as long as EU projects provided hope and evidence of modernization, southern enlargement was celebrated as a success story. This impression faded as soon as the eagerly offered loans financed with exports from the north could no longer be repaid. Unequal division of labour had thus proved disadvantageous for both importing and exporting countries alike, but resolving or dissolving it (by leaving the eurozone, for instance) was no longer possible due to the strength of the financial sector. This is why Southern Europe, most notably Greece, now finds itself in the economic and social stranglehold of austerity overseen by the EU and international financial institutions. Such austerity is masked with innocuous-sounding terms like 'rescue mechanism' and 'parachute', while the costs of refinancing the troubled banks are handed off to the taxpayers of the northern countries.[198] The southern countries have lost their function of providing northern industries with an export market in the unequal division of labour and exchange within the EU. What remains is a bank bailout which tests the union's limits as to how far social cuts can go and how much disruption the population can take when labour markets, wages, state institutions and social nets collapse and the democratic system is effectively taken over by financial commissioners. The initial intention of large-scale management of the EU internal market, namely peripheralization of the south in order to augment the global competitiveness of the north, has continued *ad absurdum*. Accordingly, views of the European Union have dimmed in the public eye, while Eurosceptic movements are multiplying. Similar developments can be observed on the North American continent in relations between the post-industrial coasts, the agricultural north and the formerly industrial interior and south. Recent referendums and elections in both the US and the EU demonstrate that while supra-nationalization wanes, regionalism, nationalism and other fundamental alternatives to the supranational hegemonic claim wax.

Large-scale connections

The destruction of domestic economic and social structures through the liberalization of global trade and the delegitimization of regional and national protectionist regulatory practices can be observed on an intercontinental scale, and manifests in the growing willingness of people in the global South to leave their homes in search of an unknown future in the global North. The swell of people flowing up through the Mediterranean and Turkey is widely perceived as a threat in the core countries, and they are now being prevented from making the crossing with the help of North African countries and the Turkish state.

Departure, exodus and illegal immigration connect the South to the North on the macro-level. These in turn result from large-scale connections which both pre-empt and lay the groundwork for further migration. The big winners of free trade impose these conditions upon the South, forcing regional structures to bow to competitive pressure and leaving flight and migration as the only hope left to the uprooted masses. A particularly drastic example is the destruction of African coastal fisheries through the expansion of international fishing zones and the flooding of local markets with cheap poultry from the North. Overfishing and predation ruin an essential occupation as well as a subsistence sector, and it thus comes as little surprise when fishermen cut off from their economic lifelines make their way to the North, or convert their fishing boats into refugee ferries. The most versatile among them can make a living from deep-sea shipping, either as hired seamen or as pirates boarding those same vessels for ransom. The extreme division of labour characteristic of global commodity production today has turned the transport sector into a crucial strategic hinge, which – if blocked – can jeopardize just-in-time commodity production. The various countermeasures designed by the North are correspondingly heavy-calibre. The presiding global authority, the International Tribunal for the Law of the Sea (1996), is headquartered in Hamburg. In 2009, the increase in kidnapping cases led to demands for the establishment of an international court dedicated to piracy.[199]

The connection to the South is not perceived exclusively as a threat in the North. 'Global buyers' spread orders for single work steps and components that go into mass consumer goods over a long chain of producers and then monopolize sales. Consumers profit from the availability of cheaper products made in low-wage countries. Mobile phones, electronics, clothing, furnishings, household items and distant travel vacations are essential items in the developed world's shopping cart. The lower one's income, the more price is valued over quality – something that can only be achieved where low-wage labour is a factor. The 200 million Chinese migrants working twelve-hour days in the coastal areas for starvation wages while living in company-owned dormitories under constant surveillance even in their free time are only the tip of an ever more vociferous iceberg.[200] The denial of their household registration in the government *hukou* system is reminiscent of certain old European states' political domicile and residency laws, of which vestiges still exist in some places today. Household registration is the prerequisite for establishing one's household or starting a family and accessing schools, health care and social institutions. In zones of intense traffic congestion like Shanghai, even use of the urban expressways is linked to household registration. For people who cannot register their household in the city where they work, the dormitory is their only option. Their rural communities of origin are responsible for all other social security needs, but are simply unprepared to deal with such burdens. Therefore supporting their migrant sons and daughters remains the responsibility of the family back home.

NICs and developing countries are not only markets for the procurement of labour forces in global location chains controlled by 'global buyers' in the form of wholesalers, retailers and trademark owners. Rather, industrial modernization and the growth of cities and transport structures also provide Western corporations with another export opportunity. While the West generally imports low-tech items, its exports consist largely of logistical development, control systems, and other functions typical of post-industrial metropolises. However, in the interest of safeguarding employment and social stability, governments of the formerly industrial countries seek to continue high-quality, value-creation-intensive research and development in certain areas of production. While the Central European consumer goods industry was largely overwhelmed by cheap labour competition in many areas, the catch-up development of the NICs has opened an expanding sales market for the machinery and automobile industries. Eastern Asian NICs, most notably China, represent a promising market for German machine- and carmakers, secured through joint ventures. In this sense, they provide a kind of development aid by contributing to higher qualification and diversification of the economic structure in the ascendant regions of the South.[201]

The pauperization and criminalization of the global South is countered by the rise of the emerging BRICS, NEXT-11 and global swing states. These countries continue to compete in the mass consumer goods segments with wage, price, social and environmental dumping practices, but in recent years have also begun to leverage economic and development policy to transform their disadvantaged role in the global economy into one of dominance. To do so, they have taken the old industrial countries' rulebook for a liberalized, globalized world economy and applied it literally, resolutely exploiting their competitive advantages against the stagnating economies of the old core. The East and South Asian industrial countries invoke their centuries-old tradition of labour-intensive industrial specialization, which was made obsolete in the nineteenth century by the Western European developmental model, achieving production growth through mechanization, centralization and monopolization. Today, these newly industrialized countries have appropriated the model and augmented it with their traditions of skill and hard work; their young populations are hungry for education and oriented towards social mobility, with an unbroken faith in the viability of progress and the right to global equity through growth.

In this phase of catch-up development, emerging countries cannot rely solely on wage restraint and low consumption, but must take measures to integrate migrant workers, the landless and day labourers into their social security systems, while facilitating social mobility for the middle classes and allowing them enrichment and consumption. All of these developments can clearly be seen in China and Brazil.[202] Both countries are no longer satisfied with their positions at the low end of the chain, characterized by contract manufacturing and consumption restraint, and have gone on the offensive in terms of education, research and development into new sectors, high tech and logistics in global commodity chains. This has been accompanied by an expansion of domestic demand, the securing of procurement and sales through acquisitions and foreign direct investment, and the lowering of production costs through inland relocation of labour-intensive work processes or outsourcing to neighbouring low-wage regions. In this way, the semi-peripheries are connecting with their own backyards and peripheries. It is not unthinkable that global capitalism, declared moribund in light of its most recent crisis-prone contradictions, may yet be saved by a new hegemonic cycle with a Chinese, East Asian or even multiple Southern cores throwing their shadow across Europe and the United States. The political turmoil in Brazil in 2016 ought to be taken as a warning that prognoses may be premature, or turn out not to be true at all. If European and American states were to become connected as semi-peripheries into a world economy under the control of the global South, they would have no other choice but to conform to the prevailing global culture of work. In the role of supplier to commodity chains controlled from elsewhere, it can be assumed that division and polarization will befall Western economic and social structures in a fashion similar to the experience of the global South under colonialism and neocolonialism.

We cannot predict the future, but it is very possible that the path to this or another future will cross a point of hegemonic succession through a military show of strength, another great war. Jean Christophe Rufin imagines how the world might look after such a showdown in his utopian novel *Globalia*, intended as a warning to its readers.[203] This work of fiction can be interpreted as a plea for a peaceful transition.

7.

Combining Labour Relations
in the *Longue Durée*

Last but not least, we will discuss sequential patterns and developmental trends in the division of labour and composition of different labour relations. First, we will turn to the quantitative side of this question in order to sum up the most important economic tendencies. In contrast to linear notions typically characteristic of scholarly thinking on global development, we look at the cyclical course of globalization, which manifests temporally in tendencies towards concentration and deglomeration, and spatially in tendencies towards expansion, contraction and displacement of leading regions and sectors. In this sense, the ever-changing combination of labour relations can be expressed in terms of simultaneity and non-simultaneity.

RELATIONS

A significant limitation to quantifying labour relations lies in the lack of reliable data. Over time, statistics on work and labour have been collected by specific actors like individual companies, guilds, lobbies, unions or government agencies. However, these never reflect the total scope of work forms in a given society at a given time, are usually focused on a single area, and employ highly divergent categories. Official statistics which introduced uniform methods of accounting in the nineteenth century improved comparability between figures, while both internal comparisons and those between states have grown more accurate through the internationalization of statistics. At the same time, however, the categories of data collection solidified into unchangeable facts, which obscured and suppressed forms of work that failed to conform to these parameters, leading the fields of planning, management and academia to leave these forms of work out of their calculations. Most notably, the coexistence of work forms combined by a single person or within families remains largely excluded even today. Either–or questions in the interest of acquiring knowledge in fact do just the opposite by excluding that which makes human cohabitation possible in the first place: cooperation and complementation of one another's strengths. They also ignore a grey area of activities in which the characters who carry them out are not obvious, and – due to the prevailing way of speaking – may not even see themselves as 'working' in the first place. A quantitative representation of changing labour relations is thus beyond the scope of this study.

Several efforts to overcome the limits of statistics can be observed in the areas of under-the-table, undeclared labour and domestic work. Here, researchers have specialized in ways of determining the extent of illegal and irregular relations of employment through estimations and by drawing on select data in order to quantify the amount of work performed which does not appear in the national product figures, and thus evades taxation.[1] In the area of household studies, calculations are carried out from various angles to determine how many working hours go unremunerated in this sphere.[2] Although these scholarly innovations are commendable, they give the (false) impression (through their restriction to partial aspects) that everything else is adequately represented in employment and national product statistics.

All the more commendable is thus the Global Collaboratory on the History of Labour Relations 1500–2000 initiated by the International Institute of Social History (IISH) in Amsterdam,[3] which is compiling a database for the comparison of labour relations worldwide. The initiative's primary merit was to create a taxonomy of labour relations and working conditions covering all existing forms of work, distinguishing between four major categories (the non-working population, and reciprocal, tributary and commodified work), which are in turn divided into subcategories.

In a further step, IISH project researchers have taken on the task of analysing available statistical sources from various countries across five historical cross-sections from 1500 to 2000 on the basis of these categories. Joint reflection on the methodological problems in collecting and assessing the sources played a decisive role in the process. The basic data points used were the proportion of economically active people (the working population) among the population as a whole and their connection to various labour relations and forms of employment, whereby the simultaneity and proportion of individual labour relations to the entirety of work performed were of particular interest. The results of this research can be viewed online. Anyone hoping to use this data to construct worldwide statistical analysis of the evolution of work, however, will be disappointed. The data provide no clear overview even on a regional level, while the degree of significance and distribution of the categories are subject to broad interpretation. As the project continues its work and approaches completion, comparability between datasets will improve to some degree. The project has already fostered a broad international discussion around the conception of work and labour relations, to which this volume contributes.

An even more complicated issue is raised by the quantification of value creation and value transfer through various forms of work. In the context of human lifeworlds, we can easily demonstrate that unpaid housework, subsistence and care activities contribute to supporting the household member who is gainfully employed, and provide, as a whole, the necessary conditions for value creation to occur in the monetary economy. Reciprocally, workers support their families with their income; state and social security systems also provide for the redistribution of worker incomes to non-workers. How hours spent carrying out various forms of work complement each other specifically, who appropriates them, and how the value and surplus value created are distributed among the parties involved are not, in factual terms, unsolvable matters. Yet major obstacles arise when attempting to quantify the hours of unpaid work that go into the production of transfer values.[4] On what basis should love or care work be evaluated? Comparable professional service providers either charge disproportionately high rates (for therapy sessions, for example), or provide cleaning services at prices so low so as to fill up some fictive work-value account of a housewife or househusband only in the most marginal sense. Such calculations help to understand labour relations and illustrate the extent of non- and underpaid activities, but cannot solve the problems of unequal workload and distribution.

This also became evident with the symbolic compensation offered by Germany and Austria to the survivors of forced labour under the Nazi regime in 2000 – compensation which only the longest-living among them were left to receive. The offer could in no way cover the loss of earnings, not to mention the years of their lives stolen from them, but laid bare an injustice that simultaneously awakened desires among a whole gamut of people pressed into forced labour who have yet to receive such recognition.

Tendencies

Looking back on the time between 1250 and today, the following tendencies emerge:

- The tendency towards the monetization of social exchange.
- The tendency towards the commodification of reciprocal work.
- The establishment of gainful employment as a separate sphere independent of life context.
- The tendency of coerced, forced, unfree labour to become free and voluntary work. Thus we also see a reduction in the proportion of tribute-based work acquired as a result of personal dependency relationships in the form of labour rents.
- The tendency towards housewife-ization – that is, the tendency of subsistence work once performed in both domestic and production contexts to transform into unpaid housework. Reciprocal work is increasingly connoted as 'women's work' or 'unproductive' even when not specifically carried out by a woman.
- Within commodified labour, the tendency of independent work to become dependent employment for someone else (proletarianization).
- Proletarianization dovetailed with the creation of a legally and socially protected sector of employment (formalization, regulation).

All of these tendencies continue to change the overall structure of social labour relations in local, regional and global respects, triggering further changes in other sectors and other regions which must be understood as simultaneously operating after-effects or countertendencies:

- Tributary work in the form of labour or product rents were replaced by monetary rents or payments to the property owner. Tribute to the nobility was replaced by state taxation.
- The emancipation realized in the abolition of slavery and serfdom was not simply a product of proletarianization – new forms of

pauperism and forced labour arose in their stead (debt bondage, new forms of slavery).

- The loss of immediate subsistence opportunities could only partially be replaced with commodities. Scarcity resulted, driving further commodification on the one hand, yet continually renewing a search for reciprocal basics in times of emergency and crisis on the other. The result of scarcity was, of course, often violent conflict over land and resources.

- The tendency towards formalization and regulation of gainful employment and social security remained limited to privileged groups both socially and regionally, and to key sectors at the cores of the global economy. They now face informalization, which is currently returning to the cores in the wake of frequent crises.

SIMULTANEITY

Observing the combination of labour relations at an individual point in time, we find specific connections at any given location. The connections we see reflect their position within the regional, national or international division of labour, while each location-specific connection links up with a broader global context. The differences between relations are what enables the cohesion of the entire system. However, due to the differential being based on continual transfer processes between regions with diverse labour portfolios, it also constantly reproduces inequality. One decisive factor for social inequality on the local level is the appropriation of surplus value from paid work by those who employ a dependent workforce, which gives the employer access to the unpaid work of the worker's family members. In international relations, transfer value from unpaid work plays a greater role than surplus value. Transfer value is incurred anywhere a region is able to disproportionately acquire unpaid work through unequal trade with another region. In the present study, this is shown in connection with interregional commodity chains whose low-end producers survive on meagre wages through the subsistence production of their families and communities, and with the example of workers migrating between regions with differing factor markets. Migrant workers often depend on the reciprocal work of family back home in order to survive in a global household. Unequal trade occurs within the monetary sphere, where products are manufactured by a paid work-force – however, every market product and every remunerated migrant worker transports unpaid work from its place of origin to its location of appropriation. Redistributive monetary flows in state and international contexts (financial compensation, regional policy and development aid, and so on) work against the value drain out of the periphery. Regardless of the difficulties posed in accounting for and evaluating these factors, they play a central role in stabilizing the foundations upon which to maintain this transfer.

Tendencies towards commercialization, commodification and pro-letarianization can be observed throughout the world, albeit often at different times. Occurring later does not signify backwardness, but is rather an expression of the simultaneous existence of differing condi-tions of production and labour relations as these unfold temporally and geographically. The analytical assumptions found in linear notions of 'catch-up' development have thus far not been confirmed. Much more likely is that transitions and sequences of unfolding conditions and relations can be conceived of as emergent phenomena that ascribe themselves into the cyclical movements of the world economy. One of these phenomena is the wave-like fluctuation between formalization and informalization. Formalization, regulation and sociopolitical safeguards of labour relations are not representative of proletarianization as such. Rather, these are the characteristics exhibited by global economic cores for roughly one hundred years between the 1880s and the 1980s. These characteristics did not transfer over to the emerging markets, where industrialization only began in the twentieth century. Instead, these countries saw their informal sectors and subsistence economies perma-nently take on a much more significant role alongside the formal sectors than was the case in the old industrial countries. The prevalence of infor-mal and subsistence sectors in newly industrializing countries translates into competitive pressures for the old industrial countries, as the com-binatory model of the NICs has an impact on labour regulations in the old cores. This dynamic began to take effect in the 1990s, and has since unleashed a wave of informalization and deregulation of labour relations hitherto taken for granted in the global economic cores.

In the wake of industrial expansion in the newly industrialized countries of Asia and Latin America, dependent gainful employment is gaining ground – bringing the core strata of the new working classes more social protections after only a few years. Additionally, the capitalist cycle was temporarily interrupted by a period of planned economics in formerly socialist states. Achievements made therein have been partially preserved and now coexist with new informal and formal occupational conditions as a segment of global commodity chains. But employment secured through legal means and collective bargaining is in decline in the old European industrial states, as well as in the post-Communist states. Unsecured, precarious occupations are growing at the expense of secured employment, both independent (self-employed) and dependent (jobs without social protections).

To the same extent that emerging economies will rise to occupy the core positions of the global economy and global swing states define the rules of the global economy, relations to the old cores are undergoing a process of reordering. When the latter lose their dominant positions in the global commodity chains and capital flows, assuming supplier roles for the new cores, the effects will be felt within the local and global composition of labour relations. New East Asian industrial powers are walking in the footsteps of the old colonial and core powers, both in terms of raw-material and foodstuff security, and in the use of extended workbenches in low-wage regions.

A continuation of non-simultaneity under new circumstances can also be expected. On the one hand, it is entirely possible that the increased desertification of reciprocity will destroy the material basis needed for the renewal of global capitalism's bases of accumulation. There are also signs, however, that under the pressure of capitalist crisis a reactivation of subsistence spheres is swelling from below, potentially allowing certain areas to escape the functionalization demanded of them by capital accumulation.

Appendix

A Lexical Comparison Across
European Languages

This overview expresses the wide-ranging lexical field with which work activities are described in select European languages. It demonstrates the diverse terminological instrumentarium by which work is distinguished according to the kind of activity (as noun, verb, and label for the person performing the activity), product, labour relations and type of identification. Common political–economic terms from the area of labour administration are also included. Terms correspond to their contemporary usage. Differences in meaning between individual languages cannot be further explored here. Moreover, divergent meanings can cause loan words to change their meaning when adopted into a foreign language.

You can read more on this in Chapter 3 (p. 39), which is dedicated to language as a tool in exploring social relations and historical transformations of labour relations.

ENGLISH	GERMAN	FRENCH	ITALIAN
Activity // verb // actor	**Tätigkeit // Verb //** AusübendeR	**Activité // verbe //** personne	**Attività // verbo //** attore
work // to work // worker	Arbeit // arbeiten // ArbeiterIn	Travail // travailler // travailleur, ouvrier	lavoro // lavorare // lavoratore/lavoratrice
(wage) labour // to labour // labourer	Lohnarbeit // (für Bezahlung) arbeiten // LohnarbeiterIn	travail salarié ou rémunéré // travailler // salarié(e), travailleur (travailleuse)	lavoro salariato (con retribuzione) // lavoratore retribuito
hard labour // to toil, to labour // unskilled labourer	Schwerarbeit // schwer arbeiten // SchwerarbeiterIn	travail pénible, labeur // homme de peine, manœuvre	lavoro di fatica, lavoro pesante //
craft, artisanry // practicing a craft // crafts(wo)man or artisan	Handwerk // Handwerk ausüben // HandwerkerIn	artisanat // artisan	lavoro artigianal // esercitare un mestiere artigianale // artigiano
housework // to do housework // housewife (househusband)	Hausarbeit // Hausarbeit leisten // Hausfrau (Hausmann)	travaux domestiques, ménage // tenir un ménage // ménagère	lavoro domestico // domestico/domestica
subsistance // to subsist // subsistence (farmer)	Selbstversorgung // sich selbst versorgen // SelbstversorgerIn	autarcie, autosuffisance // travailler en autarcie	autosufficienza, indipendenza economica
service // to serve // servant	Dienst // Dienst leisten // DienerIn, Magd, Knecht	service, domesticité // travailler au service de qqn // serviteur, domestique	servizio // prestare servizio, essere a servizio // servitore/servitrice
enterprise // to employ // employer	Unternehmen // unternehmen // UnternehmerIn, ArbeitgeberIn	entreprise // entreprendre, employer // employeur	impresa // impresario/ imprenditore, datore/ datrice di lavoro
to have hobby // leisure activity	Hobby // Hobby haben, Steckenpferd ausüben	loisir // pratiquer une activité de loisir	hobby, passatempo // coltivare un hobby
makeshift job // to get by, to do odd jobs // casual or temporary worker	// Sich-durch-Bringen	débrouille, démerde // se débrouiller par soi-même // débrouillard (adj), bricolage // bricoler // bricoleur	// arrangiarsi

SPANISH	RUSSIAN	POLISH	SERBIAN
Actividad // verbo // persona	Dejatel'nost' // glagol // ispolnitel'	Czynność // czasownik // wykonawca (wykonawczyni)	Delatnost // glagol // delatnik
trabajo // trabajar // trabajador, obrero	rabota // rabotat' // rabočij; trud // trudit'sja // trudjaščijsja ~ajasja	praca // pracować // robotnik, pracownik	rad // raditi // radnik
empleo, trabajo asalariado // trabajar // empleado, asalariado	rabota, naëmnyj trud // (tjaželo) rabotat', trudit'sja // (naëmnyj) rabočij, rabotnik	praca najemna // pracownik najemny	posao, zaposlenje // raditi // radnik, zaposleni
trabajo duro/ // trabajar forzadamente, con esfuerzo, como un negro	tjaželaja rabota // rabočij, zanjatyj na tjaželych rabotach, rabočij nekvalificirovannogo truda, raznorabočij	ciężka praca, robota (ugs.)	naporan rad, trud // naporno raditi // trudbenik
artesanía // hacer artesanías // artesano, artista, maestro	remeslo // remeslennik	rzemiosło // wykonywać rzemiosło // rzemieślnik	zanat // baviti se zanatom // zanatlija
trabajo del hogar // hacer el oficio // trabajo doméstico, ama de casa	domašnjaja rabota // domochozjajka	praca domowa // wykonywać pracę domową // gospodyni	kućni posao // raditi kućni posao // domaćica
autobastecimiento, autosuficiencia económica, subsistencia // subsistir (=am Existenzminimum leben)	natural'noe chozjastvo // žit' natural'nym chozjajstvom; podsobnoe chozjajstvo (=Subsistenzwirtschaften der Kolchoz/ Sovchozbauern oder Arbeiter mit Häuschen und Grundstück)	praca samowystarczalna //	proizvodnja za sopstvenu upotrebu, samoopskrbljivanje
servicio // servir // sirvienta/e, peón	služba // služit' // sluga, služanka, prisluga	usługa // usługiwać // sługa, chłopka, chłop	usluga, služba // vršiti uslugu, službu // sluga, sluškinja, kmet
empresa // emprender // empresario/a, patrón, empleador/a	predpijatie // predprinimatel', rabotodatel'	przedsiębiorca, pracodawca // przedsiębiorstwo	preduzeće // poslovati // preduzetnik, poslodavac
hobby (angliz.) // practicar un hobby/ tener una afición //	uvlečenie, chobbi, konëk //	hobby //	hobi // imati hobi
// sacar (se) adelante, sustentar(se)	vremennoe zanjatie // probivat'sja, probavljat'sja (vremennymi zarabotkami)	zarobić na życie	snalaziti se za posao

ENGLISH	GERMAN	FRENCH	ITALIAN
Result	**Resultat**	**Résultat**	**Risultato**
(piece of) work, workmanship	Werk, Arbeit	travail, ouvrage	opera, lavoro
service	Dienstleistung	un service	prestazione di servizio
artwork	Kunstwerk	oeuvre d'art	opera d'arte
a day's work	Tagwerk	une journée de travail	attività giornaliera
product	Produkt	produit	prodotto
commodity	Ware	marchandise	merce
output, performance, production	Leistung	rendement, production	prestazione, servizio
Labour	**Arbeitsverhältnis**	**Statut**	**Rapporto di lavoro**
employment, job	Anstellung, unselbständige Beschäftigung	travail, emploi	impiego, lavoro dipendente
self-employment, self-dependance	Selbständige Beschäftigung	travail indépendant, travail à son compte	lavoro indipendente/ autonomo
gainful employment, occupation, profession	Erwerbstätigkeit, Berufstätigkeit	profession, métier	occupazione, professione
wage labour	Lohnarbeit	travail salarié, profession	lavoro retribuito/ salariato
duty, obligation	Pflicht	tâche, fonction	dovere, obbligo, incombenza
office, position, post, job	Amt, Posten, Stellung	poste, fonction	ufficio, posto, funzione
corvée labour, servitude	Robot, Fron	corvée, servitude	servitù della gleba
slavery	Sklaverei	esclavage	schiavitù
forced / coerced labour	Zwangsarbeit, Arbeitsdienst	travail forcé	lavoro coatto
apprenticeship	Lehre	apprentissage	apprendistato
internship	Praktikum	stage non rémunéré	praticantato, stage
temp(orary) work	Leiharbeit	intérim	lavoro a tempo determinato

SPANISH	RUSSIAN	POLISH	SERBIAN
Resultado	**Rezul'tat**	**Rezultat**	**Rezultat**
obra, trabajo	trud, proizvedenie, rabota	dzieło, praca	delo, proizvod
servicio	usluga	usługa	usluga, uslužna delatnost servis
obra, obra de arte	proizvedenie iskusstva	dzieło	umetničko delo
trabajo diario, quehacer	ežednevnaja (povsednevnaja) rabota, rabota za den'	dniówka	dnevni učinak
producto	produkt, izdelie	produkt	proizvod
mercancía, artículo	tovar	towar	roba
rendimiento, eficacia, prestación, contribución	proizvedënnaja rabota, vyrabotka	świadczenie	učinak
Relación jurídica	**Trudovoe/ye (pravo) otnošenie/-ija**	**Stosunek pracy**	**Radni odnos**
empleo, contratación, puesto	rabota po najmu, zanjatie, nesamostojatel'naja rabota	praca, zatrudnienie niesamodzielne	zaposlenje
trabajo independiente	rabota ne po najmu, samostojatel'naja trudovaja dejatel'nost'	zatrudniene samodzielne	samostalna delatnost
ocupación, actividad profesional/ renumerada	zanjatic, trudovaja/ professional'naja dejatel'nost'	czynność, czynność zawodowa, zawód wykonywany	zanimanje
trabajo asalariado	naëmnyj trud	praca najemna	plaćen posao
obligación, deber, cometido	objazannosti	obowiązek	dužnost
cargo, puesto	dolžnost'	urząd, stanowisko, pozycja	služba, nameštenje
corvada, servidumbre, trabajo improbo	barščina	pańszczyzna	kuluk
esclavitud	rabstvo, rabskij trud	niewolnictwo	ropstvo
trabajo forzado	prinuditel'ny trud, prinuditel'nye raboty, trudovaja povinnost'	praca przymusowa, praca służbowa	prinudan rad
aprendizaje	obučenie	przyuczenie	obuka, ići na zanat
prácticas	dobrovol'naja rabota/služba, neoplačivaemaja stažirovka	wolontariat, praktyka bez wynagrodzenia	praksa, praktika
préstamismo (laboral), trabajo temporal/estacional	(po) vremennaja rabota, sdeľščina	praca tymczasowa	najamni rad, najam

ENGLISH	GERMAN	FRENCH	ITALIAN
to work under the table, have a side job, moonlighting, working on the black market	Schwarzarbeit	travail au noir	lavoro in nero
Identification	**Identifikation, Bestimmung**	**Identification, resenti**	**Determinazione**
profession, career	Beruf	métier, profession	mestiere
vocation	Berufung	vocation	vocazione
task, job	Aufgabe	tâche	compito
voluntary or volunteer work	Ehrenamt, Volontariat	bénévolat	volontariato
Workforce administration: polit-economic terms	**Arbeitsverwaltung: politisch-ökonomische Begriffe**	**Ressources humaines: lexique politico-économique**	**Gestione/ amministrazione del lavoro: concetti politico-economici**
labour force	Arbeitskraft	main d'œuvre	manodopera, forza-lavoro, maestranze
workforce, manpower	Verfügbare Arbeitskräfte, Arbeitspotential	personnel	manodopera disponibile, personale
workplace, job, work	Arbeitsplatz	emploi	luogo di lavoro
labour market	Arbeitsmarkt	marché de travail	mercato del lavoro
employment agency	Arbeitsagentur	agence de placement	centro per l'impiego (ex ufficio di collocamento)
use value	Gebrauchswert	valeur d'usage	valore d'uso
exchange value	Tauschwert	valeur d'échange	valore di scambio

SPANISH	RUSSIAN	POLISH	SERBIAN
trabajo ílegal/ clandestino, obra negra	levaja rabota, nelegal'naja rabota	praca na czarno	rad na crno
Identificación	Identificacija	Identyfikacja, przeznaczenie	identifikacija, određenje
profesión	professija, special'nosť	zawód	profesija, zanimanje
vocación	prizvanie	powołanie	poziv, zvanje
tarea, reto, deber	zadača, zadanie	zadanie	zadatak
cargo honorífico, voluntariado	obščestvenaja rabota, početnaja dolžnosť, rabota volonterom	urząd honorowy	počasna, dobrovoljna, volonterska služba (dužnost)
Administración laboral: términos político-económicos	Upravlenie trudovymi resursami: polit-ėkonomičeskie ponjatija	Zarządzanie: polityczno-ekonomiczne pojęcia	organizacija rada: ekonomsko-politički pojmovi
mano de obra, capacidad productiva	rabočaja sila	siła robocza	radna snaga
recursos humanos, fuerzas disponibiles	kadry, rabočaja sila	potencjał pracowniczy	ljudske radne rezerve (potencijal), raspoloživa radna snaga
lugar de trabajo, empleo, puesto	rabočee mesto	miejsce pracy	radno mesto
mercado laboral, mercado de trabajo	rynok truda	rynek pracy	tržište rada
instituto de empleo, agencia de colocación	centr zanjatosti, birža truda	agencja pracy	zavod za zapošljavanje
valor útil, valor de uso	potrebiteľskaja stojmosť	wartość użtkowa	upotrebna vrednost
valor de cambio	menovaja stojmosť	wartość wymienna	vrednost razmene

I would like to thank Dariusz Adamczyk, Kamil Dolhun, Sabine Hanisch, Gordana Ilić Marković, Alexej Klutschewsky, Stefano Petroungaro and Hervé Tilly for their assistance in compiling this table.

Notes

INTRODUCTION

1   *Translator's note*: The German term *Arbeitsverhältnisse* – literally 'labour relations' or 'relations of labour' – encompasses more than relations of employment, but rather denotes the whole ensemble of social relations and working conditions encompassing the world of work. Recently, 'labour relations' has become more common in English-language scholarship, as seen in, for example, the work of the Global Collaboratory on the History of Labour Relations discussed later in this volume. It is used here for clarity's sake. See International Institute for Social History (IISG) Amsterdam, *The Global Collaboratory on the History of Labour Relations 1500–2000*, at http://collab.iisg.nl/web/LabourRelations.

2   Janet Abu-Lughod, *Before European Hegemony: The World System A.D. 1250–1350*, Oxford, 1989.

3   Andre Gunder Frank, *ReOrient: Global Economy in the Asian Age*, Berkeley, Los Angeles and London, 1998.

4   Immanuel Wallerstein, *The Modern World-System, Volume 1: Capitalist Agriculture and the Origins of the European World-Economy in the 16th Century; Volume 2: Mercantilism and the Consolidation of the European World-Economy, 1600–1750; Volume 3: The Second Era of Great Expansion of the Capitalist World-Economy, 1730–1840s; Volume 4: Centrist Liberalism Triumphant, 1789–1914*, Berkeley, 2011.

1. TERMS AND CONCEPTS

1   Andrea Komlosy, 'Arbeitsverhältnisse und Gesellschaftsformationen', in Markus Cerman, Franz X. Eder, Peter Eigner, Andrea Komlosy and Erich Landsteiner, eds., *Wirtschaft und Gesellschaft Europa 1000–2000*, Innsbruck, 2011, 244–63, 244.

2   Werner Conze, 'Arbeit', in Reinhart Koselleck, Otto Brunner and Werner Conze, eds., *Geschichtliche Grundbegriffe: Historisches Lexikon zur politisch-sozialen Sprache in Deutschland*, Bd. 1, Stuttgart, 1972, 154–215.

3   Max Weber, *Economy and Society: An Outline of Interpretive Sociology* (1922), Berkeley, CA, 1978; Weber, *The Protestant Ethic and the Spirit of Capitalism* (1904–5), London, 2001.

4   See Herbert Applebaum, *The Concept of Work: Ancient, Medieval, and Modern*, New York, 1992; Michael S. Aßländer, *Von der vita activa zur industriellen Wertschöpfung*, Marburg, 2005; Josef Ehmer and Edith Saurer, 'Arbeit', in Friedrich Jäger, ed., *Enzyklopädie der Neuzeit*, Bd. I, Stuttgart and Weimar, 2005, 507–33; Manfred Füllsack, *Arbeit*, Vienna, 2009; Jürgen Kocka and Claus Offe, eds., *Geschichte und Zukunft der Arbeit*, Frankfurt am Main and New York, 2000.

5   For a summary of critical objections and open questions see, among others, Josef Ehmer and Catharina Lis, eds., *The Idea of Work in Europe from Antiquity to Modern Times*, Farnham, 2009.

6   Conze, 'Arbeit', 174.

7   Ibid., 175.

8   Adam Smith, *An Inquiry into the Nature and Cause of the Wealth of Nations* (1776), vol. 1, Oxford, 1976, 330.

9   David Ricardo, *On the Principles of Political Economy, and Taxation* (1821), 3rd edition, Kitchener, ON, 2001.

10 Conze, 'Arbeit', 193.

11 Andreas Heyer, *Die Utopie steht links!*, Berlin, 2006.

12 Claude Henri de Rouvroy, comte de Saint-Simon, *Doctrine de Saint-Simon: Exposition première année*, Brussels, 1831.

13 Georg Wilhelm Friedrich Hegel, *Phenomenology of Spirit* (1807), trans. A. V. Miller, Oxford, 1977.

14 Birgit van den Hoven, *Work in Ancient and Medieval Thought: Ancient Philosophers, Medieval Monks and Theologians and their Concept of Work, Occupations and Technology*, Amsterdam, 1996.

15 Ehmer and Lis, *The Idea of Work*.

16 Andrea Komlosy, *Globalgeschichte: Methoden und Theorien*, Vienna, 2011.

17 Friedrich Schiller, 'What Is, and to What End Do We Study, Universal History?' (1789), in *Friedrich Schiller: Poet of History*, Schiller Institute, 1988, 253–72, 259.

18 *Das ganze Haus*, 'the whole house', denotes the household, its attendant tasks, and the members who perform them as a single economic entity. This concept first emerged in early German social science, pioneered by figures like Otto Brunner.

19 Gisela Bock and Barbara Duden, 'Arbeit aus Liebe – Liebe als Arbeit: Zur Entstehung der Hausarbeit im Kapitalismus', in *Frauen und Wissenschaft: Beiträge zur Berliner Sommeruniversität für Frauen 1976*, Berlin, 1977, 118–99; Karin Hausen, *Geschlechtergeschichte als Gesellschaftsgeschichte*, Göttingen, 2012.

20 Komlosy, 'Arbeitsverhältnisse und Gesellschaftsformationen', 247.

21 Maria Mies, Veronika Bennholdt-Thomsen, Claudia von Werlhof, *Women: The Last Colony*, London and Atlantic Highlands, NJ, 1988.

22   Edward W. Said, *Orientalism*, New York, 1978; Dipesh Chakrabarty, *Provincializing Europe: Postcolonial Thought and Historical Difference*, Princeton, 2008.

23   Michel Cartier, ed., *Le travail et ses représentations*, Paris and Montreux 1984, 11–15; Georg Elwert, 'Jede Arbeit hat ihr Alter: Arbeit in einer afrikanischen Gesellschaft', in Kocka and Offe, *Geschichte und Zukunft der Arbeit*, 175–96; Füllsack, *Arbeit*, 13ff.

24   Gerd Spittler, 'Work: Anthropological Aspects', in Neil J. Smelser and Paul B. Baltes, eds., *Encyclopedia of the Social and Behavioral Sciences*, Amsterdam, 2001, 16561–9, 16567.

25   Marcel van der Linden, *Workers of the World: Essays toward a Global Labor History*, Leiden and Boston, 2008; Marcel van der Linden and Leo Lucassen, eds., *Working on Labor: Essays in Honor of Jan Lucassen*, Leiden, 2012; Jan Lucassen, ed., *Global Labour History: A State of the Art*, Bern, 2006; Chris Tilly and Charles Tilly, *Work under Capitalism*, Boulder, CO, 1998.

26   Wallerstein, *The Modern World-System*.

27   Alejandro Portes, Manuel Castells and Lauren Benton, *The Informal Economy: Studies in Advanced and Less Developed Countries*, Baltimore, 1989; Andrea Komlosy, Christof Parnreiter, Irene Stacher and Susan Zimmermann, eds., *Ungeregelt und unterbezahlt: Der informelle Sektor in der Weltwirtschaft*, Frankfurt am Main and Vienna, 1997.

28   Gary Gereffi, 'The Organization of Buyer-Driven Commodity Chains: How US Retailers Shape Overseas Production Networks', in Gary Gereffi and Miguel Korzeniewicz, eds., *Commodity Chains and Global Capitalism*, Westport, CT, 1994, 95–122; Nicola Yeates, *Globalizing Care Economies and Migrant Workers: Explorations in Global Care Chains*, Basingstoke, 2009.

29   Dirk Hoerder, *Cultures in Contact: World Migrations in the Second Millennium*, Durham, NC, 2002; Dirk Hoerder and Amarjit Kaur, eds., *Proletarian and Gendered Mass Migrations*, Leiden and Boston, 2013.

30   Marcel van der Linden, ed., *Grenzüberschreitende Arbeitergeschichte: Konzepte und Erkundungen*, Leipzig, 2010; van der Linden and Lucassen, *Working on Labor*; Karl-Heinz Roth, 'An Encyclopaedist of Critical Thought: Marcel van der Linden, Heterodox Marxism and Global Labour History', in Karl Heinz, Roth, ed., *On the Road to Global Labour History: A Festschrift for Marcel van der Linden*, Leiden and London, 2017, 263–351.

31   See Jan Lucassen, 'Outlines of a History of Labour', IISH-Research Paper 51, 2013.

2. WORK DISCOURSES

1   See e.g. Johann A. Schnebelin, *Das neu entdeckte Schlaraffenland: Johann Andreas Schnebelins Erklärung der Wunderseltzamen Land-Charten UTOPIAE* (1694), Bad Langensalza, 2004.

2   Paul Lafargue, 'The Right to Be Lazy' (1883), in Lafargue, *The Right to Be Lazy (Essays by Paul Lafargue)*, ed. Bernard Marszalek, Chicago, 2011, 51.

3   Heyer, *Die Utopie steht links!*, 33.

4   Most recently in Öko-Sozialismus, a 2013 special issue of the German-language magazine *Lunapark21: Zeitschrift zur Kritik der globalen Ökononomie*.

5   Christel Neusüß, *Kopfgeburten der Arbeiterbewegung oder Die Genossin Luxemburg bringt alles durcheinander*, Hamburg and Zurich, 1985.

6   Karl Marx, 'Economic and Philosophical Manuscripts' (1844), in Marx, *Early Writings*, trans. Rodney Livingstone and Gregor Benton, London, 1992, 357. Emphasis in original.

7   Conze, 'Arbeit', 203.

8   Marx Karl, *Grundrisse: Foundations of the Critique of Politicaly Economy (Rough Draft)* (1939), London, 1993, 711f.

9   Karl Marx and Friedrich Engels, 'A Critique of the German Ideology' (1845–47), in *Marx and Engels, Collected Works*, vol. 5, London, 1976, 19–539, 47.

10   Karl Marx, *Capital*, vol. 3 (1894), trans. David Fernbach, London, 1991, 958f.

11   Ibid.

12   Johann Gottlieb Fichte, *The Characteristics of the Present Age* (1806), trans. William Smith, Gloucester, 2008, 32.

13   Conze, 'Arbeit', 197; Heyer, *Die Utopie steht links!*, 7–37.

14   Written in 1863 by Georg Herwegh, set to music by Georg Eisler in 1910.

15   Written in 1867 by engraver journeyman Josef Zapf (1847–1902) for the Workers' Educational Association in Vienna-Gumpendorf, set to music by Josef Scheu.

16   Susan Zimmermann, 'Geschlechterhierarchien und Geschlechterverhält-nisse', in Cerman et al., *Wirtschaft und Gesellschaft Europa*, 365–91.

17   Louise Otto-Peters, *Das Recht der Frauen auf Erwerb* (1866), Leipzig, 1997.

18   Shulamith Firestone, *The Dialectic of Sex: The Case for Feminist Revolution*, New York, 1970.

19   Von Werlhof, Mies and Bennholdt-Thomsen, *Women*.

20   Claudia von Werlhof, *Die Verkehrung: Das Projekt des Patriarchats und das Gender-Dilemma*, Vienna, 2011.

21   Almut Bachinger, 'Der irreguläre Pflegearbeitsmarkt: Zum Transformation-sprozess von unbezahlter in bezahlte Arbeit durch die 24-Stunden-Pflege', dissertation, University of Vienna, 2009.

22   Helma Lutz, *Vom Weltmarkt in den Privathaushalt: Die neuen Dienstmädchen im Zeitalter der Globalisierung*, Opladen and Farmington Hills, 2007.

3. WORK AND LANGUAGE

1   Füllsack, *Arbeit*, 9.

2   See, for example, Hannah Arendt, *The Human Condition* (1958), 2nd edition, Chicago, 1998.

3   Richard Biernacki, *The Fabrication of Labor: Germany and Britain, 1640–1914*, Berkeley, Los Angeles and London, 1995, 253f.

4   *Oxford English Dictionary*, 2010.

5   Jacob Grimm and Wilhelm Grimm, *Deutsches Wörterbuch*, ed. Berlin-Brandenburgische Akademie der Wissenschaften, 33 vols., 1854–1971 (reprint Munich, 1999), vol. 1, col. 538.

6   *OED*, 2010.

7   Grimm and Grimm, *Deutsches Wörterbuch*, vol. 29, cols. 327–63.

8   Ibid., vol. 1, cols. 538–45.

9   Ibid., vol. 29, col. 328.

10 Ibid., vol. 29, col. 335.

11 See cnrtl.fr/definition/corvée.

12 Grimm and Grimm, *Deutsches Wörterbuch*, vol. 29, col. 347.

13 Biernacki, *The Fabrication of Labor*, 255.

14 *OED* 2010 provides the sources of the quotes.

15 Grimm and Grimm, *Deutsches Wörterbuch*, vol. 1, col. 541, provides the sources of the quotes.

16 Immanuel Kant, *Werke: Sorgfältig revidierte Gesamtausgabe in zehn Bänden*, vol. 9, Leipzig, 1838–9, 31.

17 Grimm and Grimm, *Deutsches Wörterbuch*, vol. 14, cols. 2014–31.

18 Ibid., vol. 15, cols. 1536–47.

19 Pun Ngai, *Made in China. Woman Factory Workers in a Global Workplace*, Durham, NC, 2005.

20 Pun Ngai and Chris King-Chi Chan, 'The Subsumption of Class Discourse in China', *boundary 2* (2008), 35 (2), 75–91.

21 Ibid.

22 Pun Ngai, Ching Kwan Lee et al., *Aufbruch der Zweiten Generation: Wanderarbeit, Gender und Klassenzusammensetzung in China*, Berlin, 2010; as well as personal correspondence with Felix Wemheuer and Chyi-shiow Gong.

23 Yan Hairong, *New Masters, New Servants: Migration, Development and Women Workers in China*, Durham, NC, 2008.

24 Robert Cliver, 'China', in Lex Heerma van Voss, Els Hiemstra and Elise van Nederveen Meerkerk, eds., *The Ashgate Companion to the History of Textile Workers, 1650–2000*, Aldershot, 2010, 103–40, 105ff.

25 Ibid., 129f.

26 Felix Wemheuer, 'Dining in Utopia: An Intellectual History of the Origins of the Chinese Public Dining Halls', in Matthias Middell and Felix Wemheuer, eds, *Hunger and Scarcity under State-Socialism*, Leipzig, 2012, 277–302.

27 Zhang Xia, 'Ziyou (Freedom), Occupational Choice, and Labor: Bangbang in Chongqing, PR China', *International Labor and Working Class History* (April 2008) 73, 65–84.

28 Ngai and Chan, 'The Subsumption of Class Discourse in China'.

29 Yan, *New Masters, New Servants*.

4. CATEGORIES OF ANALYSIS

1   *Encyclopedia of Religion*, ed. Lindsay Jones, 15 vols. Detroit, 2005, vol. 3, 1672ff.

2   *Encyclopedia of World Cultures*, ed. David Levinson, 10 vols., Boston, 1992–5, vol. 1.

3   Ibid., vol. 3, 57.

4   Ibid., vol. 3, 96–8.

5   Claus Offe, 'Anmerkungen zur Gegenwart der Arbeit', in Kocka and Offe, *Geschichte und Zukunft der Arbeit*, 496.

6   Susan Zimmermann, *GrenzÜberschreitungen: Internationale Netzwerke, Organisationen, Bewegungen und die Politik der globalen Ungleichheit vom 17. bis zum 21. Jahrhundert*, Vienna, 2010, 207ff.

7   Komlosy, *Globalgeschichte*, 140ff.

8   Johannes Jäger, Gerhard Melinz and Susan Zimmermann, eds., *Sozialpolitik in der Peripherie: Entwicklungsmuster in Lateinamerika, Afrika, Asien und Osteuropa*, Vienna and Frankfurt am Main, 2001.

9   Martina Kaller-Dietrich, *Ivan Illich 1926–2002: Sein Leben, sein Denken*, Vienna, 2007, 158ff.

10   Alena V. Ledeneva, *Russia's Economy of Favours: Blat, Networking and Informal Exchange*, Cambridge, 1998.

11   Sabine Kunesch, '*Blat*: Informelles Versorgungssystem in der Sowjetunion', dissertation, University of Vienna, 2013.

12   Lutz, *Vom Weltmarkt in den Privathaushalt*.

13   Ivan Illich, Irving Kenneth Zola, John McKnight, Jonathan Caplan, Harley Shaiken, *Disabling Professions*, London, 1977.

14   Grimm and Grimm, *Deutsches Wörterbuch*, vol. 12, cols. 2771–3.

15   Weber, *The Protestant Ethic and the Spirit of Capitalism*.

16   Grimm and Grimm, *Deutsches Wörterbuch*, vol. 12, col. 2773.

17   Ibid., vol. 17, cols. 1352–6.

18   Wilfried Nippel, 'Erwerbsarbeit in der Antike', in Kocka and Offe, *Geschichte und Zukunft der Arbeit*, 54–66, 57.

19   Susan Zimmermann, 'Wohlfahrtspolitik und die staatssozialistische Entwicklungsstrategie in der "anderen" Hälfte Europas im 20. Jahrhundert', in Jäger, Melinz and Zimmermann, eds., *Sozialpolitik in der Peripherie*, 211–38.

20   Sebastian Brandl and Eckhart Hildebrandt, *Zukunft der Arbeit und soziale Nachhaltigkeit: Zur Transformation der Arbeitsgesellschaft vor dem Hintergrund der Nachhaltigkeitsdebatte*, Opladen, 2002; André Gorz, *Critique of Economic Reason*, London, 1989; Jeremy Rifkin, *The End of Work: The Decline of the Global Labor Force and the Dawn of the Post-market Era*, New York, 1996.

5. DIVISIONS OF LABOUR

1   Veronika Bennholdt-Thomsen and Maria Mies, *The Subsistence Perspective: Beyond the Globalized Economy*, London and New York, 1999; Michael P. Smith and Luis E. Guarnizo, eds., *Transnationalism from Below*, New Brunswick, 1998; Joan Smith, Hans Dieter Evers and Immanuel Wallerstein, eds., *Households in the World Economy*, Beverly Hills, 1984; Joan Smith and Immanuel Wallerstein, eds., *Creating and Transforming Households: The Constraints of the World Economy*, Cambridge, 1992.

2   Karl Marx, *Capital*, vol. 1 (1867), trans. Ben Fowkes, London, 1976.

3   Karl-Heinz Roth and Marcel van der Linden, eds., *Beyond Marx: Confronting Labour History and the Concept of Labour with the Global Labour Relations of the 21st Century*, Chicago, 2014; Jason W. Moore, *Capitalism in the Web of Life: Ecology and the Accumulation of Capital*, New York and London, 2015; Andrea Komlosy, 'Re-assessing Labour and Value Transfer under Capitalism', in Roth, ed., *On the Road to Global Labour History*, 2017, 241–60.

4   Jan Lucassen and Leo Lucassen, eds., *Migration, Migration History, History: Old Paradigms and New Perspectives*, Bern, 1997; Hoerder and Kaur, *Proletarian and Gendered Mass Migrations*; Lutz, *Vom Weltmarkt in den Privathaushalt*.

5   Kunibert Raffer, *Unequal Exchange and the Evolution of the World System*, Basingstoke, 1987.

6   Gereffi, 'The Organization of Buyer Driven Commodity Chains'; Karin Fischer, Christian Reiner and Cornelia Staritz, eds., *Globale Güterketten: Weltweite Arbeitsteilung und ungleiche Entwicklung*, Vienna, 2010.

7   Pia Eberhard, 'Konzerne versus Staaten: Mit Schiedsgerichten gegen die Demokratie', *Blätter für deutsche und internationale Politik* (2013) 4, 29–33, 31.

6. HISTORICAL CROSS-SECTIONS

1   Fernand Braudel, *The Perspective of the World*, vol. 3 of *Civilisation and Capitalism, 15th–18th Century*, Berkeley and Los Angeles, 1992; Massimo Livi Bacci, *La popolazione nella historia d'Europa*, Rome and Bari, 1998.

2   Herbert Knittler, *Die europäische Stadt in der frühen Neuzeit: Institutionen, Strukturen, Entwicklungen*, Vienna and Munich, 2000; Michael Mitterauer, *Markt und Stadt im Mittelalter: Beiträge zur historischen Zentralitätsforschung*, Stuttgart, 1980.

3   Bacci, *La popolazione nella historia d'Europa*; Wolfgang Schwentker, 'Die "vormoderne" Stadt in Europa und Asien: Überlegungen zu einem strukturgeschichtlichen Vergleich', in Peter Feldbauer, Michael Mitterauer and Wolfgang Schwentker, eds., *Die vormoderne Stadt: Asien und Europa im Vergleich*, Vienna, 2002, 259–87, 274.

4   Eric H. Mielants, *The Origins of Capitalism and the 'Rise of the West'*, Philadelphia, 2007, 103.

5   For Islamic cities, see Peter Feldbauer, *Die islamische Welt 600–1250: Ein Frühfall von Unterentwicklung?*, Vienna, 1995, 154–74.

6   Bert Fragner, 'Die Mongolen und ihr Imperium', in Bert Fragner and Andreas Kappeler, eds., *Zentralasien 13. bis 20. Jahrhundert*, Vienna, 2006, 103–20.

7   Ibid., 115.

8   Abu-Lughod, *Before European Hegemony*.

9   Ibid.; Janet Lippmann Abu-Lughod, 'The World System in the Thirteenth Century: Dead-End or Precursor?', in Michael Das, ed., *Islamic & European Expansion: The Forging of a Global Order*, Philadelpha, 1993, pp. 75–101.

10   Braudel, *The Perspective of the World*.

11   Hans-Heinrich Nolte, *Kleine Geschichte Russlands*, Stuttgart, 2003, 41f.

12   Fragner, 'Die Mongolen und ihr Imperium', 112.

13   Ibid., 114.

14   Felicitas Schmieder, *Europa und die Fremden: Die Mongolen im Urteil des Abendlandes vom 13. bis in das 15. Jahrhundert*, Sigmaringen, 1994.

15   Komlosy, 'Arbeitsverhältnisse und Gesellschaftsformationen'; Otto Gerhard Oexle, 'Erwerbsarbeit in der Antike', in Kocka and Offe, *Geschichte und Zukunft der Arbeit*, 67–79; Reinhard Sieder, *Sozialgeschichte der Familie*, Frankfurt am Main, 1987.

16   Gisela Bock, *Frauen in der europäischen Geschichte vom Mittelalter bis zur Gegenwart*, Munich, 2000.

17   *Encyclopedia of World Cultures*, vol. 4.

18   Ibid.

19   Lothar Dralle, *Die Deutschen in Ostmittel- und Osteuropa: Ein Jahrtausend europäische Geschichte*, Darmstadt, 1991.

20   Nolte, *Kleine Geschichte Russlands*, 34ff.

21   Karl Kaser, *Macht und Erbe: Männerherrschaft, Besitz und Familie im östlichen Europa 1500–1900*, Vienna, Cologne and Weimar, 2000; Sieder, *Sozialgeschichte der Familie*; Reinhard Sieder, 'Haus, Ehe, Familie und Verwandtschaft', in Cerman et al., *Wirtschaft und Gesellschaft Europa 1000–2000*, 322–45, 324ff.

22   Nolte, *Kleine Geschichte Russlands*, 53.

23   Ibid., 44, 54.

24   Mielants, *Origins of Capitalism*, 133; Hans Ulrich Vogel, 'Die Stadt im vormodernen China', in Peter Feldbauer, Michael Mitterauer and Wolfgang Schwentker, eds., *Die vormoderne Stadt: Asien und Europa im Vergleich*, Vienna, 2002, 133–52, 149.

25   *Encyclopedia of Religion*, vol. 3, 1672–7.

26   Feldbauer, *Die islamische Welt 600–1250*, 376f.

27   Vogel, 'Die Stadt im vormodernen China', 145.

28   Lucassen, 'Outlines of a History of Labour', 9; Hans-Heinrich Nolte, *Weltgeschichte: Imperien, Religionen und Systeme 15.–19. Jahrhundert*, Vienna, Cologne and Weimar, 2005, 239.

29   Fragner, 'Die Mongolen und ihr Imperium', 109.

30   *Encyclopaedia of Religion*, vol. 1, 266.

31   Peter Feldbauer and Gottfried Liedl, 'Italiens Kolonialexpansion: Östlicher Mittelmeerraum und die Küsten des Schwarzen Meeres', in Peter Feldbauer, Gottfried Liedl and John Morrissey, eds., *Mediterraner Kolonialismus: Expansion und Kulturaustausch im Mittelalter*, Essen, 2005, 155–71; Peter Feldbauer and John Morrissey, *Venedig 800–1600*, Vienna, 2002.

32   Feldbauer, *Die islamische Welt 600–1250*, 376ff.

33   Uta Lindgren, *Alpenübergänge von Bayern nach Italien 1500–1850*, Munich, 1986.

34   Herbert Hassinger, 'Zollwesen und Verkehr in den österreichischen Alpenländern bis um 1300', *MIÖG* (1965), 73, 292–361.

35   Angus Maddison, *The World Economy: A Millennial Perspective*, Paris, 2001, 126.

36   Braudel, *The Perspective of the World*.

37   Feldbauer and Morrissey, *Venedig 800–1600*.

38   Abu-Lughod, 'The World System in the Thirteenth Century'; Braudel, *The Perspective of the World*.

39   Jerzy Strzelczyk, 'Ritterorden und Hanse: Mission und Expansion', in Andrea Komlosy, Hans Heinrich Nolte and Imbi Sooman, eds., *Ostsee 700–2000: Gesellschaft – Wirtschaft – Kultur*, Vienna, 2007, 49–60, 55f.

40   Hans Heinrich Nolte, 'Nations- und Staatenbildung: Parlamentarismus und Absolutismus', in Komlosy, Nolte and Sooman, *Ostsee 700–2000*, 72–90, 72.

41   Hans-Heinrich Nolte, 'Deutsche Ostgrenze, russische Westgrenze, amerikanische Südgrenze: Zur Radikalisierung der Grenzen in der Neuzeit', in Joachim Becker and Andrea Komlosy, eds., *Grenzen weltweit: Zonen, Linien, Mauern im historischen Vergleich*, Vienna, 2004, 55–74, 56.

42   Norman Foster, *Auf den Spuren der Pilger: Die großen Wallfahrten im Mittelalter*, Augsburg, 1990.

43   Reinhold Röhricht, *Deutsche Pilgerreisen nach dem Heiligen Lande*, Innsbruck, 1900, 5.

44   Ibid., 63.

45   Suraiya Faroqhi, *Pilgrims and Sultans: The Haji under the Ottomans*, London, 1994.

46   Abu-Lughod, *Before European Hegemony*; Abu-Lughod, 'The World System in the Thirteenth Century'; Wallerstein, *The Modern World-System*, vol. 1; Frank, *ReOrient*.

47   Abu-Lughod, 'The World System in the Thirteenth Century'.

48   Abu-Lughod, *Before European Hegemony*.

49   Erich Landsteiner, 'Landwirtschaft und Agrargesellschaft', in Cerman et al., *Wirtschaft und Gesellschaft Europa 1000–2000*, 178–210, 192f.

50   Peter Feldbauer and Jean Paul Lehners, eds., *Die Welt im 16. Jahrhundert*, vol. 3 of *Globalgeschichte: Die Welt 1000–2000*, Vienna, 2008.

51   Abu-Lughod, 'The World System in the Thirteenth Century'.

52   Peter Feldbauer, *Estado da India: Die Portugiesen in Asien 1498–1620*, Vienna, 2003.

53   Wallerstein, *The Modern World-System*, vol. 1.

54   Frank, *ReOrient*.

55   Ibid., 128.

56   Ibid., 185.

57   Wallerstein, *The Modern World-System*, vol. 1.

58   Andre Gunder Frank and Barry Gills, eds., *The World System: Five Hundred Years or Five Thousand?*, London and New York, 1993.

59   Birgit Van den Hoven, *Work in Ancient and Medieval Thought: Ancient Philosophers, Medieval Monks and Theologians and Their Concept of Work, Occupations and Technology*, Amsterdam, 1996.

60   Wallerstein, *The Modern World-System*.

61   Jenö Szücs, 'The Three Historical Regions of Europe', *Acta Historica Academiae Scientiarium Hungaricae* (1983), 29 (2–4), 131–84.

62   Nolte, *Weltgeschichte*, 104ff; Wallerstein, *The Modern World-System*, vol. 1.

63   Bronisław Geremek, *Geschichte der Armut: Elend und Barmherzigkeit in Europa*, Munich, 1988.

64   Edward P. Thompson, *The Making of the English Working Class*, London, 1963.

65   Landsteiner, 'Landwirtschaft und Agrargesellschaft', 194.

66   Peter Blickle, *Unruhen in der ständischen Gesellschaft, 1300–1800*, Munich, 1988, 13.

67   Landsteiner, 'Landwirtschaft und Agrargesellschaft', 193. Remember, this older form was due to the vast swathes of land that were less controllable in the last historical cross-section.

68   Nolte, *Kleine Geschichte Russlands*, 63f; Andreas Kappeler, *Die Kosaken: Geschichte und Legenden*, Munich, 2013, 17.

69   Marian Małowist, 'The Economic and Social Development of the Baltic Countries from the 15th to the 17th Centuries', *Economic History Review*, 2nd series (1959), 12 (2), 177–89.

70   Dariusz Adamczyk, *Zur Stellung Polens im modernen Weltsystem der Frühen Neuzeit*, Hamburg, 2001.

71   Horst Benneckenstein, *Waidstadt Erfurt*, Erfurt, 1991, 31.

72   Andrea Komlosy, 'Der Staat schiebt ab: Zur nationalstaatlichen Konsolidierung von Heimat und Fremde im 18. und 19. Jahrhundert', in Sylvia Hahn, Andrea Komlosy and Ilse Reiter-Zatloukal, eds., *Ausweisung – Abschiebung – Vertreibung: Europa 16.–20. Jahrhundert*, Innsbruck, 2006, 87–114, 94–102.

73   Michael Mitterauer, ed., Österreichisches Montanwesen: *Produktion, Verteilung, Sozialformen*, Vienna, 1974; Roman Sandgruber, Ökonomie und Politik: *Österreichische Wirtschaftsgeschichte vom Mittelalter bis zur Gegenwart*, Vienna, 1995, 6–79.

74   Sandgruber, *Ökonomie und Politik*, 80.

75   Komlosy, 'Arbeitsverhältnisse und Gesellschaftsformationen', 253f.

76   Bernd Hausberger, 'Wirtschaft und Wirtschaftsräume', in Friedrich Edelmayer, Bernd Hausberger and Barbara Potthast, eds., *Lateinamerika 1492–1850/70*, Vienna, 2005, 171–93, 176f.

77   Ibid., 183.

78   Ibid., 178.

79   Claus Füllberg-Stolberg, 'Transatlantischer Sklavenhandel und Sklaverei in den Amerikas', in Ulrike Schmieder and Hans-Heinrich Nolte, eds., *Altantik: Sozialgeschichte der Neuzeit*, Vienna, 2010, 86–115; Ulrike Schmieder, 'Der Lusoatlantik: Perspektiven und Debatten', in ibid., 116–37.

80   Füllberg-Stolberg, 'Transatlantischer Sklavenhandel und Sklaverei in den Amerikas', 90.

81   Braudel, *The Perspective of the World*.

82   Erich Landsteiner, 'Nichts als Karies, Lungenkrebs und Pellagra? Zu den Auswirkungen des Globalisierungsprozesses auf Europa 1500–1800', in Friedrich Edelmayer, Erich Landsteiner and Renate Pieper, eds., *Die Geschichte des europäischen Welthandels und der wirtschaftliche Globalisierungsprozeß*, Vienna and Munich, 2001, 104–39; Wallerstein, *The Modern World-System*, vol. 1.

83   Adamczyk, *Zur Stellung Polens*; Małowist, 'The Economic and Social Development of the Baltic Countries'.

84   Immanuel Wallerstein, *Historical Capitalism*, London, 1983.

85   Nolte, *Weltgeschichte*, 172.

86   Feldbauer, *Estado da India*.

87   Hoerder, *Cultures in Contact*; Lydia Potts, *Weltmarkt für Arbeitskraft: Von der Kolonisation Amerikas bis zu den Migrationen der Gegenwart*, Hamburg, 1988.

88   Sven Beckert, *The Empire of Cotton: A Global History*, New York, 2014.

89   Leopoldine Hokr, *Groß-Siegharts, Schwechat und Waidhofen/Thaya: Das Netzwerk der frühen niederösterreichischen Baumwollindustrie*, Frankfurt am Main, 2006.

90   Markus Cerman, 'Vorindustrielles Gewerbe und Protoindustrialisierung', in Cerman et al., *Wirtschaft und Gesellschaft Europa 1000–2000*, 211–27; Markus Cerman and Sheilagh C. Ogilvie, eds, *Protoindustrialisierung in Europa: Industrielle Produktion vor dem Fabrikszeitalter*, Vienna, 1994.

91   Wallerstein, *The Modern World-System*, vol. 1.

92   Dietmar Rothermund, 'Seehandel und Kolonialherrschaft', in Margarete Grandner and Andrea Komlosy, eds, *Vom Weltgeist beseelt: Globalgeschichte 1700–1815*, Vienna, 2004, 25–44, 32.

93   Wallerstein, *The Modern World-System*, vol. 3.

94   Nolte, *Kleine Geschichte Russlands*, 43ff.

95   Nolte, *Weltgeschichte*, 291.

96   Huri Islamoğlu-Inan, ed., *The Ottoman Empire and the World Economy*, Cambridge and Paris, 1987.

97   Andrea Komlosy, 'Spatial Division of Labour, Global Inter-Relations and Imbalances in Regional Development', in Lex Heerma van Voss/Els Hiemstra and Elise van Nederveen Meerkerk, eds, *The Ashgate Companion to the History of Textile Workers, 1650–2000*. Aldershot, 2010, 621–46. 629.

98   Smith, *Wealth of Nations*.

99   Komlosy, 'Re-assessing Labour and Value Transfer under Capitalism'.

100   Kirti N. Chaudhuri, *Asia before Europe: Economy and Civilisation of the Indian Ocean from the Rise of Islam to 1750*, Cambridge, 1990.

101   Peter Kriedte, Hans Medick and Jürgen Schlumbohm, *Industrialisierung vor der Industrialisierung: Gewerbliche Warenproduktion auf dem Land in der Formationsperiode des Kapitalismus*, Göttingen, 1977.

102   Barbara Duden and Karin Hausen, 'Gesellschaftliche Arbeit, geschlechts-spezifische Arbeitsteilung', in Anette Kuhn and Gerhard Schneider, eds., *Frauen in der Geschichte*, Düsseldorf, 1979, 11–33; Albert Tanner, *Das Schiffchen fliegt, die Maschine rauscht: Weber, Sticker und Unternehmer in der Ostschweiz*, Zurich, 1985.

103   Spinning contract of the Linzer Wollzeugfabrik, quoted in Andrea Komlosy, '"Wo der Webwaarenindustrie so viele fleißige und geübte Hände zu Gebote stehen": Landfrauen zwischen bezahlter und unbezahlter Arbeit', in Birgit Bolognese-Leuchtenmüller and Michael Mitterauer, eds., *Frauen-Arbeitswelten*, Vienna, 1993, 105–32, 110.

104   Cerman and Ogilvie, *Protoindustrialisierung in Europa*; Dietrich Ebeling and Wolfgang Mager, eds., *Protoindustrie in der Region: Europäische Gewerbel-andschaften vom 16. bis zum 19. Jahrhundert*, Bielefeld, 1997; Arnost Klíma, *Economy, Industry and Society in Bohemia in the 17th to 19th Centuries*, Prague, 1991; Hans Pohl, *Gewerbe-und Industrielandschaften vom Spätmit-telalter bis ins 20. Jahrhundert*, Stuttgart, 1986.

105   Andrea Komlosy, 'Austria and Czechoslovakia: The Habsburg Monarchy and Its Successor States', in Lex Heerma van Voss/Els Hiemstra and Elise van Nederveen Meerkerk, eds, *The Ashgate Companion to the History of Textile Workers, 1650–2000*, Aldershot, UK, 2010, 43–74, 49.

106   Klíma, *Economy, Industry and Society in Bohemia*.

107   Tanner, *Das Schiffchen fliegt, die Maschine rauscht*.

108   Hokr, *Groß-Siegharts, Schwechat und Waidhofen/Thaya*; Andrea Komlosy, 'Vom Kleinraum zur Peripherie: Entwicklungsphasen der wirtschaftlichen Abhängigkeit im 19. Jahrhundert', in Herbert Knittler, ed., *Wirtschaftsges-chichte des Waldviertels*, Horn-Waidhofen/Thaya, 2006, 217–340; Herbert Matis, ed., *Von der Glückseligkeit des Staates: Staat, Wirtschaft und Gesellschaft in Österreich im Zeitalter des aufgeklärten Absolutismus*, Berlin, 1981.

109   Komlosy, 'Wo der Webwaarenindustrie ...', 111.

110   Hokr, *Groß-Siegharts, Schwechat und Waidhofen/Thaya*, 47–54.

111   Islamoğlu-Inan, *The Ottoman Empire and the World Economy*.

112   Holden Fürber, *Rival Empires of Trade in the Orient, 1600–1800*, Minneapo-lis, 1976, 218ff.

113   Rainer Ramcke, *Die Beziehungen zwischen Hamburg und Österreich im 18. Jahrhundert*, Hamburg, 1969, 114.

114   Hausberger, 'Wirtschaft und Wirtschaftsräume', 173.

115   Dietmar Rothermund, *Europa und Asien im Zeitalter des Merkantilismus*, Darmstadt, 1978; Rothermund, 'Seehandel und Kolonialherrschaft'.

116   Chaudhuri, *Asia before Europe*; Dharma Kumar, ed., *The Cambridge Economic History of India*, vol. 2, *c.1757–c.1970*, Cambridge, 1983, 23.

117   John Irwin and Paul R. Schwartz, *Studies in Indo-European Textile History*, Ahmedabad, 1966, 16.

118   Rothermund, *Europa und Asien im Zeitalter des Merkantilismus*, 100.

119   Wallerstein, *The Modern World-System*, vol. 3.

120   Rothermund, 'Seehandel und Kolonialherrschaft', 39f.

121   Andrea Komlosy, 'Chinesische Seide, indische Kalikos, Maschinengarn aus Manchester: "Industrielle Revolution" aus globalhistorischer Perspektive', in Grandner and Komlosy, *Vom Weltgeist beseelt*, 103–34, 112.

122   Dixin Xu and Chengming Wu, eds., *Chinese Capitalism, 1522–1840*, Basingstoke and London, 2000.

123   Cited in Chaudhuri, *Asia before Europe*, 320f.

124   Ulrich Menzel, *Auswege aus der Abhängigkeit: Die entwicklungspolitische Aktualität Europas*, Frankfurt am Main, 1988, 283; Hans-Heinrich Nolte, 'Tradition des Rückstands: ein halbes Jahrtausend "Russland und der Westen"': *Vierteljahresschrift für Sozial- und Wirtschaftsgeschichte* (1991), 78 (3), 344–64, 349.

125   Komlosy, 'Spatial Division of Labour', 635.

126   Paul Bairoch, 'International Industrialization Levels from 1750 to 1980', *Journal of European Economic History* (1982), 11 (2), 269–334, 296.

127   Beckert, *The Empire of Cotton*, ch. 4, 5; Dale Tomich, *Through the Prism of Slavery: Labor, Capital, and the World Economy*, Lanham, MD, 2004.

128   Rothermund, *Europa und Asien im Zeitalter des Merkantilismus*, 117f.

129   Andrea, 'Chinesische Seide, indische Kalikos, Maschinengarn aus Manchester', 105f.

130   Maddison, *The World Economy*, 261.

131   Beckert, *The Empire of Cotton*, ch. 5.

132   Arno Sonderegger, 'Sklaverei und Sklavenhandel: Zum Beziehungswandel zwischen Europa und Afrika im 18. und 19. Jahrhundert', in Birgit Englert, Inge Grau and Andrea Komlosy, eds., *Nord–Süd-Beziehungen: Kolonialismen und Ansätze zu ihrer Überwindung*, Vienna 2006, 29–50, 38f.

133   Matthias Middell, 'Revolutionsgeschichte und Globalgeschichte: Transatlantische Interaktionen in der zweiten Hälfte des 20. Jahrhundert', in Grandner and Komlosy, *Vom Weltgeist beseelt*, 135–60, 150.

134   Sonderegger, 'Sklaverei und Sklavenhandel', 44.

135   Beckert, *The Empire of Cotton*, ch. 4.

136   See the section on 1500.

137   See the section on 1700; Nolte, *Kleine Geschichte Russlands*, 54.

138   Karl H. Schneider, *Geschichte der Bauernbefreiung*, Stuttgart, 2010.

139   Nolte, *Kleine Geschichte Russlands*, 151.

140   Komlosy, 'Wo der Webwaarenindustrie …', 112.

141   Komlosy, 'Vom Kleinraum zur Peripherie', 262ff.

142   Wolfgang Kaschuba and Carola Lipp, *Dörfliches Überleben*, Tübingen, 1982;

Wolfgang Kaschuba, 'Vom Heimweber zum Arbeiterbauern: Aufstieg und Niedergang der ländlichen Leinenindustrie im Gebiet der Schwäbischen Alb', in Andrea Komlosy, ed., *Spinnen – Spulen – Weben: Leben und Arbeiten im Waldviertel und anderen ländlichen Textilregionen*, Krems-Horn, 1991, 77–89.

143 Andrea Komlosy, *Grenze und ungleiche regionale Entwicklung: Binnenmarkt und Migration in der Habsburgermonarchie*, Vienna, 2003, 255ff; Jan Lucassen, *Migrant Labour in Europe: The Drift to the North Sea*, London and Sydney, 1987; Leslie Page Moch, 'Dividing Time: An Analytical Framework of Migration History Periodization', in Jan Lucassen and Leo Lucassen, eds., *Migration, Migration History, History: Old Paradigms and New Perspectives*, Bern, 1997, 41–56; Saskia Sassen, *Guests and Aliens*, New York, 1999.

144 Lucassen, *Migrant Labour in Europe*, 209f.

145 Lucassen, *Migrant Labour in Europe*; Heinz Noflatscher, 'Arbeitswanderung in Agrargesellschaften der frühen Neuzeit', *Geschichte und Region* (1993) 2 (2), 63–98.

146 Keely Stauter-Halsted and Nancy Wingfield, eds, 'Sexual Deviance and Social Control in Late Imperial Eastern Europe', special issue of the *Journal of the History of Sexuality* (May 2011), 20 (2).

147 Komlosy, *Grenze und ungleiche regionale Entwicklung*, 172, 261ff; Page Moch, 'Dividing Time'; Sassen, *Guests and Aliens*.

148 Komlosy, *Grenze und ungleiche regionale Entwicklung*, 100f.

149 Ibid., 318–47.

150 Annemarie Steidl, *Auf nach Wien! Die Mobilität des mitteleuropäischen Handwerks im 18. und 19. Jh. am Beispiel der Haupt- und Residenzstadt*, Vienna and Munich, 2003, 67ff; Andreas Weigl, *Demographischer Wandel und Modernisierung in Wien*, vol. 5 of *Kommentare zum Historischen Atlas der Stadt Wien*, Vienna, 2000, 132f.

151 Hans-Christian Maner, *Galizien: Eine Grenzregion im Kalkül der Donaumonarchie im 18. und 19. Jahrhundert*, Munich, 2007, 49–52.

152 Lars Olsson, 'Labor Migration as a Prelude to World War I', *International Migration Review* (1996), 30, 875–900, 876.

153 Komlosy, 'Chinesische Seide, indische Kalikos, Maschinengarn aus Manchester', 120–4; Komlosy, 'Spatial Division of Labour', 636.

154 Rothermund, 'Seehandel und Kolonialherrschaft', 40.

155 Ranajit Guha, *Elementary Aspects of Peasant Insurgency in Colonial India*, Durham and London, 1999.

156 Fikret Adanir, 'Bevölkerungsverschiebungen, Siedlungspolitik und ethnisch-kulturelle Homogenisierung: Nationsbildung auf dem Balkan und in Kleinasien, 1878–1923', in Sylvia Hahn, Andrea Komlosy and Ilse Reiter-Zatloukal, eds., *Ausweisung, Abschiebung, Vertreibung in Europa, 16.–20. Jahrhundert*, Innsbruck, 2006, 172–92, 176ff.

157 Sonderegger, 'Sklaverei und Sklavenhandel', 42f.

158 Füllberg-Stolberg, 'Transatlantischer Sklavenhandel und Sklaverei in den Amerikas', 103f.

159   Klaus J. Bade, *Migration in European History*, Malden, MA, 2003; Hoerder, *Cultures in Contact*.

160   Annemarie Steidl, 'On Many Roads: Internal, European, and Transatlantic Migration in the Habsburg Monarchy, 1850–1914', habilitation, University of Vienna, 2014, 194.

161   Potts, *Weltmarkt für Arbeitskraft*, 83–90.

162   Andreas Eckert, 'Transatlantischer Sklavenhandel und Sklaverei in Westafrika', in Andreas Eckert, Ingeborg Grau and Arno Sonderegger, eds., *Afrika 1500–1900: Geschichte und Gesellschaft*, Vienna, 2010, 72–88.

163   Bairoch, 'International Industrialization Levels', 298.

164   Bade, *Migration in European History*.

165   Sebastian Conrad, Elisio Macamo and Bénédicte Zimmermann, 'Die Kodifizierung der Arbeit: Individuum, Gesellschaft, Nation', in Kocka and Offe, *Geschichte und Zukunft der Arbeit*, 449–75, 454.

166   See http://pow.univie.ac.at.

167   Alexander Mejstrik, Sigrid Wadauer and Thomas Buchner, eds., *Die Erzeugung des Berufs/Production of 'Beruf'*, Österreichische Zeitschrift für Geschichtswissenschaft (2013) 24 (1).

168   Wallerstein, *The Modern World-System*, vol. 4.

169   Susan Zimmermann, *Divide, Provide and Rule: An Integrative History of Poverty Policy, Social Policy, and Social Reform in Hungary under the Habsburg Monarchy*, Budapest and New York, 2011.

170   Susan Zimmermann, 'Geschützte und ungeschützte Arbeitsverhältnisse von der Hochindustrialisierung bis zur Weltwirtschaftskrise: Österreich und Ungarn im Vergleich', in Komlosy et al., *Ungeregelt und unterbezahlt*, 87–116, 91.

171   *Bericht der k. k. Gewerbeinspectoren über die Heimarbeit in Österreich* (1900), 1, 315.

172   Komlosy, *Grenze und ungleiche regionale Entwicklung*, 269.

173   Olsson, 'Labor Migration as a Prelude to World War I'; Page Moch, 'Dividing Time'; Sassen, *Guests and Aliens*.

174   Olsson, 'Labor Migration as a Prelude to World War I', 880.

175   Ibid., 887.

176   Ibid., 888; Leopold Caro, *Auswanderung und Auswanderungspolitik in Österreich*, vol. 131 of *Schriften des Vereins für Socialpolitik*, Leipzig, 1909, 39.

177   Karl Englisch, 'Die oesterreichische Auswanderungsstatistik', *Statistische Monatsschrift*, new series (1913), 18, 65–167, 91–7.

178   Bade, *Migration in European History*.

179   Henning Melber, 'Koloniale Grenzziehungen und afrikanischer Nationalstaat', in Arno Sonderegger, Inge Grau and Birgit Englert, eds., *Afrika im 20. Jahrhundert*, Vienna, 2011, 27–39, 33.

180   Caro, *Auswanderung und Auswanderungspolitik in Österreich*, 144; Olsson, 'Labor Migration as a Prelude to World War I', 889.

181   Frank-Johnson Alison, 'The Children of the Desert and the Law of the Sea:

Austria, Great Britain, the Ottoman Empire, and the Mediterranean Slave Trade in the Nineteenth Century', in *American Historical Review*, 117, 2 (April 2012), 415–26.

182   Mechthild Leutner and Klaus Mühlhahn, eds., *Kolonialkrieg in China: Die Niederschlagung der Boxerbewegung 1900–1901*, Berlin, 2007.

183   Georg Lehner and Monikam Lehner, eds., Österreich-Ungarn und der *'Boxeraufstand' in China*, Vienna, 2002 (Mitteilungen des Österreichischen Staatsarchivs Sonderband 6).

184   Raymond Dumett, ed., *Mining Tycoons in the Age of Empire 1870–1945: Entrepreneurship, High Finance, Politics and Territorial Expansion*, Basingstoke, 2008.

185   Iván Berend, *Central and Eastern Europe 1944–1993: Detour from the Periphery to the Periphery*, Cambridge, 1996.

186   Robert Kappel, 'Der Aufstieg der BRICS und Europas Zukunft in der Weltwirtschaft', *Wirtschaftspolitische Blätter* (2013), 2, 193–208.

187   Joachim Hirsch, *Herrschaft, Hegemonie und politische Alternativen*, Hamburg, 2002.

188   Lutz, *Vom Weltmarkt in den Privathaushalt*.

189   Bachinger, 'Der irreguläre Pflegearbeitsmarkt'.

190   Christian Brütt, 'Von Hartz zu Agenda 2010: Die Realpolitik im "aktivierenden Sozialstaat"', *Prokla: Zeitschrift für kritische Sozialwissenschaft* (2003), 133, 645–66.

191   See de.wikipedia.org/wiki/Reallohn.

192   See sozialhilfe24.de/hartz-iv-4-alg-ii-2/1-ein-euro-job.html.

193   Ivan Illich, *Shadow Work*, London, 1981.

194   Average gross monthly wages in euros (2012): Bulgaria: 397, Romania: 466, Hungary: 771, Slovakia: 805, Czech Republic: 999, Germany: 2,412.

195   Hannes Hofbauer, *EU-Osterweiterung: Historische Basis – ökonomische Triebkräfte – soziale Folgen*, Vienna, 2007, 258ff; Bettina Musiolek, *Made in … Osteuropa: Die neuen 'fashion Kolonien'*, Berlin, 2002.

196   World Bank, *World Development Report 1995*, Washington, DC, 1995, 131.

197   Bachinger, 'Der irreguläre Pflegearbeitsmarkt'; Lutz, *Vom Weltmarkt in den Privathaushalt*.

198   Roth, 'An Encyclopaedist of Critical Thought'.

199   Barbara Bartels-Leipold, 'Internationaler Gerichtshof für Piraterie', dissertation, Universität der Bundeswehr München, 2012.

200   Pun and Chan, 'The Subsumption of Class Discourse in China'.

201   Kappel, 'Der Aufstieg der BRICS'.

202   Georg Egger, Daniel Fuchs, Thomas Immervoll, Lydia Steinmassl, eds, *Arbeitskämpfe in China: Berichte von der Werkbank der Welt*, Vienna, 2013; Viktor Krasilshchikov, 'Brasilien und Russland: Ähnlichkeiten und Unterschiede der Entwicklungslinien', *Zeitschrift für Weltgeschichte* (2012) 13 (2), 123–50.

203   Jean-Christophe Rufin, *Globalia*, Paris, 2004.

7. COMBINING LABOUR RELATIONS IN THE *LONGUE DURÉE*

1   Friedrich Schneider, *Kompaktwissen Schattenwirtschaft und Steuermoral*, Zurich, 2008.
2   Norbert Neuwirth and Stefanie Gude, *Unternehmen Haushalt: Dynamik und makroökonomische Bewertung haushaltsrelevanter Tätigkeiten*, Vienna, 2003 (Österreichisches Institut für Familienforschung).
3   See http://collab.iisg.nl/web/LabourRelations.
4   Komlosy, 'Re-assessing Labour and Value Transfer under Capitalism'.

Index